PENGUIN BOOKS

3,096 Days

Natascha Kampusch was born on 17 February 1988 in Vienna and became victim, at the age of ten, to what proved to be one of the longest abductions in recent history. She finally gained her freedom in 2006. On the day she escaped, her abductor, Wolfgang Priklopil, committed suicide by throwing himself under a train. *3,096 Days* is her own account of her ordeal.

Natascha, now aged twenty-two, lives in Vienna, where she is continuing her studies.

3,096 Days

NATASCHA KAMPUSCH

With Heike Gronemeier and Corinna Milborn

Translated by Jill Kreuer

PENGUIN BOOKS

PENGUIN BOOKS

Published by the Penguin Group

Penguin Books Ltd, 80 Strand, London WC2R ORL, England

Penguin Group (USA) Inc., 375 Hudson Street, New York, New York 10014, USA

Penguin Group (Canada), 90 Eglinton Avenue East, Suite 700, Toronto, Ontario, Canada M4P 2Y3
(a division of Pearson Penguin Canada Inc.)

Penguin Ireland, 25 St Stephen's Green, Dublin 2, Ireland (a division of Penguin Books Ltd)

Penguin Group (Australia), 250 Camberwell Road, Camberwell, Victoria 3124, Australia
(a division of Pearson Australia Group Pty Ltd)

Penguin Books India Pvt Ltd, 11 Community Centre, Panchsheel Park, New Delhi – 110 017, India

Penguin Group (NZ), 67 Apollo Drive, Rosedale, North Shore 0632, New Zealand
(a division of Pearson New Zealand Ltd)

Penguin Books (South Africa) (Pty) Ltd, 24 Sturdee Avenue, Rosebank,
Johannesburg 2196, South Africa

Penguin Books Ltd, Registered Offices: 80 Strand, London WC2R ORL, England
www.penguin.com

3,096 Tage first published in Germany by Ullstein Buchverlage 2010
First published in English by Penguin 2010

1

Grateful acknowledgement is made for permission to reproduce the following copyright
material: quotation on p. v is from *Trauma and Recovery* by Judith Herman, copyright © Judith
Herman, 1992, reprinted with permission from Basic Books, a member of the Perseus Books Group;
the poem on pp. 87–8 is from *Winnetou*, by Karl May, copyright © Karl May, 2006, reprinted by
permission of The Continuum International Publishing Group

Set in 11/13 pt Monotype Dante
Typeset by Ellipsis Book Limited, Glasgow
Printed in Great Britain by Clays Ltd, St Ives plc

ISBN: 978-0-670-91999-4

www.greenpenguin.co.uk

Penguin Books is committed to a sustainable future
for our business, our readers and our planet.
The book in your hands is made from paper
certified by the Forest Stewardship Council.

'Psychological trauma is an affliction of the powerless. At the moment of trauma, the victim is rendered helpless by overwhelming force. When the force is that of nature, we speak of disasters. When the force is that of other human beings, we speak of atrocities. Traumatic events overwhelm the ordinary systems of care that give people a sense of control, connection and meaning.'
Judith Herman, *Trauma and Recovery*

Dear Reader

To get a deeper insight into my biography you can find a 2D-Code at the end of each chapter. By scanning the 2D-Code, you will receive video, text, picture and audio information about my childhood and captivity on your mobile phone. Also you would be welcome to send me any questions or to request a dedicated autograph card.

All my best
Natascha Kampusch

Point on a Code   Take a Picture   Decoding   Content

How to Get Started

Please send an SMS with the keyword *nkuk* to the following number: +43 676 800 92 022.

Follow the link in the reply SMS to download the free 2D-Reader.

Free Content. Data-transfer and SMS costs are according to your mobile phone contract.

Questions, dedicated autograph, etc.

My mobile site

Contents

I

My Crumbling World

My Childhood on the Outskirts of Vienna

My mother lit a cigarette and took a deep puff. 'It's already dark outside. Think of all the things that could've happened to you!' She shook her head.

My father and I had spent the last weekend of February 1998 in Hungary, where he had purchased a holiday house in a small village not far from the border. It was a complete dump, with damp walls where the plaster was crumbling off. Over the years he had renovated the house, furnishing it with beautiful old furniture, making it nearly inhabitable through his efforts. Still, I was not particularly fond of going there. My father had a number of friends in Hungary with whom he spent a great deal of time, always drinking a little bit too much thanks to the favourable currency exchange rate. In the bars and restaurants we visited in the evenings, I was the only child in the group. I would sit there saying nothing, bored.

I had reluctantly gone with him to Hungary on this occasion as well. Time seemed to move incredibly slowly, and I was angry that I was still too young and had no say in how I spent my time. Even when we visited the thermal spa in the area that Sunday, I was less than overjoyed. In a rotten mood, I was strolling through the spa premises when a woman I knew asked me, 'Would you like to have a soda with me?' I nodded and followed her into the café. She was an actress and lived in Vienna. I admired her because she always exuded great serenity and seemed so self-assured.

Besides, I had always secretly dreamed of being an actress. After a while, I took a deep breath and said, 'You know, I would like to become an actress too. Do you think I could do that?'

She beamed a smile at me. 'Of course you could, Natascha! You'd be a great actress if that's what you really want!'

My heart leapt at that. I had truly expected not to be taken seriously or even to be laughed at – as had happened many times before.

'When you're ready, I'll help you,' she promised me, putting her arm around my shoulders.

On the way back to the swimming area, I bounded about in high spirits, humming to myself, 'I can do anything if I want it enough and believe in myself enough.' I felt more light-hearted and untroubled than I had in a long time.

However, my euphoria was cut short. The afternoon was already getting on, but my father wasn't making any move to leave the spa. When we finally returned to his holiday house, he again didn't seem to be in any great hurry. Just the opposite. He even wanted to lie down for a short while. I glanced nervously at the clock. We had promised my mother that we would be home by seven o'clock, because the next day was a school day. I knew that there would be a heated discussion if we didn't get back to Vienna on time. While he lay snoring on the couch, the clock kept ticking away inexorably. It was already dark when my father finally woke up and we began the trip home. I sat in the back seat pouting and saying nothing. We wouldn't make it on time, my mother would be angry, and everything that had been so pleasant this afternoon would be ruined in one fell swoop. As always, I would be caught in the middle. Adults always ruined everything. When my father stopped at a petrol station and bought me a chocolate bar, I crammed the whole thing into my mouth at once.

It wasn't until 8.30, one and a half hours late, that we arrived

at the Rennbahnsiedlung council estate. 'I'll let you
home quickly,' said my father and gave me a kiss.

'I love you,' I muttered as always when saying goodbye. T
I ran through the dark courtyard to our stairway and unlocked the
door. In the foyer there was a note from my mother next to the
telephone: 'I've gone to the cinema. Be back later.' I put my bag
down and hesitated a moment. Then I scribbled a short note to
my mother that I would wait for her at our neighbour's flat, one
floor below ours. When she came to pick me up there a while
later, she was beside herself.

'Where is your father?' she barked at me.

'He didn't come with me. He dropped me off out the front,' I
said quietly. It wasn't my fault we were late and it wasn't my fault
that he hadn't walked me to our front door. But still I felt guilty.

'Jesus Christ! You are hours late. Here I've been, worrying. How
could he let you cross the courtyard by yourself? In the middle of
the night? Something could have happened to you. I'll tell you one
thing: You are not to see your father any more. I'm so sick and
tired of this and I won't put up with it any longer!'

When I was born on 17 February 1988, my mother was thirty-eight
years old and already had two grown-up daughters. She had had
my first half-sister when she was just eighteen years old and the
second came about a year later. That was at the end of the 1960s.
The two small children were more than my mother, who was on
her own, could handle. She and the girls' father had divorced soon
after the birth of my second half-sister. It was not easy for her to
make a living for her small family. She had to struggle, took a
pragmatic approach to things, was somewhat tough on herself
and did everything in order to get her children through. There was
no place in her life for sentimentality or a lack of assertiveness,
for leisure or lightness. At thirty-eight, now that both girls were
grown up, she was free from the obligations and worries of raising

a long while. It was exactly at that
mother had not counted on getting

born into was actually in the process of
gain. I turned everything on its head. All of
be brought out of storage, and daily life had
time to the needs of an infant. Even though I
was ╌╌╌╌ with joy and spoilt like a little princess by everybody, as a ╌╌╌ I sometimes felt like the third wheel. I had to fight
to establish myself in a world where all the roles had already been
assigned.

When I was born, my parents had been together for several
years. A customer of my mother's had introduced them. As a
trained seamstress, my mother had earned a living for herself and
her two daughters by selling and altering clothing for the women
in the neighbourhood. One of her customers was a woman from
the town of Süssenbrunn bei Wien, who ran a bakery and a small
grocery store with her husband and her son. Ludwig Koch Junior
accompanied his mother sometimes when she came to try on the
clothes and always stayed a bit longer than necessary to chat with
my mother. She soon fell in love with the young, handsome baker
who made her laugh with his stories. After a while, he moved in
with her and her two girls, into her flat in the large block of council
flats situated on the northern outskirts of Vienna.

Here, the edge of the city bleeds into the flat countryside of
the Marchfeld plain, unable to decide what exactly it wants to be.
It is an incongruous area with no centre and no identity, where
everything seems possible and chance reigns supreme. Commercial areas and factories stand surrounded by fallow fields where
dogs from the neighbouring council estates roam the unmowed
grassy areas in packs. In the midst of this, the nuclei of former
villages struggle to maintain their identities, which are peeling
away just as the paint slowly flakes off from the façades of the

small Biedermeier-era houses. They are relics of bygone days, slowly replaced by innumerable council flat buildings, utopias of social housing construction, set down in the middle of a green field with a grand gesture and left to fend for themselves. I grew up in one of the largest of these council estates.

The council flats located on Rennbahnweg were designed on a drawing board in the 1970s and built as the stony embodiment of urban planners' vision, urban planners looking to create a new environment for new people: happy, industrious families of the future, lodged in modern satellite cities characterized by clean lines, shopping centres and excellent public transport into Vienna.

At first glance, the experiment seems to have been successful. The council estate consists of 2,400 flats housing over 7,000 people. The courtyards between the tower blocks are generously proportioned and shaded by large trees. Playgrounds alternate with areas of concrete and large grassy sections. You can picture very clearly how urban planners placed miniatures of mothers with prams and children playing in their mock-ups and were convinced that they had created a space for an entirely new kind of shared environment. The flats, stacked one on top of the other in towers of up to fifteen storeys, were – compared to the stuffy and substandard tenement buildings closer to the centre – airy and well-proportioned, equipped with balconies and appointed with modern bathrooms.

But from the beginning the council estate was a catch-all for people originating from outside Vienna who had wanted to move to the city but had never quite made it that far: blue-collar workers from other Austrian provinces, such as Lower Austria, Burgenland and Styria. Slowly but surely, immigrants moved in as well with whom the other residents squabbled daily about minor issues, such as cooking smells, playing children and varying opinions regarding noise levels. The atmosphere in the area became more and more aggressive, and the nationalistic and xenophobic graffiti slogans increased. Shops with cheap merchandise opened up in the shopping centres, and milling about in the large squares in front of these were teenagers and people without jobs who drowned their frustrations in alcohol.

Today the council estate has been renovated, the tower blocks gleam in bright new colours and the Vienna underground station nearby has finally been completed. But when I lived there as a child, the Rennbahnsiedlung estate was viewed as a typical hotspot for social problems. It was considered dangerous to walk through the area at night, and during the day it was awkward having to pass the groups of teenagers who spent their time hanging around the courtyards and shouting dirty comments at women. My mother always hurried through the courtyards and stairwells holding tight to my hand. Despite being a resolute, quick-witted woman, she hated the coarse remarks she was subjected to at Rennbahnweg. She tried as best she could to protect me; she explained why she did not like it when she saw me playing in the courtyard and why she found the neighbours vulgar. Of course, as a child I was unable to really understand what she meant, but most of the time I did what she told me.

I vividly remember as a small girl how I resolved time and again to go down into the courtyard anyway and to play there. I spent hours getting ready, imagining what I would say to the other kids, and changed my clothes over and over. I chose toys for the sandbox and tossed them aside. I thought long and hard about what doll it would be best for me to take in order to make friends. But when I actually made it down to the courtyard, I never stayed longer than just a few minutes: I could never shake off the feeling that I didn't belong. Despite my lack of understanding, I had internalized my parents' negative attitude to such an extent that my own council estate remained unfamiliar territory. I preferred instead to escape in daydreams, lying on my bed in my room. That room – with its pink painted walls, light-coloured wall-to-wall carpet and patterned curtain sewn by my mother that was never opened even during the day – enshrouded me protectively. Here I forged great plans and spent hours thinking about where my path in life would likely lead. At any rate, I knew that I did not want to put down any roots here on the council estate.

For the first few months of my life I was the centre of our family. My sisters took care of the new baby as if they were practising for later in life. While one fed and changed my nappies, the other took me with her in the baby sling into the city centre to stroll up and down along the streets of Vienna's shopping districts where passers-by stopped to admire my wide smile and my pretty clothes. My mother was overjoyed when they told her about what had happened. She worked hard to make sure I looked good and out-fitted me from infancy with the prettiest clothes, which she spent long evenings sewing for me herself. She chose special fabrics, leafed through fashion magazines to find the latest sewing patterns or bought little accessories for me in boutiques. Everything was colour-coordinated, even my socks. In the midst of a neighbour-hood where many women went about wearing curlers in their hair and most men shuffled to the supermarket in shell-suit bottoms, I was turned out like a mini fashion model. This over-emphasis on outward appearances was not only an act of dis-tancing ourselves from our environment, it was also my mother's way of demonstrating how much she loved me.

Her brisk, resolute nature made it difficult for her to allow herself to show her emotions. She was not the type of person who was always hugging and cuddling a child. Tears and gushing pro-nouncements of love alike always made her uncomfortable. My mother, whose early pregnancies had forced her to grow up so quickly, had developed a thick skin over the years. She allowed herself no 'weaknesses' and refused to tolerate them in others. As a child I often watched her gain the upper hand on colds through sheer willpower and observed with fascination as she removed steaming hot dishes from the dishwasher without wincing. 'An Indian knows no pain' was her credo – a certain amount of toughness doesn't hurt, but actually helps you assert yourself in the world.

My father was just the opposite. He opened his arms wide when I wanted to cuddle him and had great fun playing with me – that is, when he was awake. During the time when he still lived with us, he was asleep more often than not when I saw him. My father loved going out at night, drinking copious amounts of alcohol with his friends. Consequently, he was ill suited to his trade. He had taken over the bakery from his father without ever really having any great interest in it. But having to get up so early in the morning caused him the greatest suffering. He stayed out in bars until midnight, and when the alarm clock rang at two in the morning it was extremely difficult to wake him. Once all of the rolls had been delivered, he lay on the couch for hours snoring. His enormous round belly raised and lowered formidably before my fascinated child's eyes. I played with the large sleeping man, placed teddy bears against his cheek, decorated him with ribbons and bows, put bonnets on him and painted his fingernails. When he awoke in the afternoon, he tossed me through the air, producing small surprises from his sleeves as if by magic. Then he would go out once again to make his rounds of the bars and cafés in town.

My grandmother became the most important point of reference for me during this time. With her – she ran the bakery together with my father – I felt completely safe and at home. She lived just a few minutes away from us by car and yet it was like another world. Süssenbrunn, situated on the northern outskirts of the city, is one of the oldest villages in Vienna, and the ever-encroaching city has never been able to destroy its rural character. The peaceful side streets are lined with old single-family dwellings with gardens where people still grow vegetables. My grandmother's house, which also included a small grocery and the bakery, still looked as nice as it did during the Austro-Hungarian empire.

My grandmother was originally from the Wachau, a picturesque region in the Danube valley where vineyards stretch across sunny terraced slopes. Her parents had been winegrowers and, as was the custom back then, my grandmother had to help out in the vineyards even at a very young age. She always spoke nostalgically of her childhood in the Wachau, made famous in Austria by the Hans Moser films from the 1950s, which romanticized the region as a dulcet idyll. In reality, her life in this panoramic landscape had mainly centred round work, work and more work. One day, on a ferry shuttling people to the other bank of the Danube, she met a baker from Spitz. She seized her opportunity to flee her predetermined life and married him. Ludwig Koch Senior was twenty-four years older than her, and it is difficult to imagine that love was the only motivation for her decision to marry. But as long as she lived she always spoke of her husband with great affection. I never got to know him, as he died shortly after I was born.

Even after all her years living in the city, my grandmother remained a rather eccentric country woman. She wore wool skirts and, over them, flowered aprons. She twisted her hair into curls and she smelled of a mixture of kitchen and *Franzbranntwein**, which enveloped me whenever I pressed my face into her skirts. I even liked the slight odour of alcohol that surrounded her. As the daughter of winegrowers, she always drank a large glass of wine at every meal as if it were water, without ever showing any

---

* A kind of rubbing alcohol made of camphor, menthol and various fragrances, such as spruce or pine needle oil.

signs of drunkenness. She remained true to her traditions, cooking meals on an old wood-fired stove and scouring her pots with an old-fashioned wire brush. She tended her flowers with particular devotion. Innumerable pots, pails and a long, old dough trough stood on exposed aggregate concrete slabs in the large courtyard behind her house, turning into islands of purple, yellow, white and pink blossoms every spring and summer. Apricots, cherries, plums and currants grew in the adjoining fruit orchard. The contrast between her house and our council estate at Rennbahnweg couldn't have been greater.

During the first years of my life, my grandmother was the epitome of 'home' for me. I often spent the night at her house, allowed her to spoil me with chocolate and cuddled up with her on her old couch. In the afternoons, I would visit a friend of mine in the village whose parents had a small swimming pool in their garden. I rode my bike through the village with the other children living on the streets and explored with curiosity an environment where I was free to wander as I pleased. My parents had opened a shop nearby and I sometimes rode my bike the short distance to my grandmother's house to surprise her with a visit. I still remember that she would often be sitting under the hairdryer, which drowned out the doorbell and my knocking. Then I would climb over the fence, sneak up to her from behind and have great fun startling her. She would laugh and shoo me through the kitchen with curlers still in her hair – 'Just you wait till I get my hands on you!' – and sentence me to work in the garden as 'punishment'. I loved picking dark red cherries with her off the tree or snapping the over-full branches of currants carefully from the bushes.

My grandmother not only provided me with a small slice of a carefree and loving childhood, but I also learned from her how to create space for feelings in a world that did not allow emotions to come to the surface. On my visits, I accompanied her nearly daily to a small cemetery a little outside the village, surrounded by a wide-open field. My grandfather's grave, with its shiny black tombstone, was located all the way at the back along a newly created gravel pathway near the cemetery wall. During the summer the sun beats down on the graves, and except for the occasional passing car along the main street, the only thing you can hear is the humming of the crickets and the flocks of birds flying above the fields. My grandmother would place fresh flowers on the grave, crying softly to herself. When I was small, I always tried to comfort her, saying, 'Don't cry, Grandma – Grandpa wants to see you smile!' Later, when I was old enough to go to primary school, I understood that the women in my family, unwilling to show any weakness in their daily lives, needed a place where they could let their emotions run free. A protected place that belonged only to them.

When I was older, the afternoons spent with my grandmother's friends, who often joined us in visiting the cemetery, began to bore me. Though I had once loved being fed cakes and asked questions by old ladies about anything and everything, I had now reached the age when I simply had no more desire to sit in old-fashioned living rooms full of dark furniture and lace doilies, where you were not allowed to touch anything, while the ladies bragged about their grandchildren. At the time, my grandmother felt insulted when I 'turned away from her'. 'I'll just go and find myself another granddaughter,' she informed me one day. I was deeply hurt when she actually began to give ice cream and sweets to another, smaller, girl who came into her shop regularly.

Although that disagreement was soon cleared up, from then on my visits to Süssenbrunn grew less frequent. My mother had an uneasy relationship with her mother-in-law anyway, so it was not inconvenient for her that I was no longer to spend the night there so often. But even though the relationship became less close when I began primary school, as is the case with most grandmothers and grandchildren, she always remained my touchstone.

For she gave me the sense of safety and security that I lacked at home.

Three years before I was born, my parents opened a small grocery with a *Stüberl*, an adjoining café, in the Marco-Polo-Siedlung council estate, about fifteen minutes by car from Rennbahnweg. In 1988, they took over yet another grocery located on Pröbstlgasse in Süssenbrunn, situated on the main road running through the village and just a few hundred metres from my grandmother's house. In a single-storey, antique pink corner house with an old-fashioned door and a shop counter from the 1960s, they sold baked goods, ready-to-eat foods, newspapers and special magazines for lorry drivers, who made their final stop here on this arterial road on the outskirts of Vienna. The shelves were stocked with the small things required for everyday life that people still bought from the corner grocery even though they now had access to the local supermarket: small cardboard packages with laundry detergent, noodles, instant soups and, most of all, sweets. An old cold storehouse painted pink stood in the small back courtyard.

These two shops later became the central pillars of my childhood, in addition to my grandmother's house. I spent countless afternoons after kindergarten or school at the shop in the Marco-Polo-Siedlung while my mother balanced the accounts or waited on customers. I played hide-and-seek with the other children or rolled down the small sledding hill the municipality had made. The council estate was smaller and quieter than ours; I was free to explore as I pleased and found it easy to make friends. From the shop I was able to observe the customers in the café: housewives, men coming home from work, and others who began drinking beer even in the late morning, ordering a grilled cheese sandwich to go with it. Such shops were slowly disappearing from the cities and, with their longer opening hours, the serving of alcohol and their personal atmosphere, my parents' shops filled an important niche for many people.

My father was responsible for the bakery and for delivering the baked goods, while my mother took care of everything else. When I was about five years old, he began to take me with him on his delivery rounds. We drove in the van through the rambling suburbs and villages, stopping in restaurants, bars and cafés, at hotdog stands and in smaller shops as well. For that reason I probably became better acquainted with the area north of the Danube than any other kid my age – and spent more time in bars and cafés than was perhaps appropriate. I enjoyed spending so much time with my father immensely and felt like I was very grown up and being taken seriously. But our delivery rounds had their downside as well.

'What a sweet girl!' I probably heard that a thousand times. I don't have pleasant memories of it, although I was on the receiving end of compliments and the centre of attention. The people who pinched my cheeks and bought me chocolate were unfamiliar. Besides, I hated being pushed into a spotlight that I had not sought out myself. It left in me only a deep-seated feeling of embarrassment.

My father was a jovial man who loved to make a grand entrance. His little daughter in her freshly pressed dresses was the perfect accessory and he enjoyed showing me off to his customers. He had friends everywhere – so many that even as a child I recognized that not all of these people could really be close to him. Most of them let him buy them a drink, or borrowed money from him. In an effort to fulfil his need for approval, he was happy to pay.

I sat on barstools in these smoky pubs and listened to grown-ups whose interest in me quickly dissipated. A large number of them were unemployed and had failed at life, spending their days drinking beer and wine and playing cards. Many of them had

had a profession at one time, had been teachers or civil servants, and had just fallen through the cracks of life. Today we call that 'burnout syndrome'. Back then this was part of the normal fabric of life on the outskirts of the big city.

Only rarely did someone ask me what I was doing in these places. Most of them just took it for granted and were friendly to me in an exaggerated way. 'My big girl,' said my father approvingly, patting my cheek with his hand. When someone bought me sweets or a soft drink, payment in kind was expected in return: 'Give Uncle So-and-So a kiss. Give Aunty here one too.' I resisted such close contact with strangers, who I resented for stealing my father's attention, attention that was supposed to be mine. These delivery rounds were a constant emotional roller-coaster: one moment I was the centre of attention, presented to the group and given a sweet, while the next I was ignored so completely that I could have been run over by a car and it not be noticed. This fluctuation between attention and neglect in a world of superficial interactions chipped away at my self-esteem. I learned to play-act my way to the centre of attention and keep myself there for as long as possible. Only nowadays have I begun to understand that this attraction I have for the stage, the dream of acting that I had nurtured from my earliest days, did not come from within me. It was my way of imitating my extrovert parents – and a way to survive in a world in which you were either admired or ignored.

Just a little while later, this roller-coaster ride of attention and neglect began to extend to my closest environment. The world of my early childhood slowly began to crack. At first, only small cracks appeared, barely noticeable in the familiarity of my surroundings so that I still took little notice of them, blaming myself as the cause of all the discord. But then the cracks grew bigger until our entire family structure imploded. My father realized much too late that he had pushed things a little too far and that my mother had already long made up her mind to leave him. He continued to behave extravagantly, like a king of the urban fringe area, who went from bar to bar and bought himself large expensive cars time and again. The Mercedes or Cadillacs were meant to impress his 'friends'. He borrowed the money to buy them. Whenever he gave me a small allowance, he would borrow it right back again to buy cigarettes or to go out for coffee. He took out so many loans on my grandmother's house that it was seized as payment. By the mid 1990s he had accumulated so much debt that it endangered the existence of our family. In the process of his debt-restructuring, my mother took over the grocery in Süssenbrunn and the shop in the Marco-Polo-Siedlung. But the cracks went far beyond finances. At some point my mother had just had enough of a man who liked to party, but who had no idea of the meaning of dependability.

The gradual separation of my parents changed my entire life. Instead of being pampered and spoilt, I got left by the wayside. My parents spent hours arguing loudly. They took turns locking themselves in the bedroom, while the other would continue to shout in the living room. When I timidly tried to ask what was going on, they put me in my room, closed the door and continued fighting. I felt caged up in there and didn't know what the world was coming to. I buried my head in my pillow to try to shut out the loud rows and transport myself back to my earlier, carefree childhood. Only rarely was I able to do this. I simply could not understand why my once beaming father now seemed helpless and lost, unable to produce little surprises from his sleeve as if by magic to cheer me up. His inexhaustible supply of gummi bears seemed to have suddenly dried up.

After one heated quarrel, my mother even left the flat, not returning for several days. She wanted to show my father how it felt to have no idea where your partner was. For him, one or two nights away from home was nothing unusual. But I was much too young to understand her ulterior motives, and I was afraid. At that age you have a different sense of time and my mother's absence seemed interminable to me. I had no idea whether she would ever come back at all. The feeling of abandonment, of being rejected, became deep-seated within me. A phase of my childhood began in which I was no longer able to find my place, in which I no longer felt loved. The small, self-assured person I had been was gradually transformed into an insecure girl who ceased to trust the people closest to her.

It was during these difficult times that I started pre-school, or *Kindergarten* as we call it. This was a moment when other people's control over my life, which I had such difficulty coping with as a child, reached a high point.

My mother had registered me at a private pre-school close to where we lived. From the very beginning I felt misunderstood and so unaccepted that I began to hate pre-school. The very first day I experienced something that laid the cornerstone for these feelings. I was outside with the other children in the garden and I discovered a tulip that held great fascination for me. I bent over the flower, pulling it carefully towards me with my hand in order to take a sniff. The teacher must have thought that I was about to pick the flower. With one sharp movement, she slapped the back of my hand. I called out indignantly, 'I'm going to tell my mother!' However, that evening I was forced to realize that now she had delegated authority over me to someone else, my mother was no longer on my side. When I told her about the incident, convinced that she would defend me in solidarity and admonish the teacher the very next day, she merely said that that was the way things were in school, that you had to follow the rules. And, moreover, 'I'm just not going to get involved, because I wasn't even there to see it.' This statement became her standard answer when I came to her with problems I had with the pre-school teachers. And whenever I told her about bullying by the other kids, she merely said, 'Then you just have to hit back.' I had to learn to overcome difficulties by myself. The time I spent in pre-school was a tough period in my life. I hated the strict rules. I rebelled at having to lie down after lunch with the other kids in the nap room although I wasn't at all tired. The teachers went about their daily routines without expressing any particular interest in us. While they kept one eye on us, they read novels and magazines with the other, gossiping and painting their fingernails.

I was only able to make friends with the other children very slowly, and though surrounded by kids the same age I felt lonelier than before.

> Risk factors, primarily with secondary enuresis, are links to a sense of loss in the broadest sense, such as parents' splitting up, divorce, death, the birth of a sibling, extreme poverty, delinquency on the part of parents, deprivation, neglect, a lack of support for developmental milestones.

This is the dictionary definition for the causes of the problem I was forced to deal with during that time. I went from being a precocious child, who had quickly been able to do without nappies, to a bed-wetter. Bed-wetting became a stigma that blighted my life. The wet patches in my bed every night were the source of never-ending scolding and ridicule.

When I had wet my bed for the nth time, my mother reacted in a manner that was common at the time. She thought it was wilful behaviour on my part that could be trained out of a child by force and punishment. She spanked my behind and asked angrily, 'Why are you doing this to me?' She railed, despaired and was powerless to do anything. And I continued to wet my bed night after night. My mother bought rubber sheets and put them on my bed. It was a humiliating experience. From discussions with friends of my grandmother I knew that rubber pads and special sheets were used for the old and infirm. I just wanted to be treated like a big girl. But I couldn't stop. My mother woke me up during the night to put me on the toilet. But I wet the bed anyway, and she changed my sheets and my pyjamas, swearing all the while. Sometimes I would wake up dry in the mornings and proud of it, but she quickly put a damper on my happiness, bluffing, 'You just can't remember that I had to change you once again in the middle of the night. Just look at the pyjamas you're wearing.' These were accusations I was unable to counter. She punished me with disdain and ridicule. When I asked for undergarments for my Barbie doll, she laughed at me, saying that I would just wet them anyway. I was so embarrassed I wished the ground would swallow me up.

Finally she began to monitor how much I was drinking. I had always been a thirsty child, drinking copiously and frequently. But now my drinking was precisely regulated. I was only given a little to drink during the day and nothing more at night. The more prohibited water or juices became, the greater my thirst, until I could think of nothing else. Every swallow, every trip to the toilet, was observed and commented on, but only when we were alone – otherwise what would people think.

In pre-school, the bed-wetting took on a new dimension. I began to wet myself during the day as well. The other children laughed at me, and the teachers simply egged them on, embarrassing me time and again in front of the group. They probably thought that the ridicule would make me control my bladder better. But every humiliation only made it worse. A trip to the toilet or a drink of water became torture. They were forced upon me when I did not want them and denied me when I desperately needed them. We had to ask for permission to go to the toilet and in my case, every time I asked, I was told, 'But you just went. Why do you have to go again?' Vice versa, they forced me to go to the toilet before any outings, before eating, before my afternoon nap, and monitored me while I did it. Once, when the teachers suspected me of having wet myself again, they even forced me to show all the other children my knickers.

Each time I left the house with my mother, she always brought along a bag with a change of clothes. The bundle of clothing reinforced my feelings of shame and insecurity. It was as if the adults seemed to expect me to wet myself. And the more they expected it, and the more they scolded and ridiculed me, the more they were proven right. It was a vicious circle that I could not find a way out of throughout primary school. I remained a ridiculed, humiliated and perpetually thirsty bed-wetter.

After two years of quarrelling and a number of attempts at reconciliation, my father finally moved out for good. I was now five years old and I had gone from being a cheerful toddler to an insecure, taciturn person who no longer liked life and sought out various ways to protest. Sometimes I withdrew, sometimes I screamed, vomited and had outbursts of crying from the pain and the feeling of being misunderstood. I once suffered with gastritis for weeks.

My mother, who was also reeling from the break-up, transferred her way of dealing with it to me. Just as she swallowed the pain and uncertainty and carried on bravely, she demanded that I keep a stiff upper lip as well. She had a very difficult time understanding that, as a small child, I was completely incapable of doing so. When I became too emotional for her, she reacted aggressively to my outbursts. She accused me of feeling sorry for myself and either tried to tempt me with treats or threatened punishment if I didn't stop.

My anger at a situation that was incomprehensible to me gradually turned against the one person who had remained after my father had moved out: my mother. More than once I was so angry at her that I resolved to move out. I packed a few of my things in my gym bag and said farewell to her. But she knew that I wouldn't get any further than the door and remarked on my behaviour with a wink, saying, 'OK, take care.' Another time I removed all of the dolls that she had given me from my room and placed them in a row in the hallway. I meant for her to see that I had resolved to lock her out of the realm that was my room. But, of course, these attempts to outmanoeuvre my mother were not a solution to my actual problem. When my parents split up, I had lost the anchors of stability in my life and was unable to continue relying on the people who had previously always been there for me.

The disregard I suffered slowly destroyed my self-esteem. When you think of violence perpetrated on children, you picture systematic, heavy blows that result in bodily injuries. I experienced none of that in my childhood. It was rather a mixture of verbal oppression and occasional 'old school' slaps across the face that showed me that as a child I was the weaker one.

It was not anger or cold calculation that drove my mother to do it, but rather an aggression that flared up, shot out of her like a flash and was doused just as quickly. She slapped me when she felt overburdened or when I had done something wrong. She hated it when I whined, asked her questions or queried any of her explanations – that too earned me another slap.

At that time and in that area it was not unusual to treat children that way. Quite the contrary – I had a much 'easier' life than many of the other kids in my neighbourhood. In the courtyard I was able to observe time and again mothers screaming at their children, pushing them to the ground and pummelling them. My mother would never have done such a thing, and her way of casually slapping me across the face would certainly not have shocked anyone. When she slapped me in public, nobody intervened – though, for the most part, she was too much of a lady to even risk being observed. Open violence, that was something the other women in our council estate engaged in. I was required to wipe away my tears or cool my cheek before I left the house or climbed out of the car.

At the same time, my mother also tried to assuage her guilty conscience with gifts. She and my father competed to buy me the prettiest clothes or to take me on outings at the weekend. But I didn't want any gifts. At that phase of my life the only thing I needed was someone to give me unconditional love and support, something my parents were not able to do.

A memory from my primary school years demonstrates the extent to which I had internalized the fact that I could expect no help from adults. I was about eight years old and had travelled with my class to spend a week on a school retreat to the country in the province of Styria. I was not an athletic child and did not dare play any of the wild games that other children liked to play. But I wanted to brave at least one attempt on the playground.

The pain shot sharply through my arm as I fell from the monkey bars and hit the ground. I tried to sit up, but my arm gave out, causing me to fall back. The cheerful laughter from the children all around me on the playground rang hollowly in my ears. I wanted to scream. Tears ran down my cheeks, but I couldn't make a sound. It wasn't until a schoolmate of mine came over that I was able to ask her to get the teacher. The girl ran to her, but the teacher sent her back to tell me that I had to come over myself if I wanted something.

I struggled once again to get up, but I hardly had to move for the pain in my arm to return. I remained helplessly lying on the ground. It wasn't until sometime later that the teacher from another class helped me up. I clenched my teeth and didn't complain. I didn't want to be any trouble to anyone. Later my teacher noticed that something was wrong with me. She suspected that I was bruised from the fall and permitted me to spend the afternoon in the television room.

That night I lay in my bed in the dormitory, and the pain was so bad I could hardly breathe. Still, I didn't ask for help. It wasn't until late the next day when we were visiting the Herberstein zoological park that my teacher realized I had seriously injured myself and took me to the doctor. He immediately sent me to the hospital in Graz. My arm was broken.

My mother came with her boyfriend to pick me up from the hospital. The new man in her life was well known to me – my godfather. I didn't like him. The ride to Vienna was a hellish ordeal. For three long hours my mother's boyfriend complained that they had to drive such a long way just because of my clumsiness. My mother tried to lighten the mood, but she couldn't make him cease his criticisms. I sat in the back seat and cried softly to myself. I was ashamed that I had fallen, and I was ashamed of the trouble I was causing everyone. *Don't make trouble. Don't make a scene. Don't be hysterical. Big girls don't cry.* These mantras from my childhood, heard a thousand times, had enabled me to bear the pain of my broken arm for a day and a half. Now, as we drove along the motorway, a voice inside my head was repeating them in between the tirades my mother's boyfriend was letting loose.

My teacher had to face disciplinary proceedings because she had failed to take me to the hospital immediately. It was certainly true that she had neglected her duty to supervise me. But I was myself largely responsible for the neglect. My confidence in my own perceptions was so minimal that not even with a broken arm did I have the feeling that I was allowed to ask for help.

In the meantime, I only saw my father at the weekends or when he took me with him on his delivery routes. He too had fallen in love again after separating from my mother. His girlfriend was nice, but reserved. Once she mused to me, 'Now I know why you are so difficult. Your parents don't love you.' I protested loudly, but the observation haunted my wounded childish soul. Maybe she was right? After all, she was a grown-up, and grown-ups were always right.

I couldn't shake the thought for days.

When I was nine I began using food to compensate for my frustrations. I had never been a thin child and had grown up in a family where food played a major role. My mother was the kind of woman who could eat as much as she wanted without gaining a pound. It might have been due to hyperactivity of the thyroid or just her active nature. She ate slices of bread with lard and cake, roast pork with caraway and ham sandwiches. She didn't gain any weight and never got tired of emphasizing that to others: 'I can eat whatever I want,' she piped, holding a slice of bread with a fatty spread on it in her hand. I inherited her lack of moderation with food, but not her ability to burn up all those calories.

On the other hand, my father was so fat that I was embarrassed as a child to be seen with him. His stomach was enormous and the skin stretched as taut as the belly of a woman eight months pregnant. When he lay on the couch, his stomach jutted upwards like a mountain, and as a child I often patted it, asking, 'When's the baby due?' My father would just laugh good-naturedly. Piles of meat were always stacked on his plate, and he had to have several large dumplings, which swam in a veritable ocean of sauce. He devoured huge portions and continued to eat even when he was no longer hungry.

When we went on our family daytrips at the weekend – first together with my mother, later with his new girlfriend – everything centred around food and eating. While other families went hiking in the mountains, biking or visited museums, we headed to culinary destinations. He drove to a new wine tavern or went on trips to country inns located in castles, not for the historical guided tours, but to take part in medieval-style banquets: piles of meat and dumplings that you pushed into your mouths with your hands, mugs of beer to wash them down – this was the kind of daytrip that appealed to my father.

And I was constantly surrounded by food in the two shops, the one in Süssenbrunn and the one in the Marco-Polo-Siedlung that my mother had taken over after splitting up with my father. When my mother picked me up from afterschool care and took me to the shop, I kept boredom at bay by eating: an ice cream, gummi bears, a piece of chocolate, a pickle. My mother usually gave in – she was too busy to pay close attention to everything I was stuffing into my mouth.

Now I began to overeat systematically. I would devour an entire packet of Bounty chocolate bars, drink a large bottle of Coke, and then top it off with more chocolate until my stomach was stretched ready to burst. When I was barely able to put anything more in my mouth, I began eating again. The last year before my abduction I gained so much weight that I had gone from being chubby to being a really fat young girl. I exercised even less, and the other kids teased me even more. And I compensated for my loneliness by eating all the more. On my tenth birthday I weighed forty-five kilos.

My mother would frustrate me further by saying, 'I like you anyway, no matter what you look like.' Or: 'You only have to put an ugly child in a pretty dress.' When I became offended, she laughed and said, 'Don't think I mean you, sweetie. Don't be so sensitive.' 'Sensitive' – that was the worst. You were not allowed to be sensitive. Today I am often surprised at how positively the word 'sensitive' is used. When I was a child, it was an insult for people who were too soft for this world. Back then I wished I could have been allowed to be softer. Later on, the toughness that chiefly my mother had imposed on me probably saved my life.

Surrounded by sweets of all sorts, I spent hours alone in front of the television or in my room with a book in my hand. I wanted to flee from this reality, which held nothing but humiliations in store for me, to other worlds. At home our TV had all of the channels available and nobody really paid any attention to what I was watching. I flipped through the channels aimlessly, watching kids' programmes, news and crime stories that frightened me, and still I soaked them up like a sponge. In the summer of 1997 one issue dominated the media: in the Salzkammergut, one of Austria's lake districts predominantly located in Upper Austria, the police discovered a child pornography ring. Horrified, I heard on the TV that seven grown men had lured an unknown number of small boys into a specially equipped room in a house by offering them small amounts of money. There, they molested them and made videos of what they did that were sold all over the world. On 24 January 1998 yet another scandal shook Austria. Videos of the molestation of girls between the ages of five and seven had been sent out through the mail. One video showed a man luring a seven-year-old girl from her neighbourhood into an attic room, where he had severely molested her.

Even more disturbing to me were the reports of girls who had been murdered by a serial killer in Germany. To my recollection, hardly a month went by during my primary school years that the media didn't report yet another abducted, raped or murdered girl. The news programmes spared almost no detail describing the dramatic search operations and police investigations. I saw sniffer dogs in forests and divers who combed lakes and ponds for the bodies of the missing girls. Again and again I listened to the horrific stories of the family members: how the girls had disappeared while playing outdoors or simply failed to come home from school; how their parents had desperately searched for them until they received the terrible news that they would never see their children alive again.

The reports throughout the media at the time were so pervasive that we discussed them in school as well. The teachers explained to us how we could protect ourselves from attacks. We watched films where girls were molested by their older brothers, or where boys learned to say 'No!' to their grabby fathers. And our teachers reiterated the warnings that had been hammered into us children repeatedly at home: 'Never go anywhere with strangers! Never get into a strange car. Never accept sweets from a stranger. And cross to the other side of the street if something seems strange to you.'

When I look at the list of cases that occurred during those years, I'm as shaken as I was back then:

- Yvonne (twelve years old) was beaten to death in July 1995 on Lake Pinnow (Brandenburg) because she resisted the man trying to rape her.
- Annette (fifteen years old), from Mardorf on Lake Steinhude, was found naked, sexually molested and murdered in 1995 in a cornfield. The perpetrator was not caught.
- Maria (seven years old) was abducted, molested and thrown into a pond in Haldensleben (Sachsen-Anhalt) in November 1995.
- Elmedina (six years old) was abducted, molested and suffocated in February 1996 in Siegen.
- Claudia (eleven years old) was abducted, molested and burned to death in Grevenbroich in May 1996.
- Ulrike (thirteen years old) never returned from an outing on a pony-drawn carriage on 11 June 1996. Her body was found two years later.
- Ramona (ten years old) disappeared without a

     trace from a shopping centre on 15 August 1996 in
     Jena. Her body was found in January 1997 near
     Eisenach.

- Natalie (seven years old) was abducted,
  molested and murdered by a 29-year-old man
  on 20 September 1996 in Epfach in Upper
  Bavaria on her way to school.
- Kim (ten years old), from Varel in Frisia, was
  abducted, molested and murdered in January 1997.
- Anne-Katrin (eight years old) was found beaten to
  death on 9 June 1997 near her parents' house in
  Seebeck in Brandenburg.
- Loren (nine years old) was molested and murdered
  in the basement of her parents' house in Prenzlau
  by a 20-year-old man in July 1997.
- Jennifer (eleven years old) was lured by her uncle
  into his car, molested and strangled on 13 January
  1998 in Versmold near Gütersloh.
- Carla (twelve years old) was attacked on her way to
  school on 22 January 1998 in Wilhermsdorf near
  Fürth, molested and thrown unconscious into a
  pond. She died five days later in a coma.

The cases involving Jennifer and Carla hit me particularly hard.
Jennifer's uncle confessed after his arrest that he wanted to sexually
molest the girl in his car. When she resisted, he strangled her and
hid her body in the woods. The reports really got under my skin.
The psychologists interviewed on TV advised us back then not to
resist the attackers so as not to risk being killed. Even more horrific
were the TV reports about Carla's murder. I can still see the
reporters in my mind's eye; I can picture them standing in front
of the pond in Wilhermsdorf, explaining that the police could tell
from the churned-up earth just how much the girl had resisted.
The funeral service was broadcast on television. I sat in front of

my TV with eyes wide open in fear. Only one thing calmed me when I saw her pictures in the news: I was not the blonde, delicate girl that child molesters seemed to prefer.

I had no idea how wrong I was.

2

What Could Happen Anyway?

The Last Day of My Old Life

The day after returning from my father's weekend house, I woke up angry and sad. The anger at my mother's wrath, which was aimed at my father but had been taken out on me, made my chest tighten. I was even more upset at the fact that she had forbidden me from ever seeing him again. It was one of those decisions that adults make over the heads of children, out of anger or caused by a sudden mood, without thinking that it isn't just about them, but rather about the deepest needs of those who are helplessly faced with such pronouncements.

I hated this feeling of powerlessness – a feeling that reminded me that I was still a child. I wanted to finally be more grown up in the hope that these altercations with my mother wouldn't get under my skin so much. I wanted to learn how to swallow my feelings, including those deep-seated fears that fights between parents always trigger in children.

As of my tenth birthday I had put the first and least self-sufficient phase of my life behind me. The magic date that was to officially mark my independence was drawing closer: just eight more years to go, then I would move out and get a job. Then I would no longer be dependent on the decisions of grown-ups around me who cared more about their petty quarrels and jealousies than my needs and wants. Just eight more years that I would take advantage of to prepare myself for a life in which I would make the decisions.

I had already taken an important step towards independence several weeks earlier: I had convinced my mother to allow me to walk to school by myself. Although I was in the fourth grade, she had always driven me to school, dropping me off in front of the building. The trip didn't take more than five minutes. Every day I was embarrassed in front of the other kids for my helplessness, on display to everyone as I got out of the car and my mother gave me a goodbye kiss. I had been negotiating with her for quite a while that it was high time for me to get the hang of walking to school alone. I wanted to show not just my parents, but also myself, that I was no longer a little child. And that I could conquer my fears.

My insecurity was something that rankled me deep down inside. It would come over me even as I was making my way down the stairwell. It grew as I crossed the courtyard and became a dominating emotion as I ran through the streets of the council estate at Rennbahnsiedlung. I felt unprotected and tiny, and hated myself for feeling that way. That day I made a resolution: I wanted to try to be strong. I wanted that day to be the first day of my new life and the last day of my old one. Looking back, it seems rather ironic that it was precisely that day my life as I knew it actually *did* end, albeit in a way that I could not possibly have imagined.

Decisively, I pushed the patterned duvet aside and got out of bed. As always, my mother had laid out the clothes I was supposed to put on: a dress with a denim top and a skirt made of grey tartan flannel. I felt shapeless in it, constrained, as if the dress was holding me down tightly in a stage that I had long wanted to grow out of.

Grumbling, I slipped it on, then passed though the hallway into the kitchen. My mother had prepared my packed sandwiches and left them on the table wrapped in the napkin which bore the logo from the small café in the Marco-Polo-Siedlung and her name. When it was time to leave the house, I put on my red anorak and my rucksack. I petted the cats and said goodbye to them. Then I opened the door to the stairwell and went out. Almost out the door, I stopped and hesitated, thinking of what my mother had told me a dozen times before: 'You must never part in anger. You never know if we'll ever see each other again!' She could be angry, she was impulsive, and she would often slap me on the spur of the moment. But when it was time to say goodbye she was always very loving. Should I really leave without saying a word? I turned round, but then inside me rose the feeling of disappointment that the previous evening had left behind. I would not give her any more kisses and would instead punish her with my silence. Besides, what could happen anyway?

'What could happen anyway?' I mumbled half to myself. My words echoed down the staircase with its grey tiling. That question became the mantra that accompanied me out on to the street and through the block of houses to school. My mantra, arming me against my fear and my guilty conscience for not having said goodbye.

I left the council block, ran along an endless wall and waited at the pedestrian crossing. A tram rattled past, stuffed to the brim with people heading to work. My courage evaporated. Everything around me suddenly seemed much too big. The argument with my mother weighed on me, and the feeling that I was sinking in this new labyrinth of relationships between my quarrelling parents and their new partners, who did not accept me, made me fearful. I had wanted to feel the sensation of embarking on something new that day, but that once again gave way to the certainty that I would have to struggle to find my place in this entangled network of relationships. And how would I ever be able to change my life if a mere pedestrian crossing loomed before me like an insurmountable obstacle?

I began to cry and felt the overpowering desire to simply disappear and vanish into thin air. I let the traffic flow by and imagined myself walking into the street and being hit by a car. It would drag me along for a few metres, and then I would be dead. My rucksack would be lying right next to me and my red jacket would be like a stop light on the asphalt, crying out, 'Just look at what you've done to this girl!' My mother would come running out of the building, cry over me and realize all of her mistakes. Yes, she would. For certain.

Of course, I did not jump in front of a car, nor in front of the tram. I would never have wanted to draw so much attention to myself. Instead I pulled myself together, crossed the street and walked down Rennbahnweg towards my primary school, located on Brioschiweg. My route took me through a couple of quiet side streets lined with small family houses built in the 1950s with modest front gardens. In an area characterized by industrial buildings and residential estates with prefabricated concrete tower blocks, they seemed anachronistic and yet calming. As I turned on to Melangasse, I wiped the remaining tears from my face and trotted along with my head down.

I don't remember any longer what caused me to lift my head. A noise? A bird? In any case, my eyes focused on a delivery van. It was parked alongside the street on the right-hand side and seemed strangely out of place in these peaceful surroundings. A man was standing in front of the delivery van. He was lean, not very tall, seemed young and somehow glanced around aimlessly, as if he were waiting for something and didn't know what.

I slowed my pace and stiffened. A fear that I could hardly put my finger on returned instantly, making the hair on the back of my neck stand up and covering my arms with goose bumps. Immediately I felt the impulse to cross to the other side of the street. A rapid sequence of images and fragments of sentences raced through my head: don't talk to strange men . . . don't climb into strange cars . . . abduction . . . child molestation . . . the many horror stories I had heard on the TV about girls being abducted.

But if I really wanted to be grown up, I couldn't allow myself to give in to my impulse. I had to overcome my fear and I forced myself to keep walking. What could happen after all, I asked myself. The walk to school was my test. I would pass it without deviating.

Looking back, I can no longer say why the sight of the delivery van set off alarm bells inside me: it might have been intuition, although it is likely that any man I had encountered in an unusual situation on the street would have frightened me. Being abducted was, in my childish eyes, something that was a realistic possibility – but deep down inside it was still something that happened only on TV, and certainly not in my neighbourhood.

When I had come within about two metres of the man on the street, he looked me right in the eye. At that moment my fear vanished. He had blue eyes, and with his almost too-long hair he looked like a university student from one of those old made-for-TV movies from the 1970s. His gaze seemed strangely empty. That is one poor man, I thought, because he gave me the feeling that he was in need of protection; at that very moment I felt the desire to help him. That may sound odd, like a child holding tight at all costs to the naive belief that there is good in everyone. But when he looked at me squarely for the first time that morning, he seemed lost and very vulnerable.

Yes, I would pass this test. I would walk by him, giving him the berth the narrow pavement afforded. I did not like bumping into people and wanted to move out of his way far enough so that I could avoid touching him.

Then everything happened so fast.

The very moment I lowered my eyes and went to walk past the man, he grabbed me by the waist and threw me through the open door into his delivery van. Everything happened in one fell swoop, as if it had been a choreographed scene, as if we had rehearsed it together. A choreography of terror.

Did I scream? I don't think so. And yet everything inside me was one single scream. It pushed upwards and became lodged far down in my throat: a silent scream as if one of those nightmares had become reality where you try to scream but no sound comes out; where you try to run but your legs move as if trapped in quicksand.

Did I fight back? Did I get in the way of his perfect choreography? I must have fought back, because the next day I had a black eye. I can't remember the pain inflicted by that blow, only the feeling of paralysing helplessness. The kidnapper had an easy time of it with me. He was 1.72 metres tall, while I was only 1.45 metres. I was plump and not particularly quick anyway. Plus, my heavy school bag hindered my mobility. The whole thing had only taken a few seconds.

The moment the delivery van door closed behind me I was well aware of the fact that I had been kidnapped and that I would probably die. In my mind's eye I saw the images from Jennifer's funeral. Jennifer had been molested in a car and killed when she tried to escape. Images of Carla's parents waiting for word of their daughter. Carla, who had been molested, was found unconscious floating in a pond and died a week later. I had wondered back then what that would be like: dying and what comes after. Whether you felt pain just before, and whether you really see a light.

These images mixed with the jumble of thoughts that flashed through my mind at the same time. *Is this really happening? To me?* asked one voice. *What a completely off-the-wall idea, kidnapping a child. That never turns out well*, said another. *Why me? I'm short and chubby, I don't really fit the profile of a typical abduction victim*, pleaded another.

The kidnapper's voice brought me back to the present. He ordered me to sit down on the floor at the back of the van and barked at me not to move. If I didn't do what he said, I would be in for a nasty surprise. Then he climbed over the front seat and drove off.

Because the cab and the back of the delivery van were not separated, I was able to see him from the back. And I heard him frantically punching numbers into his car phone. But he couldn't seem to reach anyone.

In the meantime the questions continued to pound in my head: *Will he blackmail my family for ransom? Who will pay it? Where is he taking me? What kind of car is this? What time is it?* The windows of the delivery van were blacked out with the exception of a narrow strip along the upper edge. From the floor of the van I couldn't tell where we were going, and I didn't dare lift my head to look out of the windows. It seemed we had been driving for quite some time and were not headed anywhere in particular. I quickly lost any sense of space or time. But the treetops and the utility poles that kept whizzing by made me feel like we were driving around in circles in my neighbourhood.

Talk. You have to talk to him. But how? How do you talk to a criminal? Criminals don't deserve any respect, so it didn't seem appropriate to address him using the *Sie* form in German used for strangers and persons of respect. So I decided on *du*, the form of address that had, until now, been reserved for people who were close to me.

Absurdly enough, I asked him first what size shoes he wore. I had remembered that from watching TV shows like *Aktenzeichen XY ungelöst**. You had to be able to give an exact description of the perpetrator; even the slightest detail was important. Naturally, I didn't get an answer. Instead the man snapped at me to be quiet and nothing would happen to me. Even today I don't know how

---

* A German television show produced in cooperation with the Swiss and Austrian public service broadcasters describing unsolved crimes and eliciting help from viewers in finding the perpetrator(s); similar to the BBC programme *Crimewatch*.

I managed to get up enough courage to disregard his order. Maybe because I was certain that I was going to die anyway – that things couldn't get any worse.

'Are you going to molest me?' was my next question.

This time I got an answer. 'You're too young for that,' he said. 'I would never do that.' Then he made another phone call.

After he had hung up he said, 'I'm going to take you to a forest and turn you over to the others. Then I'll be able to wash my hands of this business.' He repeated that sentence several times, rapid-fire and agitated: 'I will turn you over, and then I'll have nothing more to do with you. We'll never see each other again.'

If he had intended to scare me, then he had found exactly the right words. The pronouncement that he was going to hand me over to 'others' took my breath away. I went rigid with fear. He didn't need to say anything more; I knew what he meant. Child pornography rings had been all over the media for months. Since last summer hardly a week had gone by without some discussion of the people who abducted and molested children while filming it on video. In my mind's eye I saw everything perfectly: groups of men would pull me into a basement and grope me all over while others took pictures. Up until that moment I had been convinced that I was soon going to die. What seemed in store for me now appeared even worse.

I don't remember how long we drove until we came to a stop. We were in a pine forest like the many found on the outskirts of Vienna. The kidnapper turned off the engine and made another phone call. Something appeared to have gone wrong. 'They're not coming. They're not here!' he cursed to himself. He seemed frightened, agitated. But maybe that was also just a trick: maybe he wanted me to take his side against these 'others' he was supposed to hand me over to and who had left him hanging; maybe he had just made them up to increase my fear and to paralyse me.

The kidnapper got out and ordered me not to move. I obeyed

silently. Hadn't Jennifer wanted to flee from such a car? How had she tried to do that? And what had she done wrong? My thoughts were all jumbled up inside my head. If he hadn't locked the door, I could maybe open it. But then what? In just two strides he'd be on me. I couldn't run very fast. I had no idea what forest we were in and what direction I should run in. And then there were the 'others' who were supposed to come and get me, who could be anywhere. I pictured it vividly in my mind, how they would chase me, grab me and throw me to the ground. And then I saw myself as a corpse in the woods, buried under a pine tree.

I thought of my parents. My mother would come to pick me up from afterschool care in the afternoon. And the woman who ran the programme would say to her, 'But Natascha hasn't been here!' My mother would be beside herself and I had no way to protect her. It cut my heart to think of her coming to get me and not finding me. 'What could happen anyway?' I had thought as I had left that morning without saying a word of goodbye, without giving her a kiss. *You never know if we'll see each other again.*

The kidnapper's words made me jump. 'They're not coming.' Then he got back in the car, started the engine and drove off again.

This time I recognized the gables and rooftops of the houses that I could just make out through the narrow strips of window along the sides. I could tell where he was steering the car to – back to the edge of the city and then on to the arterial road leading towards the town of Gänserndorf.

'Where are we going?' I asked.

'To Strasshof,' the kidnapper said forthrightly.

As we drove through Süssenbrunn, a deep sadness engulfed me. We passed my mother's old shop, which she had recently closed down. Just three weeks before she would have been sitting here at the desk in the mornings, doing the office work. I could still picture her and I wanted to cry out, but I only produced a weak whimper when we drove by the street that led to my grandmother's house. Here I had spent the happiest moments of my childhood.

The car came to a standstill in a garage. The kidnapper ordered me to remain lying down on the floor in the back and turned the engine off. Then he got out, fetched a blue blanket, threw it over me and wrapped me up tight. I could hardly breathe, and I was surrounded by absolute darkness. When he picked me up like a wrapped package and carried me out of the car, panic struck me. I had to get out of that blanket. And I had to go to the toilet.

My voice sounded muffled and foreign under the blanket when I asked him to put me down and let me go to the toilet. He stopped for a moment, then unwrapped me and led me through a hallway to a small guest toilet. From the hallway I was able to catch a glimpse of the adjoining rooms. The furnishings appeared fusty and expensive – yet another indication to me that I had really fallen victim to a crime. In the TV police shows that I knew, criminals always had large houses with expensive furnishings.

The kidnapper stood in front of the door and waited. I immediately locked the door and breathed a sigh of relief. But the moment of relief lasted only a few seconds. The room had no windows and I was trapped. The only way out was through the door and I couldn't stay locked behind that door forever. Especially as it would have been easy for him to break it open.

When I came out of the toilet after a while, the kidnapper wrapped me up in the blanket again: darkness, stuffiness. He lifted me up and I felt him carry me several steps downwards: a cellar? Once at the bottom of the stairs, he laid me on the floor, pulled on the blanket to move me forward, threw me again over his shoulder and continued onwards. It seemed an eternity before he put me down again. Then I heard his footsteps moving away from me.

I held my breath and listened. Nothing. There was absolutely nothing to hear. Still, it was a long time before I dared to cautiously peel the blanket off. There was absolute darkness all around. It smelled of dust and the stale air was strangely warm. Beneath me I could feel the cold, naked floor. I rolled myself into a ball on the blanket and whimpered softly. My own voice sounded so peculiar in the silence that I became frightened and stopped. I don't remember how long I remained lying there. At first I tried to count the seconds and the minutes. *Twenty-one, twenty-two . . .* I mumbled to myself, to time the length of the seconds. I tried to keep track of the minutes on my fingers. I kept losing count, and I couldn't allow that to happen, not now! I had to concentrate, remember every detail! But I quickly lost all sense of time. The darkness, the odour that caused disgust to well up in me – all of this lay upon me like a black cloth.

When the kidnapper came back, he had brought a light bulb that he screwed into a fixture on the wall. The harsh light that blazed outwards so suddenly blinded me and brought no relief – because now I could see where I was. The room was small and empty, the walls covered with wood panelling; a bare pallet bed was affixed to the wall on hooks. The floor was light-coloured laminate. A toilet with no lid stood in the corner and a double stainless-steel sink was along one wall.

Was this what a criminal gang's secret hiding place looked like? A sex club? The walls covered in light-coloured wood reminded me of a sauna and triggered a chain of ideas: sauna in the basement – child molester – criminal. I pictured fat, sweaty men setting upon me. For me a sauna in the basement was the place people like that lured their victims in order to molest them. But there was no stove and none of those wooden buckets that you usually see in saunas.

The kidnapper instructed me to stand in front of him at a certain distance and not to move. Then he began to remove the wooden pallet bed and to unscrew from the wall the hooks that had been holding it up. During all of this, he spoke to me in a voice that people usually reserve for household pets: gentle and placating. I was not to be afraid, everything was going to be all right, if only I would do what he told me. He looked at me the way the proud owner looks at his new car; or worse – like a child eyeing his new toy, full of anticipation and at the same time uncertain of everything he can do with it.

After some time my panic began to subside and I got up the courage to address him. I begged him to let me go: 'I won't tell anybody anything. If you let me go, nobody will notice anything. I'll just say that I ran away. If you don't keep me overnight, nothing will happen to you.' I tried to explain to him that he had just committed a grave mistake, that they were already looking for me and were certain to find me. I appealed to his sense of responsibility and I begged for sympathy. But it was no use. He made it unequivocally clear to me that I would be spending the night in this dungeon.

Had I been able to foresee that this room would be both my refuge and my prison for 3,096 nights, I don't know how I would have reacted. Looking back today, I realize that just knowing I would have to remain in the basement that first night triggered a reaction that probably saved my life – and was dangerous as well. What appeared to be outside the realm of the thinkable was now a fact: I was locked in the basement of a criminal and I was not going to be freed, at least not today. A shockwave passed through my world, and reality shifted just a little. I accepted what had happened and, instead of railing against my new situation with desperation and indignation, I acquiesced. As an adult you know that you give up a little piece of yourself whenever you have to tolerate circumstances that, before they occur, are completely outside the realm of the imagination. A crack appears in the foundation on which your own personality rests. And yet adapting is the only correct response, as it ensures your survival. Children act more intuitively. I was intimidated and did not resist, but rather I began to make myself at home – at least for one night.

With hindsight it seems to me quite bizarre how my panic gave way to a kind of pragmatism. How quickly I comprehended that my pleading would be futile and every additional word would bounce right off this strange man. How instinctively I felt that I had to accept the situation in order to get through this one endless night in the cellar.

When the kidnapper had unscrewed the pallet bed from the wall, he asked me what I required. An absurd situation, as if I were staying the night in a hotel and had forgotten my toiletries. 'A hairbrush, a toothbrush, toothpaste and a toothbrush cup. An empty yogurt cup will do.' I was functioning.

He explained to me that he would have to go to Vienna to fetch a mattress for me from his flat there.

'Is this your house?' I asked, but received no answer. 'Why can't you keep me in your flat in Vienna?'

He said that it would be too dangerous: thin walls, nosy neighbours, I might scream. I promised him I would be quiet if he would only take me to Vienna. But it was no use.

The moment he left the room, walking backwards, and locked the door, my survival strategy started to waver. I would have done anything to get him to stay or take me with him; anything so as not to be alone.

I crouched on the floor. My arms and legs felt strangely numb and it was difficult to unstick my tongue from the roof of my mouth. My thoughts centred on school, as I sought to impose a chronological structure that I could hold on to. But I had long lost any sense of time. What subject would be being taught right now? Was the long lunchtime break over already? When did they notice that I wasn't coming today? And when would they realize that I wouldn't be coming any more? Would they tell my parents? How would they react?

The thought of my parents brought tears to my eyes. But I

mustn't cry. I had to be strong, remain in control. An Indian knows no pain and, besides, tomorrow everything would most certainly be over. And then everything would be all right again. Moved by the shock of almost having lost me, my parents would get back together and treat me with love. I pictured them sitting together eating at the table, full of pride and admiration as they asked me how I had coped so well with everything. I imagined my first day back at school. Would they laugh at me? Or would they celebrate me as a miracle because I had escaped while all the others who had had similar experiences had ended up as corpses in a pond or in the woods? I imagined how triumphant it would be – and also a bit embarrassing – when they all crowded around me, tirelessly asking, 'Did the police rescue you?' Would the police be able to rescue me at all? How would they be able to find me? 'How were you able to escape?' 'Where did you get the courage to escape?' Would I even *have* the courage to escape?

Panic was once again creeping up inside me. I had no idea how I was supposed to get out of here. On TV you just 'overpowered' criminals. But how? Would I even have to kill him perhaps? I knew that you could die from a stab to the liver. I had read that in the newspaper. But where was the liver exactly? Would I be able to find the right location? What was I supposed to stab with anyway? And was I capable of doing it? Killing a person, me, a little girl? My thoughts turned to God. Would it be permissible in my situation for me to kill someone, even if I had no other choice? *Thou shalt not kill*. I tried to remember whether we had discussed that commandment in religion classes – and whether there were exceptions in the Bible. I couldn't think of any.

A muffled noise tore me from my thoughts. The kidnapper was back.

He had with him a narrow, approximately eight-centimetre-thick foam mat that he placed on the floor. It looked as if it were Austrian army issue, or a cover from a sun lounger. When I sat down on it, the air immediately came whooshing out of the thin fabric, and I once again felt the hard floor beneath me. The kidnapper had brought me everything I had asked for. Even biscuits. Butter biscuits with a thick layer of chocolate on them. My favourite biscuits, which I was actually no longer allowed to eat because I was too chubby. I associated these biscuits with an unbridled longing and a series of humiliating moments: that look when somebody said to me, 'But you weren't going to eat *that*. You're too plump anyway;' the shame, when all the other children reached for one and my hand was held back; and the feeling of pleasure when the chocolate slowly melted in my mouth.

My hands began to shake as the kidnapper opened the packet of biscuits. I wanted to have them, but my mouth went completely dry out of fear and nervousness. I knew that I would not be able to get them down. He held the package under my nose until I took one out, which I crumbled up into small pieces. As I did so, a couple of pieces of chocolate broke off, which I put in my mouth. I could not eat any more than that.

After a while, the kidnapper turned away from me and walked over to my school bag, which lay on the floor in a corner. When he picked it up and got ready to go, I begged him to leave me the bag – the thought of losing the only personal items I had with me in this unsettling environment made me feel completely at sea. He stared at me with a confused expression on his face, saying, 'You could have hidden a transmitter in there and you could use it to call for help. You're trying to trick me and you're playing the innocent on purpose! You're smarter than you admit to!'

The sudden change in his mood frightened me. Had I done something wrong? And what kind of transmitter was I supposed to have in my bag, which contained only my packed snacks, aside from a couple of books and writing utensils? At the time I had no clue why he was behaving so strangely. Today I realize that those words were the first indication that the kidnapper was paranoid and mentally ill. Back then there were no such transmitters that children could have been given so that they could be located – and even today, where the possibility exists, it is highly unusual. However, the kidnapper believed there was a real danger that I could have had such a futuristic means of communication hidden in my bag. So real that in his delusion he was afraid that a small child would bring tumbling down the world that existed only in his head.

His role in that world shifted lightning fast: one moment he seemed to want to make my forced incarceration in his basement as pleasant as possible; the next moment he saw me – a small girl with no strength, no weapon and certainly no transmitter – as an enemy who was out to get him. I had fallen victim to a crazy person and had become a play figure in the sick world inside his head. But back then I did not recognize that. I knew nothing about mental illness, about compulsions and delusional disorders that create a different reality within the person suffering from them. I treated him like any other adult whose thoughts and motives I would never have been able to see through as a child.

My begging and pleading was futile; the kidnapper took my rucksack and turned to the door. It opened inwards and had no handle on the inside of the dungeon, but rather a small, round knob so loosely attached to the wood that you could even pull it out.

As the door clicked shut, I began to cry. I was all alone, locked in a bare room somewhere beneath the earth. Without my rucksack, without the sandwiches my mother had made for me just hours before. Without the napkins they were wrapped up in. It felt as if he had torn a piece of me away, as if he had cut off my connection to my mother and my old life.

I cowered in a corner on the mattress and whimpered softly to myself. The wood-panelled walls seemed to be moving in on me, the ceiling seemed to be caving downwards. My breathing was rapid and shallow – I could hardly get any air – while my fear kept closing in around me. It was a horrific feeling.

As an adult I've often reflected on how I managed to live through that moment. The situation was so frightening that it could have shattered me. But the human mind can cope with the most astonishing situations – by tricking itself and withdrawing so as not to have to capitulate when faced with circumstances that cannot be logically comprehended.

Today I know that I regressed psychologically. The mind of the ten-year-old girl I was regressed back to that of a small child four or five years of age. A child that accepted the world around her as a given, for whom not the logical perception of reality, but rather the small rituals of a child's daily life offered the fixed points of reference that we require in order to have that feeling of normality – to keep from completely breaking down. My situation was so far out of the scope of anything anyone could possibly fathom that I subconsciously regressed to that stage: I felt small, at the mercy of someone else and free of responsibility. That person who was later to return to my dungeon was the only adult present and therefore the person of authority who would know what was to be done. I would only have to do what he asked and everything would be all right. Then everything would proceed as it always did: the bedtime ritual, my mother's hand on my duvet, the goodnight kiss and an attachment figure who would leave a night-light on and quietly tiptoe out of the room.

This intuitive withdrawal into the mental state of a small child was the second important transformation that took place the first day of my imprisonment. It was the desperate attempt to create a small, familiar oasis in a hopeless situation. When the kidnapper came back to the dungeon later, I asked him to stay with me, to put me to bed properly and to tell me a goodnight story. I even asked him for a goodnight kiss like my mother used to give me before softly closing the door to my room behind her. Everything to preserve the illusion of normality. And he played along. He took a reader with fairy tales and short stories out of my book bag, which he had put down somewhere in the dungeon, laid me down on the mattress, covered me with a thin blanket and sat down on the floor. Then he began to read *The Princess and the Pea, Part 2*. In the beginning he kept stumbling over the words. Almost timidly and in a soft voice, he told me the story of the prince and the princess. At the end he kissed my forehead. For a moment I felt like I was lying in a soft bed in a safe child's bedroom. He even left the light on.

It was only when the door closed behind him that the protective illusion burst like a bubble.

I could not sleep that night. I tossed and turned uneasily on the thin mattress in the clothes that I had not wanted to take off. The outfit that made me look so shapeless was the last thing that remained of my life from that day on.

3

Hoping in Vain for Rescue

My First Weeks in the Dungeon

'The Austrian authorities are focusing on the disappearance of a girl, the ten-year-old Natascha Kampusch. Natascha was last seen on 2 March. Her route to school, where she was last seen, is relatively long. Reportedly, a girl in a red anorak was pulled into a white van.'

Aktenzeichen XY ungelöst, 27 March 1998

I had listened to the kidnapper for quite some time before he came into the dungeon the next day. Back then I did not know how well the entrance was secured – but I could tell from the sounds gradually coming nearer that it took him a long time to open my dungeon.

I was standing in the corner, my eyes glued to the door, when he entered the room which measured five square metres. He seemed younger than on the day of my abduction: a lanky man with soft, youthful features. His brown hair was neatly parted, like a model pupil at a proper university-preparatory school. His face was gentle and at first glance seemed to promise nothing evil. It was only when you observed him for a longer period of time that you noticed the traces of madness that lurked behind his conservative, bourgeois exterior, an exterior that wouldn't begin to show deep cracks until later.

I immediately pelted him with questions:

'When are you going to let me go?'

'Why are you keeping me here?'

'What are you going to do with me?'

He gave me one-syllable answers and registered each one of my movements as you would if you were keeping an eye on a captive animal. Not once did he turn his back on me, and I always had to keep a distance of about one metre between him and me.

I tried to threaten him. 'If you don't let me go immediately, you're going to be in big trouble! The police have been out looking for me. They are going to find me and be here very soon! And then you'll have to go to jail! You don't want that, do you? Let me go and everything will be all right. Please, you'll let me go?'

He promised to let me go soon. As if with that he had answered all my questions, he turned round, pulled the knob out of the door and bolted it from the outside.

I listened in desperation in the hope that he would come back to me. Nothing. I was completely cut off from the outside world. No sounds penetrated, not one flicker of light peeped through the cracks in the wall panelling. The air was musty and covered my skin like a damp film that I could not brush off. The only sound to keep me company was the rattling of the fan that blew air from the attic via the garage into my dungeon through a pipe in the ceiling. The noise was pure torture: day and night it continued to whir throughout the tiny room until it became unreal and shrill, forcing me to press my hands to my ears in despair to block out the noise. When the fan overheated, it began to smell and the blades warped. The scraping noise got slower and a new sound was added: tock, tock, tock. Interrupted only by the scraping. There were days when that torturous noise filled not only every corner of the room, but also every corner of my mind.

During my first few days in the dungeon the kidnapper left the light on round the clock. I had asked him to because I was afraid to be alone in the total darkness the dungeon was plunged into as soon as he unscrewed the light bulb. But the constant, glaring light was nearly as bad. It hurt my eyes and forced me into an artificial state of wakefulness that I couldn't shake. Even when I pulled the blanket over my head to soften the brightness of the light, my sleep was superficial and disturbed. My fear and the harsh light never allowed me to do more than doze lightly, and I always started awake with the feeling that it was bright daylight outside. But in the artificial light of the hermetically sealed basement there was no difference between day and night.

Today I know that it was, and in some countries still is, a widespread means of torture to constantly subject prisoners to artificial light. Plants shrivel up when exposed to the extreme and constant effects of light, and animals die. For people it is perfidious torture, more effective than physical violence. It destroys biorhythms and sleep patterns to such an extent that the body reacts as if paralysed by deep exhaustion, and the brain can no longer function correctly even after only a few days. Just as cruel and effective is the torture of bombarding someone continuously with inescapable noise. Like a scraping, whirring fan.

I felt as if I had been preserved alive in an underground safe. My prison was not entirely square, measuring about 2.70 metres long and 1.80 wide and just under 2.40 high. Eleven and a half cubic metres of stuffy air. Not quite five square metres of floor, across which I paced like a tiger in a cage, from one wall to the other. Six small steps one way, six steps back, was the length. Four steps one way and four back was the width. I could walk around the perimeter in twenty paces.

Pacing dampened my panic only slightly. As soon as I remained standing, as soon as the sound of my feet hitting the floor faded, my panic rose again. I was nauseated and I was afraid of losing my mind. What was going to happen anyway? *Twenty-one, twenty-two . . . sixty.* Six forward, four to the left. Four to the right, six back.

The feeling that there was no way out gripped me again and

again. At the same time I knew that I couldn't allow myself to be smothered by my fear, that I had to do something. I took one of the mineral water bottles, in which the kidnapper had brought me fresh tap water, and hammered with all my might against the wooden panelling. First rhythmically, then energetically until my arm went numb. In the end it was no more than a desperate drumming mixed in with my cries for help. Until the bottle slipped out of my hand.

No one came. No one had heard me, perhaps not even the kidnapper. I collapsed on the mattress exhausted and curled up like a small animal. My cries were transformed into sobs. Crying gave release to my despair at least for a short time and calmed me. It reminded me of my childhood, when I would cry over nothing – and then quickly forget the reason why.

The previous evening my mother had notified the police. When I didn't come home at the usual time, she first called afterschool care, then the school. Nobody could explain my disappearance. The next day, the police began looking for me. From old newspaper articles I know that hundreds of police officers searched the area around my primary school and my council estate using dogs. There were no clues that would have justified limiting the radius of the search. Back courtyards, side streets and parks were combed, as were the banks of the Danube. Helicopters flew overhead and posters were hung up at every school. Every hour people called with tips, purportedly having seen me in various places. However, none of these tips led in the right direction.

In the first few days of my imprisonment I tried again and again to imagine what my mother must have been doing at that moment. How she would be looking for me everywhere, and how her hope would dwindle from day to day. I missed her so much that the loss I felt threatened to eat me up inside. I would've given anything to have had her with me with her power and strength.

Looking back, I am amazed how much importance the media has attached to my argument with my mother in the interpretation of my case. As if my leaving without saying goodbye provided insights into my relationship with my mother. Even though I'd felt rejected and disregarded, especially during my parents' draining separation, it should have been clear to anyone that any child in such an extreme situation would almost automatically be crying out for his or her mother. Without my mother or father, I was without protection, and knowing that they had no news of me saddened me deeply. There were days that my anxious worrying about my parents put a greater strain on me than my own fear. I spent hours thinking about how I might at least communicate to them that I was still alive. So that they wouldn't completely despair. And so that they wouldn't give up looking for me.

During the initial time I spent in the dungeon, I hoped every day, every hour, that the door would open and someone would rescue me. The hope that someone couldn't possibly make me disappear so easily carried me through the endless hours in the cellar. But days and days passed, and no one came. Except for the kidnapper.

Looking back, it seems obvious that he had been planning the abduction for a long time: otherwise why else would he have spent years building a dungeon that could only be opened from the outside and was just barely large enough to allow a person to survive in there? But the kidnapper was, as I witnessed over the years of my imprisonment, a paranoid, fearful person, convinced that the world was evil and that people were after him. It could be just as true that he built the dungeon as a bunker in preparation for a nuclear strike or World War III, as his own place of refuge from all of those he thought were pursuing him.

Nobody today can tell us which answer is the right one. Even statements made by his former co-worker Ernst Holzapfel allow for both interpretations. In a statement to the police, he later said that the kidnapper had once asked him how to soundproof a room so that not even a hammer drill could be heard anywhere in the house.

To me, at least, the kidnapper did not behave like a man who had been preparing for years to abduct a child and whose long-cherished wish had just been fulfilled. Quite the opposite: he seemed like someone whom a distant acquaintance had suddenly saddled with an unwanted child, and who did not know what to do with this little creature that had needs he didn't know how to cope with.

In my first days in the dungeon, the kidnapper treated me like a very small child. I found this accommodating, as I had inwardly regressed to the emotional level of a kindergarten-aged child. He brought me anything I wanted to eat – and I behaved as if I were spending the night with a distantly related great aunt who could be credibly convinced that chocolate was an appropriate breakfast food. The very first morning, he asked me what I wanted to eat. I wanted fruit tea and croissants. In fact, the kidnapper came back with a thermos filled with rosehip tea and a brioche croissant from one of the most well-known bakeries in town. The printing on the paper bag confirmed my suspicions that I was being held somewhere in Strasshof. Another time I asked for salty sticks with honey and mustard. This 'order' was also promptly delivered. It seemed very strange to me that this man fulfilled my every request, given that he had taken everything else away from me.

His penchant for treating me like a small child also had its downside. He would peel every orange for me and put it in my mouth piece by piece, as if I were unable to feed myself. Once, when I asked for chewing gum, he refused – for fear that I would choke on it. In the evenings he forced my mouth open and brushed my teeth as one would a three-year-old who cannot yet hold her toothbrush. After a few days he grabbed my hand roughly and, gripping it tightly, cut my fingernails.

I felt pushed aside, as if he had taken the remaining dignity I was trying to preserve in that situation. At the same time I also knew that I was largely responsible for finding myself on this level, a level that protected me to a certain extent. Because the very first day I had realized how widely the kidnapper fluctuated in his paranoia, between treating me as if I were too small on the one hand or too independent on the other.

I acquiesced in my role, and when the kidnapper returned to the dungeon the next time to bring me food, I did everything I could to keep him there. I pleaded. I begged. I vied for his attention so that he would occupy himself with me, play with me. My time in the solitary dungeon was driving me mad.

So there we were after a few days; I was sitting with my kidnapper in my jail playing Chinese checkers, Nine Men's Morris, Parcheesi. The situation seemed unreal to me, as if taken from an absurd film. Nobody in the world outside would believe that an abduction victim would do anything to make her kidnapper play Parcheesi. But the world outside was no longer my world. I was a child and alone, and there was only one person who could relieve this oppressive loneliness.

I sat on the mat with my kidnapper, rolled the dice and moved the pieces. I stared at the patterns on the playing board, at the small colourful pieces, and tried to forget about my surroundings and imagine the kidnapper as a fatherly friend who was generous in taking time to play with a child. The better I succeeded in allowing myself to be absorbed by the game, the further away the panic receded. I knew that it was lurking in a corner somewhere, always ready to pounce. And when I was about to win a game, I would surreptitiously make a mistake so as to put off the threat of being alone.

In those first days, the presence of the kidnapper seemed to me a guarantee that I would be spared the final cruelty. Because in all his visits he talked about the people who had supposedly 'ordered' my kidnapping and with whom he had spoken on the telephone so frantically during my abduction. I continued to assume that they must have something to do with a child pornography ring. He repeatedly mumbled something about people who would come to take pictures of me 'and do other things as well', which confirmed my fears. The fact that the stories he was feeding me didn't agree at all, that these ominous people probably didn't even exist, were thoughts that went through my head sometimes. It is likely that he made up these people supposedly behind the kidnapping to intimidate me. But I couldn't know for sure, and even if they were invented, they fulfilled their purpose. I lived in constant fear that at any moment a horde of evil men would come into my dungeon and attack me.

The images and the scraps of stories that I had snapped up over the last few months from the media coalesced into ever-more frightening scenarios. I attempted to push them to the back of my mind – and pictured at the same time everything that the kidnapper might do with me. How that was supposed to work with a child. What objects they would use. Whether they would do it right here in the dungeon, or take me to a villa, a sauna or an attic room, like in the case that had most recently been portrayed in the media.

When I was alone, I tried to position myself at all times so that I could keep an eye on the door. At night I slept like a caged animal, closing only one eye, constantly on the alert. I didn't want to be surprised while I was defencelessly sleeping by the men that I was supposedly to be handed over to. I was tense every second, pumped full of adrenaline and driven by a fear that I was unable to escape in that small room. The fear of my supposed 'true kidnappers' made the man who abducted me at their behest appear to offer caring, friendly support; as long as I was with him, the anticipated horror would not take place.

*

In the days after my abduction, my dungeon began to fill up with all sorts of objects. First, the kidnapper brought me some fresh clothes. I had only what I was wearing: knickers, tights, dress, anorak. He had burned my shoes in order to erase any possible traces of me. Those were the shoes with the thick platform soles that I had got for my tenth birthday. When I had walked into the kitchen that day, a cake with ten candles was sitting on the table, next to it a box wrapped in shiny, coloured paper. I took a deep breath and blew the candles out. Then I pulled off the tape and tore the paper aside. For weeks I had been bugging my mother to buy me shoes like the ones everybody else was wearing. She had categorically refused, saying that they were inappropriate for children and that you couldn't walk properly in them. And now, there they were in front of me: black suede ballerinas with a narrow strap across the instep; underneath, a thick corrugated rubber platform sole. I was delighted! Those shoes, which immediately added three centimetres to my height, would most certainly pave the way for my new self-assured life to begin.

My last present from my mother. And he had burned them. In doing so, he had not only taken from me yet another link to my old life, but also a symbol of the strength that I had hoped to glean from those shoes.

Now the kidnapper gave me one of his old jumpers and khaki-green fine-rib T-shirts that he had obviously kept from his military conscription. It mitigated the outer cold in the night. To protect myself against the cold that seized me on the inside, I continued to wear one of my own items of clothing.

After two weeks he brought me a sunlounger to replace the thin foam mat. The reclining surface was suspended on metal springs that squeaked at the slightest movement. For the next half-year this sound would be my companion during the long days and nights in my dungeon. Because I froze so – it was chilly in the dungeon all year round – the kidnapper dragged a large, heavy electric heater to the tiny room. And he brought my school things back. The bag, so he told me, had been burned along with my shoes.

My first thought was to send my parents a message. I took out paper and a pen and began to write to them. I spent many hours carefully wording that letter – and even found a way to tell them where I was. I knew that I was being held somewhere in Strasshof, where my sister's parents-in-law lived. I hoped that the mention of her family would be enough to put my parents – and the police – on the right trail.

To prove that I had written the letter myself, I enclosed a photograph from my pencil case, of me ice-skating the previous winter, wrapped up in thick overalls, a smile on my face and my cheeks red. It seemed a snapshot from a world very far away, a world filled with the loud laughing of children, pop music from rattling loudspeakers and vast swathes of cold, fresh air. A world where, after spending an afternoon on the ice, you could go home, take a hot bath and watch TV while drinking hot chocolate. I stared at the photograph for minutes on end, memorizing every detail so as never to forget the feeling I associated with that outing. I probably knew that I would have to preserve every single happy memory in order to recall them in the darkest moments. Then I placed the photograph with the letter and made an envelope from another sheet of paper.

With a mixture of naivety and confidence, I waited for the kidnapper.

When he came, I made an effort to be calm and friendly. 'You have to send this letter to my parents so that they know that I'm alive!' He opened the envelope, read what I had written, and refused. I begged and pleaded with him not to leave my parents in the dark much longer. I appealed to the conscience I presumed him to have. 'You mustn't turn into such a bad person,' I told him.

What he had done was wrong, but making my parents suffer was much worse. I kept searching for new reasons why and wherefore, and assured him that nothing could happen to him as a result of the letter. He had read it himself and could see that I had not betrayed him . . . The kidnapper said 'no' for a long time – then suddenly gave in. He assured me that he would post the letter to my parents.

It was completely naive of me, but I so wanted to believe him. I lay down on my sunlounger and imagined how my parents would open the letter, how they would find the hidden clues and rescue me. Patience, I just had to have a little patience, and then this nightmare would be over.

The next day, my fantasy came crashing down like a house of cards. The kidnapper came into my dungeon with an injured finger, claiming that 'someone' had torn the letter from him in a dispute, injuring him as he fought to get it back. He hinted that it had been the people who supposedly had ordered my abduction and who didn't want me to contact my parents. The fictitious 'bad guys' from the pornography ring became threateningly real. At the same time, the kidnapper donned the role of protector. After all, he had wanted to grant my request and had made such a great effort that he had been hurt in the process.

Today I know that he had never intended to post that letter and had probably burned it, just like all the other objects that he had taken from me. Back then I wanted to believe him.

In the first few weeks the kidnapper did everything to avoid destroying his image as my purported protector. He even fulfilled my greatest wish: a computer. It was an old Commodore C64 with very little memory capacity. But it came with a few floppy disks with games I could use to distract myself. My favourite was an 'eating' game. You moved a small man through an underground labyrinth in order to avoid monsters and 'eat up' bonus points. It was a somewhat more sophisticated version of Pac-Man. I spent hours and hours scoring points. When the kidnapper was in the dungeon, we sometimes played together on a split screen. Back then he often let me, the small child, win. Today I see the analogy to my own situation in the cellar, where monsters were able to penetrate at any time, monsters that you had to run away from. My bonus points were rewards, like the computer, 'won' by 'impeccable' behaviour.

When I got tired of that one, I switched to Space Pilot, where you had to fly through space and shoot alien spaceships. The third game on my C64 was a strategic game called *Kaiser*, or Emperor. In it, you ruled over people and challenged others to become Emperor. He liked that game best. He would send his people to war with enthusiasm. He would also let them starve or make them perform forced labour as long as it served to increase his power and wouldn't decimate the hordes he needed for his armies.

All of this still took place in a virtual world. But it wouldn't take long for him to show me his other face.

'If you don't do what I tell you, I will have to turn your light off.'

'If you're not good, then I'll have to tie you up.'

In my situation I had absolutely no chance of not being 'good', and I didn't know what he meant. Sometimes a sudden movement on my part was enough to cause his mood to change. Or when I looked directly at him, despite his order that I should keep my eyes strictly on the floor. Everything that didn't fit the fixed template that he had prescribed for my behaviour spurred his paranoia. Then he would berate me and accuse me time and time again of only wanting to trick him, deceive him. It was in all likelihood the uncertainty about whether I really could communicate with the outside world that drove him to abuse me verbally like that. He did not like it when I insisted on my point of view that he was wrongly accusing me. He wanted recognition when he brought me something, praise for the effort that he had had to undertake on my account – for example, in dragging the heavy heater down into the dungeon. Even back then he began to demand gratitude from me. And even back then I tried to deny it to him as much as I could, saying, 'I'm only here because you've locked me up.' Secretly, I couldn't do anything but rejoice when he brought me food and other items I desperately needed.

Today, as an adult, it seems amazing to me that my fear, my recurrent panic, was not directed towards the kidnapper's person. It may have been my reaction to his nondescript appearance and his insecurity, or his strategy aimed at giving me as much of a sense of security as possible in this unbearable situation by making himself indispensable as an attachment figure. The threatening part of my situation was the dungeon under the earth, the closed-in walls and locked door, and the people who had supposedly ordered my abduction. The kidnapper himself created the impression sometimes that his crime had been merely a pose that he had struck, but which did not fit with his personality. In my childish imagination, he had decided at some point to become a criminal and commit an evil deed. I never doubted that his actions constituted a crime that had to be punished. But I separated the crime distinctly from the person who had committed it. The bad guy was most certainly a role he was only playing.

'From now you'll have to cook for yourself.'

One morning during the first week, the kidnapper came into the dungeon carrying a box made out of dark plywood. He put it up against the wall, put a hotplate and a small oven on it and plugged both of them in. Then he disappeared again. When he came back, he was carrying a stainless-steel pot and a pile of ready-to-eat food: tins of beans and goulash, and a selection of those instant meals that come in small white plastic dishes and colourful cardboard packages and are warmed using steam. Then he explained to me how the hotplate worked.

I was happy to have got back a small piece of my independence. But when I poured the first tin of beans into the small pot and placed it on the hotplate, I didn't know how hot to make it or how long it would take for the food to cook. I had never cooked anything before, and I felt alone and out of my depth. And I missed my mother.

Looking back, it seems astonishing to me that he let a ten-year-old cook, especially as he was otherwise so keen to see me as the small, helpless child. But from then on, I warmed one meal a day on the hotplate myself. The kidnapper came to the dungeon every morning and then one more time, either at noon or in the evening. In the morning he brought me a cup of tea or hot chocolate, a piece of cake or a bowl of cereal. At noon or in the evening, depending on when he had time, he would come with tomato salad and cold-cut sandwiches, or with a hot meal that he shared with me. Noodles with meat and sauce, a rice dish with meat, Austrian home-style cooking that his mother had made for him.

Back then I had no idea where the food came from or how he lived. Or whether he even had a family who was in on his crime and sat comfortably with him in his living room, while I lay on my thin mattress in the basement. Or whether the people who had supposedly ordered my abduction lived up in the house with him, only sending him down to bring me proper supplies. In fact, he made certain that I ate healthy food and regularly brought me dairy products and fruit.

One day he brought me a couple of lemons, which gave me an idea. It was a childish and naive plan, but it seemed ingenious to me at the time: I was going to fake an illness which would force the kidnapper to take me to a doctor. I had always heard my grandmother and her friends tell stories about the time during the

Russian occupation in eastern Austria after World War II, how the women avoided being raped or carried off, which was the order of the day back then. One of their tricks was to smear red jam into their face so that it looked like an awful skin disease. Yet another trick involved lemons.

Once I was alone again, I took my ruler and carefully separated the razor-thin skin from the fleshy part of the lemon and carefully glued it to my arm using lotion. It looked disgusting, as if I truly had a purulent infection. When the kidnapper came back, I held up my arm to him and faked terrible pain. I whimpered and asked him to please take me to the doctor. He stared at me steadfastly, then with one gesture he wiped the lemon skin from my arm.

That day he turned my light off. Lying in the darkness, I racked my brains to think of more ways I could try to force him to let me go. I couldn't think of any.

My only hope in those days rested with the police. At that point I was still counting on being freed and hoped that my rescue would take place before he handed me over to the ominous people who had ostensibly ordered my abduction – or found somebody else who could figure out what to do with an abducted girl. Every day I waited for men in uniform to break down the walls of my dungeon. In fact, in the world outside the large-scale search for me had been called off after only three days. The search of the surroundings had been unsuccessful and now the police were questioning all the people closest to me. Only the media issued daily requests for information, with my picture and always the same description:

> The girl is about 1.45 metres tall, weighing forty-five kilograms and has a plump stature. She has straight, light-brown hair with a fringe and blue eyes. At the time of her disappearance, the ten-year-old was wearing a red ski jacket with a hood, a denim dress with a top

whose sleeves are grey-and-white checked, light blue tights and black suede shoes size 34. Natascha Kampusch wears glasses with light-blue plastic oval frames and a yellow nose bridge. According to the police, she has a slight squint. The girl was carrying a blue plastic rucksack with a yellow cover and turquoise straps.

From the case file I know that over 130 tips had been received after four days. People said they had seen me with my mother in a supermarket in Vienna, alone at a motorway rest stop, once in the town of Wels and three times in the province of Tyrol. The police in Kitzbühel, Tyrol, searched for me for days. A team of Austrian law enforcement officers travelled to Hungary where somebody reported having seen me in Sopron. The small Hungarian village where I had spent the previous weekend with my father at his holiday house was searched systematically from top to bottom by the Hungarian police. A neighbourhood watch was set up, and my father's house was placed under surveillance, because it was thought that I still had my child's photo identification with me from the weekend and could have run away there. One man called the police and demanded a ransom of one million Austrian schillings for me. A copycat and a con-artist, like so many to come.

Six days after my abduction, the head of the investigation told the media, 'In Austria, as in Hungary, uniformed police officers are searching for Natascha by putting up posters. No one is giving up. However, the hope of finding the child alive has vanished.' Not one of the many tips turned out to lead to a hot trail.

And yet, the police failed to pursue the one tip that would have led them to me: on Tuesday, one day after my abduction, a twelve-year-old girl reported having seen a child abducted in a white delivery van with darkened windows on Melangasse. However, the police did not at first take this piece of information seriously.

In my dungeon I had no idea that the outside world had already begun grappling with the thought that I could be dead. I was convinced that the large-scale search was still underway. Whenever I lay on my sunlounger, staring at the low, white ceiling with the bare bulb, I imagined the police talking to each one of my school-mates, and played their answers through in my mind. I pictured the women who supervised afterschool care, as they described again and again when and where they had seen me for the last time. I considered who of our many neighbours would have watched me leave the house, and if anyone had witnessed the abduction and seen the white delivery van on Melangasse.

Even more intensely, I pondered fantasies that the kidnapper had demanded a ransom after all and would let me go once the money was handed over. Every time I warmed my food on the hotplate, I carefully tore off the small pictures of the meals and hid them in the pocket of my dress. I knew from films that kidnap-pers sometimes had to prove that their victims were still alive for the ransom to be handed over. I was prepared: with the pictures I could prove that I had regularly had something to eat. And I could also use them to prove to myself that I was still alive.

To be on the safe side, I chipped off a small piece of the veneer from the hotplate and placed it in my dress pocket as well. That way nothing could go wrong. I imagined that the kidnapper would drop me off at an undisclosed location after the payment of the ransom and leave me alone there. My parents would be told of my location and come to get me. Afterwards we would alert the police, and I would hand over the veneer chip to the officers. Then all the police would have to do would be to search all of the garages in Strasshof for basement dungeons. The hot-plate with the missing chip from its veneer would be the vital piece of evidence.

In my head I stored every detail I knew about the kidnapper so that I could describe him after I was set free. I was largely limited to outside appearance, which disclosed little about him. When he visited me in the dungeon, he wore old T-shirts and Adidas tracksuit bottoms – practical clothing so that he could fit through the narrow passageway which led to my prison.

How old did I think he was? I compared him to the adults in my family: younger than my mother, but older than my sisters who, back then, were around thirty. Although he looked young, one time I came straight out and said, 'You are thirty-five.' I didn't find out until much later that I was correct.

But I did, in fact, find out his name – only to immediately forget it. 'Look, that's my name,' he said once, annoyed by my constant questions, holding his business card in front of my face for a number of seconds. 'Wolfgang Priklopil' it said. 'Of course, that's not really my name,' he quickly added, laughing. I believed him. It didn't seem credible that a dangerous criminal would have such a mundane name as 'Wolfgang'. I could hardly decipher his last name so quickly anyway. It is difficult and hard for an overwrought child to remember. 'Or maybe my name is Holzapfel,' he asserted, before he closed the door behind him once again. At the time I had no idea what that name was supposed to mean. Today I know that Ernst Holzapfel was something akin to Wolfgang Priklopil's best friend.

The closer 25 March came, the more nervous I grew. Since my abduction I had asked Priklopil every day what the date and time were in order to keep from becoming completely disorientated. For me there was no day or night, and although spring had sprung outside, my dungeon became freezing cold as soon as I turned off the heater. One morning he answered, 'Monday, 23 March.' I had not had even the slightest contact with the outside world for three weeks. And my mother's birthday was in two days.

That date was highly symbolic for me. If I was forced to see it go by without wishing my mother a happy birthday, my imprisonment would have gone from a temporary nightmare to something undeniably real. Until now I had only missed a few days of school. But not being home for an important family celebration would be a significant milestone. 'That was the birthday Natascha wasn't here,' I heard my mother telling her grandchildren, looking back. Or even worse: 'That was the first birthday Natascha wasn't here.'

It troubled me deeply that I had left her in anger and now I could not even tell my mother on her birthday that I hadn't meant it and loved her after all. I tried to stop time in my head, tried in desperation to think of how I could send her a message. Maybe it would work out this time, unlike with my letter. I would forgo leaving any hidden hints of my location in the letter. A sign of life for her birthday, that was all I wanted.

At our next meal together, I pleaded with the kidnapper for so long that he said he would bring a cassette recorder to the dungeon the next day. I would be able to record a message for my mother!

I gathered up all my strength to sound cheerful on the tape: 'Dear Mummy. I am fine. Don't worry about me. Happy birthday. I miss you enormously.' I had to stop several times because tears were pouring down my cheeks and I didn't want my mother to hear me sob.

When I was finished, Priklopil took the cassette and assured me that he would call my mother and play it for her. I didn't want anything more than to believe him. For me it was an immense relief that my mother would now not have to worry so much about me.

She never heard the tape.

For the kidnapper, his assertion that he had played the recording for my mother was an important manoeuvre in his manipulative bid for dominance, because shortly thereafter he changed his strategy. He no longer spoke of the people who had supposedly ordered my abduction, but rather of a kidnapping for ransom.

He maintained again and again that he had contacted my parents, but they obviously had no interest in seeing me freed:

'Your parents don't love you at all.'

'They don't want you back.'

'They are happy to finally be rid of you.'

These statements were like acid, penetrating the open wounds of a child who had previously felt unloved. Although I never once believed that my parents did not want to see me free, I knew that they didn't have much money. But I was completely convinced that they would do everything they could to come up with the ransom somehow.

'I know my parents love me. They've always told me so,' I told him, bravely resisting the kidnapper's malicious remarks, the kidnapper who very much regretted unfortunately never having received an answer from them.

But the doubts that had been planted before my imprisonment cropped up.

He systematically undermined my belief in my family, and with it an important pillar of my already tattered self-esteem. The certainty of having my family behind me, a family that would do everything to rescue me, slowly faded. Because days and days passed, and nobody came to free me.

Why had I, of all people, become a victim of such a crime? Why had he picked me out and locked me up? Those questions began to torture me, and they still occupy my thoughts today. It was so difficult to comprehend the reasons for his crime that I cast about desperately for an answer. I wanted the abduction to have some kind of meaning, a clear logic that had remained hidden to me up until that point, which would make it more than just a random attack against me. Even today it is difficult to cope with knowing that I forfeited my youth just to a whim and the mental illness of one single man.

I never received an answer to that question from the kidnapper himself, although I continued to probe time and again. Only once did he say, 'I saw you in a school picture and picked you out.' But then he immediately retracted his statement. Later he would say, 'You came to me like a stray cat. Cats you are allowed to keep.' Or, 'I saved you. You should be grateful.' Towards the end of my imprisonment, he was probably the most honest: 'I always wanted to have a slave.' But years would pass before he would say those words.

I have never found out why he chose to abduct me of all people. Because it seemed the obvious choice to select me as a victim? Priklopil grew up in the same district of Vienna as I did. During the time I accompanied my father on his delivery rounds to the bars, he was a young man at the end of his twenties, moving in the same shady circles that we did. During my primary school years I was amazed again and again at how many people greeted me so cheerfully because they recognized me from my father's delivery round. He may have been one of the men who noticed me then.

It is possible, however, that other people brought me to his attention. Perhaps his story about the pornography ring was true. Back then there were enough such organizations in Germany and Austria which would not have hesitated to abduct children for their cruel purposes. And the discovery of a dungeon in Marc Dutroux's house in Belgium had been made only two years previously. Still, I do not know even today whether Priklopil – as he continued to claim in the beginning – had kidnapped me on the orders of others, or whether he acted alone. It is too frightening to speculate that somewhere out there the true culprits are still free. However, during my imprisonment there was no indication of any criminal accomplices, aside from the initial references made by Priklopil.

Back then, I had a very clear picture of what abduction victims looked like. They were blonde girls, small and very thin, nearly transparent, who floated helplessly and angelically through the world. I imagined them as creatures whose hair was so silky that one absolutely had to touch it. Their beauty intoxicated sick men, making them commit crimes of violence just to be near them. I, on the other hand, was dark-haired, and felt cloddish and unattractive. And more so than ever on the morning of my abduction. I didn't fit my own image of a kidnapped girl.

Looking back, I know that this image was skewed. It is the nondescript children with very little self-esteem that criminals choose to prey on. Beauty is not a factor in abduction or sexual violence. Studies have shown that mentally and physically disabled persons, as well as children with few family connections, run a higher risk of falling victim to a criminal. Next in the 'rankings' come children such as I was on the morning of 2 March: I was intimidated, afraid and had just stopped crying. I was insecure, walking to school on my own for the first time, and my small steps were hesitant. Perhaps he saw that. Perhaps he noticed how worthless I felt and decided spontaneously that day that I was to be his victim.

Lacking any outward indication as to why I of all people had become his victim, back in the dungeon I began to blame myself. The arguments with my mother the evening before my abduction ran on endless repeat before my eyes. I was afraid of the thought that the abduction had been my punishment for having been a bad daughter, for having left without making any attempt at reconciliation. I turned everything over and over in my head. I examined my past for all the mistakes I had made. Every little unkind word. Every situation in which I had not been polite, good or nice. Today I know that it is common for victims to blame themselves for the crime perpetrated against them. Back then it was a maelstrom that swept me along and I could do nothing to resist it.

The excruciating brightness that had kept me awake during my first few nights had given way to total darkness. When the kidnapper unscrewed the light bulb in the evening and closed the door behind him, I felt as if I had been cut off from everything: blind, deaf from the constant whirring of the fan, unable to orientate myself spatially or sometimes even sense myself. Psychologists call this 'sensory deprivation'. Being cut off from all sensory input. Back then the only thing I knew was that I was in danger of losing my mind in that lonely darkness.

From the moment when he left me alone in the evening until breakfast the next day, I was trapped in a state of uncertainty, completely devoid of light. I could do nothing other than lie there and stare into the darkness. Sometimes I still screamed or beat against the walls in the desperate hope that somebody would hear me.

In all my fear and loneliness, I had to rely only on myself. I tried to buck myself up and fight back my panic using 'rational' means. These were words that saved me back then. Like others who crochet for hours and have a fine doily to show for their efforts, I wove words together in my head, writing long letters to myself and short stories that nobody would put on paper.

The point of departure for my stories was mainly my plans for the future. I imagined every detail of how life would be after my rescue. I would do better at all of my subjects at school and overcome my fear of other people. I promised myself to exercise more and lose weight so that I could take part in the other children's games. I pictured myself going to another school once I was freed – after all, I was in fourth grade* – and how the other kids would react to me. Would they know me from the reports of my abduction? Would they believe me and accept me as one of their

---

* In the Austrian school system, fourth grade marks the end of the primary school phase, after which the pupils switch schools, choosing which kind of educational path to take, i.e. either aimed at learning a trade or eventually going to university.

own? What I liked best was to imagine myself reuniting with my parents. How they would take me in their arms, how my father would lift me up and toss me through the air. How the intact world of my earlier childhood would return, making me forget the period of quarrelling and humiliation.

Other nights, such visions of the future were not enough. Then I took on the role of my absent mother, in a way splitting myself into two parts and giving myself encouragement: 'This is just like a holiday. Although you're away from home, on holiday you can't just call on the telephone. There is no telephone on holiday, and you can't interrupt a holiday just because you've had one bad night. And when the holiday's over, you'll come back home to us, and then school will be starting up again.'

During these monologues I pictured my mother in front of me. I heard her say with a determined voice, 'Get yourself together, there's no point in getting all worked up. You have to get through this, and afterwards everything will be okay again.' Yes. If I could only be strong, everything would be okay again.

And when none of that helped, I tried to recall a situation in which I had felt safe and loved. A bottle of *Franzbranntwein* that I had asked the kidnapper to get for me helped. My grandmother had always rubbed it on her skin. The sharp, fresh odour immediately transported me to her house in Süssenbrunn and gave me a warm sense of security. When my brain was no longer enough, my nose took over, helping me not to lose my connection to myself – and my mind.

Over time I tried to become accustomed to the kidnapper. I intuitively adapted myself to him, the way you adapt to the incomprehensible customs of people in a foreign country.

Today I think the fact that I was still a child may have helped me. As an adult, I don't think I would have been able to get through, even partially intact, this extreme form of being told exactly what to do and the psychological torture I was subjected to as a prisoner in the cellar. From the very beginning of their lives children are programmed to perceive the adults closest to them as unquestioned authorities, who provide orientation and set the standards for what is right and what is wrong. Children are told what to wear and when to go to bed. They are to eat what is put on the table, and anything undesirable is suppressed. Parents are always denying their children something they want to have. Even when adults take chocolate away from children, or the few euros they received from a relative for their birthday, that constitutes interference. Children must learn to accept that and trust that their parents are doing the right thing. Otherwise the discrepancy between their own desires and the discouraging behaviour of their loved ones will break them.

I was used to following instructions from adults, even when it went against the grain. If it had been up to me, I never would have gone to afterschool care. Particularly to one which dictated to children when they were allowed to take care of their most basic bodily functions, i.e. when they could eat, sleep or go to the toilet. And I would not have gone to my mother's shop every day after afterschool care, where I attempted to stave off boredom by eating ice cream and pickles.

Even robbing children of their freedom, at least temporarily, was to me nothing outside the realm of the conceivable, although I had never experienced it myself. Back then in some families it was still common to punish unruly children by locking them in a dark cellar. And old women on the tram scolded mothers of misbehaving children by saying, 'Well, if it was mine, I would lock it up.'

Children can adapt even to the most adverse circumstances. In the parents who beat them, they still see the part that loves them, and in a mouldy shack they see their home. My new home was a dungeon, my attachment figure, the kidnapper. My whole world had veered off course, and he was the only person in this nightmare which had become my world. I was completely dependent on him, as only infants and toddlers are on their parents. Every gesture of affection, every bite of food, light, air – my entire physical and psychological survival depended on the one man who had locked me in his basement dungeon. And in claiming that my parents failed to respond to his demands for ransom, he made me emotionally dependent on him as well.

If I wanted to survive in this new world, I had to cooperate with him. For somebody who has never been in such an extreme situation of oppression, this may be difficult to comprehend. But today I am proud of the fact that I was able to take this step towards the person who had robbed me of everything. Because that step saved my life, even though I had to dedicate more and more energy to maintaining this 'positive approach' to the kidnapper. He successively transformed himself into a slave driver and dictator. But I never departed from my image of him.

Still, his outward show of playing benefactor by trying to make my life in the dungeon as pleasant as possible remained intact. In fact, a kind of daily routine developed. Several weeks after the abduction, Priklopil brought into the dungeon a patio table, two folding chairs, a dishtowel I was permitted to use as a tablecloth and some dishes. When the kidnapper arrived with food, I would put the dishtowel on the table. I would place two glasses on it and put the forks neatly next to the plates. The only thing missing was serviettes, which he was too miserly to provide. Then we would sit down together at the folding table, eat the pre-cooked meal and drink fruit juice. At that time he was not yet rationing anything and I enjoyed being able to drink as much as I wanted. A kind of cosiness set in and I began to look forward to these meals together with the kidnapper. They broke up my loneliness. They became important to me.

These situations were so entirely absurd that I was unable to put them in any sort of familiar category from my world up until that point in time – this small, dark world that suddenly held me captive had in every way so little in common with any standard of normality. I had to create new standards. Perhaps I was in a fairy tale? In a place taken from the imaginings of the Brothers Grimm, far away from the normal world? Of course. Hadn't an aura of evil already enshrouded Strasshof from before? My sister's despised in-laws lived in a section of Strasshof called 'Silberwald', literally 'Silver Forest'. As a small child, I had been afraid of meeting them during their visits to my sister's flat. The place name and the negative atmosphere in that family had already turned Silberwald – and therefore Strasshof – into a forest under a witch's spell even before my kidnapping. Yes, I had certainly ended up in a fairy tale, whose deeper meaning was unknown to me.

The only thing that did not sit well with the evil fairy tale was the bathing in the evening. I couldn't remember ever reading anything about bathing in fairy tales. The dungeon had only a double stainless-steel sink and cold water. The hot water pipes the kidnapper had installed were not yet functional, which is why he brought me warm water in plastic bottles. I had to undress, sit in one of the sinks and put my feet in the other. In the beginning he simply poured warm water over me. Later I came up with the idea of punching small holes in the bottles to make a kind of shower. Because there was very little room to move about, he had to help me wash. I was unaccustomed to being naked in front of him, a strange man. What was he thinking all the while? I eyed him uncertainly, but he scrubbed me down like a car. There was neither anything tender nor anything salacious in his gestures. He attended to me as one would maintain a household appliance.

It was exactly at the time when the image of the evil fairy tale imposed itself on my reality that the police finally began to follow up the tip provided by the girl who had witnessed my abduction.

On 18 March the statement of that single witness was published, together with the announcement that the owners of 700 white delivery vans would be examined over the next few days. The kidnapper had enough time to prepare.

On Good Friday, the thirty-fifth day of my imprisonment, the police came to Strasshof and demanded that Wolfgang Priklopil show them his car. He had filled it with construction debris and told the police that he was using the delivery van for renovation work on his house. On 2 March, Priklopil said, according to police records, he had spent the whole day at home and that there were no witnesses. The kidnapper had no alibi, a fact that the police continued to cover up even years after I had escaped.

The police were satisfied and decided to forgo searching the house, which Priklopil supposedly freely invited them to do. While I sat in the dungeon, waiting to be rescued and trying not to lose my mind, they merely took a few Polaroid photographs of the car I had been kidnapped in and added them to my case files. In my rescue fantasies down in the cellar, specialists combed the area, looking for traces of my DNA or tiny pieces of fabric from my clothing. But, above ground, things were different; the police did none of that. They apologized to Priklopil and left without ever having examined the car or the house any more closely.

I didn't find out until after I had escaped how close the kidnapper had come to being arrested if only the police had truly taken the matter seriously. However, only two days later it became clear to me that I would never go free.

In 1998 Easter Sunday fell on 12 April. The kidnapper brought me a small basket with colourful chocolate eggs and a chocolate Easter bunny. We 'celebrated' Christ's resurrection in the light of the bare light bulb, sitting at a small patio table in my airless dungeon. I was happy to receive the goodies and tried with all my might to push aside my thoughts of the outside world, of Easter celebrations in previous years. Grass. Light. Sun. Trees. Air. People. My parents.

That day the kidnapper told me that he had given up hope of ransoming me, because my parents had still not got in touch with him. 'Obviously they don't care about you enough,' he said. Then came the judgement. A life sentence. 'You've seen my face and you know me already too well. Now I can no longer let you go. I will never take you back to your parents, but I will take care of you here as well as I can.'

All my hopes were dashed at a stroke that Easter Sunday. I cried and begged him to let me go. 'But I have my whole life ahead of me. You can't just lock me up here! What about school, what about my parents?' I swore to God and everything that I held sacred that I wouldn't betray him. But he didn't believe me, saying that once free I would forget my oath only too quickly, or give in to pressure from the police. I tried to make it clear to him that he didn't want to spend the rest of his life with a crime victim in the cellar, and begged him to blindfold me and take me far away. I would never find the house again and I had no name that would lead the police to him. I even made plans for him to escape. He could go abroad; after all, life in another country would be much better than locking me away forever in a dungeon and having to take care of me.

I whimpered, begged and at some point I began to scream, 'The police will find me! And then they will lock you up. Or shoot you dead! And if not, then my parents will find me!' My voice cracked.

Priklopil remained completely calm. 'They don't care about you, have you already forgotten? And if they come to the house, I will kill them.' Then he left the dungeon backwards, closing the door from the outside.

I was alone.

It wasn't until ten years later, two long years after my escape and in the wake of a police scandal centring on the errors in the investigation and their cover-up that I found out I had come close to being rescued a second time that Easter holiday without even knowing it. On 14 April, the Tuesday after Easter, the police made public yet another tip. Witnesses had told them that they had seen a delivery van with darkened windows in the vicinity of my council estate the morning of my abduction. The number plate read 'Gänserndorf', the administrative district where Strasshof was located.

However, the police did not make public a second tip. A member of the Vienna police's canine unit had called the police station. The officer on duty recorded the following report from him verbatim:

On 14 April 1998 at 2.45 p.m. an unknown person called and reported the following information:

Regarding the search for a white delivery vehicle with darkened windows in the district of Gänserndorf and with regards to the disappearance of Kampusch, Natasche [*sic!*], there is a person in Strasshof/Nordbahn who could be connected to her disappearance and owns a white delivery van, model Mercedes, with darkened windows. This man is known as a 'loner' who has extreme difficulties relating to his environment and problems dealing with other people. He is said to be living with his mother in Strasshof/Nordbahn, Heinestrasse 60 (single-family dwelling), which is fully equipped with an electric alarm system. The man reportedly may have weapons in the house. His white delivery van, model Mercedes, number plate unknown, has often been seen in front of his house at Heinestrasse 60 with completely darkened windows along the sides and in the back. The man was previously employed by SIEMENS as a communication engineer and may still be working there. It is possible that the man lives in the house with his elderly mother and is said to have a penchant for 'children' with regard to his sexuality. It is unknown whether he has any prior police record in that regard.

The man's name was not known to the caller, who only knows him from the neighbourhood. The man is approximately thirty-five years old, has blond hair, is lanky and 175–180 centimetres tall. The anonymous caller was not able to provide any information that was more specific.

4

Buried Alive

The Nightmare Begins

The rabbit-hole went straight on like a tunnel for some way, and then dipped suddenly down, so suddenly that Alice had not a moment to think about stopping herself before she found herself falling down what seemed to be a very deep well. [. . .] Down, down, down. Would the fall *never* come to an end? [. . .]

'Come, there's no use in crying like that!' said Alice to herself, rather sharply. 'I advise you to leave off this minute!' She generally gave herself very good advice (though she very seldom followed it), and sometimes she scolded herself so severely as to bring tears into her eyes; and once she remembered trying to box her own ears for having cheated herself in a game of croquet she was playing against herself, for this curious child was very fond of pretending to be two people. 'But it's no use now,' thought poor Alice, 'to pretend to be two people! Why, there's hardly enough of me left to make *one* respectable person!'

Lewis Carroll, *Alice's Adventures in Wonderland*

One of the first books I read in the dungeon was *Alice's Adventures in Wonderland* by Lewis Carroll. The book touched me in an unpleasant, spooky way. Alice, a girl probably my age, follows a talking white rabbit into its hole in a dream. As soon as she enters, she falls down into the depths and lands in a room with doors all around. She's trapped in an in-between world under the earth, and the way up is blocked. Alice finds a key to the smallest door and a small bottle with a magic potion that makes her shrink. She has hardly gone through the tiny opening when the door closes behind her. In the underground world she has now entered, nothing seems right. Sizes change constantly, the talking animals she meets there do things that defy all logic. But nobody seems to be bothered by it. Everything is madly off-kilter, off-balance. The entire book is one single, lurid nightmare, in which all of the laws of nature have been suspended. Nothing and no one is normal. The girl is all alone in a world that she does not understand, where she has no one to confide in. She has to buck herself up, forbid herself to cry and act according to the rules of others. She attends the Mad Hatter's endless tea parties where all sorts of crazy guests cavort, and takes part in the Queen of Heart's cruel game of croquet, at the end of which all the other players are sentenced to death. 'Off with their heads!' shouts the Queen, laughing madly.

Alice is able to leave this world deep below the earth because she wakes up from her dream. When I opened my eyes after just a few hours of sleep, my nightmare was still there. It was my reality.

The entire book seemed like an exaggerated description of my own situation. I too was trapped beneath the ground in a room that the kidnapper had secured against the outside world with a number of doors. And I too found myself trapped in a world where all the rules I was familiar with no longer applied. Everything that had held true in my life until that point was meaningless here. I had become part of a psychopath's sick fantasy, a fantasy I did not understand. Could not understand. There was no link any more to the other world I had just recently been a part of. No familiar voice, no familiar sounds that would prove to me that the world up above was still there. How was I supposed to maintain a link to the real world and to myself in that situation?

I hoped against hope that I, like Alice, would suddenly awake. In my old room, amazed at my crazy, frightening dream that had nothing in common with my 'real world'. But it wasn't my dream

I was trapped in, it was my kidnapper's. And he wasn't sleeping either, but had dedicated his life to turning a terrible fantasy into reality, a fantasy from which there was no escape, not even for him.

From that time on I ceased all attempts to persuade the kidnapper to let me go. I knew that there was no point.

The world I was living in had shrunk to five square metres. If I wasn't to go crazy in it, I would have to try to conquer it for myself. And not wait, trembling, for the cruel call 'Off with her head!' like the playing card people from *Alice in Wonderland*; and not submit like all the other fantasy creatures from that twisted reality. But rather try to create a refuge in this dark place, which the kidnapper could infiltrate but within which I could weave as much as possible of myself and my old world around me – like a protective cocoon.

I began to make myself at home in the dungeon and turn the kidnapper's prison into *my* space, into *my* room. The first things I asked for were a calendar and an alarm clock. I was trapped in a time warp where the kidnapper alone was the master of time. The hours and minutes blurred into a thick mass that weighed dully on everything. Like a deity, Priklopil had the power over light and darkness in my world. 'God spoke: Let there be light. And there was light. And God called the light Day and the darkness he called Night.' A bare bulb dictated to me when I was to sleep and when I was to be awake.

I had asked the kidnapper every day what day of the week it was, what the date was. I don't know whether he lied to me, but that didn't matter. The most important thing for me was to feel a connection to my former life 'up there'. Whether it was a school day or a weekend off. Whether bank holidays or birthdays I wanted to spend with my family were drawing near. Measuring time, I learned back then, is probably the most important anchor you can have in a world in which you run the risk of otherwise simply dissolving. The calendar helped me to regain a modicum of orientation – and images that the kidnapper had no access to. I now knew whether other children would be getting up early or were allowed to sleep in. In my imagination I followed my mother's daily routine. Today she would go to the shop. Tomorrow she might visit a friend. And at the weekend she might go on an outing with her boyfriend. In this way the sober numbers and names of the days of the week took on a life of their own, giving me support and structure.

Almost more important was the alarm clock.

I asked for one of those old-fashioned ones that mark the passing of the seconds with a loud monotone ticking sound. My beloved grandmother had such an alarm clock. When I was younger, I had despised the loud ticking that bothered me when I was trying to fall asleep and even crept into my dreams. Now I held tight to that ticking like somebody under water clings on to her last straw in order to get just a little bit of air from above into her lungs. With every tick-tock that alarm clock proved to me that time had not come to a standstill and the earth had continued to turn. In stasis, without any sense of time or space, the alarm clock was my ticking connection to the real world outside.

When I really tried, I could concentrate so intensely on that noise that at least for a couple of minutes I was able to block out the tedious whirring of the fan that filled my room to the threshold of pain. In the evening, as I lay on my lounger unable to fall asleep, the ticking of the alarm clock was like a long lifeline which I could use to climb out of my dungeon and slip into my childhood bed in my grandmother's home. There I was able to fall asleep peacefully in the knowledge that she was in the next room watching over me. On evenings such as these I would often rub some *Franzbranntwein* on my hand. When I held it up to my face and the characteristic smell rose into my nose, a feeling of closeness would course through me. Just like back when I would bury my face in my grandmother's apron as a child. In this way I was able to fall sleep.

Throughout the day I busied myself by making the tiny room as habitable as possible. I asked the kidnapper to bring me cleaning supplies so as to ward off the damp smell of cellar and death that hung over everything. A fine, black mould had formed on the floor of the dungeon from the additional moisture caused by my presence. That mould made the air even more stale and breathing even more difficult. In one spot the laminate was moist because dampness had risen up from the ground. The spot was a constant, painful reminder that I was apparently far beneath the earth's surface. The kidnapper brought me a red broom and dustpan set, a bottle of 'Pril' washing-up liquid, an air freshener and exactly those cleaning wipes scented with thyme that I had seen before in television commercials.

Now I carefully swept every corner of my dungeon and wiped the floor clean. I began my scrubbing at the door. The wall there was only slightly wider than the narrow door. From there the wall led at an oblique angle to the part of the room where the toilet and the double sink were. I would spend hours using decalcifying cleaning materials to wipe away the small traces of water drops on the metal of the sink until it took on a brilliant shine, and wipe the toilet so clean that it rose out of the floor like a valuable porcelain flower. Then I worked my way carefully from the door through the rest of the room: first along the longer wall, and then along the shorter one until I reached the narrow wall opposite the door. Finally, I would push my lounger aside and clean the centre of the room. I was very careful not to use too many cleaning wipes so as not to make the damp worse.

When I was finished, a chemical version of freshness, nature and life hung in the air that I soaked up greedily. If I then sprayed a bit of air freshener, I could let myself go for a moment. The lavender scent did not smell particularly good, but it gave me the illusion of meadows in bloom. And when I closed my eyes, the picture printed on the spray can became a set that dropped down in front of the walls of my prison. In my thoughts I ran along the endless, blue-violet rows of lavender, felt the earth beneath my feet and smelled the tangy scent of the flowers. The warm air was filled with the buzzing of bees and the sun burned down on the back of my neck. Above me, the cerulean sky, endlessly high, endlessly wide. The fields extended to the horizon, with no walls, with no limitations. I ran so fast that I had the feeling that I could fly. And nothing in this blue-violet endlessness stopped me.

When I opened my eyes again, the bare walls brought me back from my fantasy journey with a thud.

Images. I needed more images, images from *my* world that *I* could shape. That did *not* fit the kidnapper's sick fantasy that jumped out at me from every corner of the room. Slowly but surely I began to turn the tongue-and-groove wood panels covering the walls into colourful pictures using the crayons from my school bag. I wanted to leave something of me behind, the way prisoners write on the walls of their cells. Drawing images and making notches for every single day, and writing sayings. Prisoners don't do that out of boredom, I now understood. Drawing is a way to counter the feeling of powerlessness and of being at the mercy of others. They do it to prove to themselves and all those who ever enter that cell that they exist – or at least had once existed.

Drawing my murals served another purpose: I created a film set in which I could imagine that I was home. First I tried to draw the entryway to our apartment. I drew a long door handle on the door to the dungeon, the small dresser that still stands in the hallway in my mother's flat today on the wall next to it. Meticulously I outlined it and drew the handles of the drawers. I didn't have enough crayons to draw more, but it was enough to create the illusion. Now when I lay on my lounger looking at the door, I could imagine that it would open at any moment and my mother would walk in to greet me, placing her key on the dresser.

The next thing I drew on the wall was a family tree. My name was all the way at the bottom, then came the names of my sisters, their husbands and children, then my mother's and her boy-friend's, my father's and his girlfriend's, and then the names of my grandparents. I spent a lot of time designing my family tree. It gave me a place in the world and assured me that I was part of a family, part of a whole unit, and not a free-floating atom meandering in space outside the real world – the way I often felt I was.

I drew a large car on the wall opposite. It was supposed to be a Mercedes SL in silver, my favourite car. I even had a model at home and planned to buy one someday when I was an adult. It had large, full breasts instead of wheels. I had seen that once in some graffiti painted on a concrete wall near our council estate. I don't know exactly why I chose that motif. Apparently I wanted something that was strong and presumably grown-up. Over the last few months in primary school I had provoked my teachers at times. Before school started, we were allowed to write on the blackboard with chalk if we erased it in time for class to start. While other children drew flowers and comic characters, I scribbled 'Protest!', 'Revolution!' or 'Teachers out!' It was not behaviour that seemed appropriate in that small classroom of twenty children where we learned our school subjects, sheltered as if in an eternal kindergarten environment. I don't know whether I was further along the path towards puberty than my classmates, or whether I just wanted to show off to those who otherwise only teased me. At any rate, in the dungeon the small rebellion that lay in that drawing gave me strength. Just like the swear word that I wrote on the wall in small letters in a hidden spot: 'a—'. I wanted to show my power to resist; I wanted to do something forbidden. I don't appear to have impressed the kidnapper with it. At least, he refrained from commenting on the picture.

The most important change came as a result of the arrival in my dungeon of a television set and a video recorder. I had asked Priklopil repeatedly for them, and one day he did bring them for me, placing them next to the computer on the dresser. After weeks in which 'life' appeared to me in only one form, namely in the person of the kidnapper, I was now able to bring a colourful imitation of human company into my dungeon with the help of the television screen.

In the beginning, the kidnapper had simply recorded at random the television programmes on a given day. But it was probably too much effort to edit out the news programmes which still reported on the search for me. He never would have allowed me to receive any hint that people in the world outside had not forgotten me. The image that my life was of no value to anyone, particularly to my parents, was, after all, one of the most important psychological instruments he had to keep me pliable and dependent on him.

For that reason he later only recorded individual shows or brought me old video cassettes with films that he had recorded in the early 1990s. The furry alien in *ALF*, *I Dream of Jeannie*, Al Bundy in *Married with Children* and the Taylors from *Home Improvement* became replacements for family and friends. Every day I looked forward to meeting them again, and observed them probably more closely than any other television viewer. Every facet of their interactions, every scrap of dialogue, no matter how minuscule, fascinated and interested me. I analysed every detail of the set backdrops which demarcated the horizon at my disposal. They were my only 'windows' into other homes, and yet were crafted in such a thin and paltry way that the illusion that I had access to 'real life' quickly caved in. Perhaps that was also one of the reasons why I later found science fiction so gripping: *Star Trek*, *Stargate*, *Back to the Future*, etc . . . anything that had to do with space or time travel fascinated me. The heroes in those films strike out to discover new territory, unknown galaxies. And, unlike me, they had the technical means to simply beam themselves away from difficult locations and life-threatening situations.

One spring day that I knew only from the calendar, the kidnapper brought a radio to the dungeon. Inside, I leapt with joy. A radio – that would truly mean a link to the real world! News, the familiar morning shows that I had always listened to in the kitchen while eating breakfast, music – and perhaps an off-hand clue that my parents had not forgotten me after all.

'Of course, you cannot listen to any Austrian stations,' said the kidnapper, destroying my illusions with one casual remark as he plugged the radio into the socket and turned it on. Still, I was able to hear music. But when the announcer said something, I couldn't understand a word. The kidnapper had manipulated the radio so that I could only receive Czech stations.

I spent hours fiddling with the small radio that could have been my gateway to the world outside. Always in the hope of finding a German word, a familiar jingle. Nothing. Only a voice I did not understand. This, on the one hand, gave me the impression that I was not alone, but on the other hand reinforced my feelings of alienation, of being excluded.

Desperate, I turned the knob back and forth, millimetre by millimetre, readjusting the antenna again and again. But outside that one frequency, the only thing I could hear was static.

Later on the kidnapper gave me a Walkman. Because I suspected that he had music from older bands at home, I asked for tapes of The Beatles and Abba. When the light was turned off in the evening, I now no longer had to lie in the darkness with my fear, but could listen to music, as long as the batteries held out. The same songs over and over.

The most important means I had at my disposal for combating boredom and for keeping me from going crazy was books. The first book the kidnapper brought me was *The Flying Classroom* by Erich Kästner, followed by a series of classics, such as *Uncle Tom's Cabin*, *Robinson Crusoe*, *Tom Sawyer*, *Alice in Wonderland*, *The Jungle Book*, *Treasure Island* and *Kon-Tiki*. I devoured the paperback comic books with stories of Donald Duck, his three nephews, his miserly Uncle Scrooge and the inventive Professor Ludwig von Drake. Later I asked for Agatha Christie, whose books I was familiar with from my mother, and read whole piles of crime novels, like *Jerry Cotton*, and science-fiction stories. The novels catapulted me into another world and absorbed my attention to such an extent that I forgot where I was for hours. And that is precisely what made reading so significant to my survival. While television and radio allowed me to bring the illusion of the company of others into my dungeon, reading enabled me to leave it for hours in my thoughts.

The books by Karl May held a particular importance for me during my initial time in captivity when I was still a ten-year-old girl. I devoured the adventures of Winnetou and Old Shatterhand, and read the stories about the North American Wild West. A song sung by German settlers for the dying Winnetou touched me so deeply that I copied it word for word and pasted the paper to the wall using Nivea lotion, as I had neither Sellotape nor any other adhesive or glue in the dungeon. It is a prayer to Mary the mother of God:

> The light of day seeks to depart;
> Now the quiet night is falling.
> Oh, if only the heart's suffering
> Could pass just like the day!

I lay my plea at your feet;
Oh carry it upwards to God's throne
And, Madonna, be saluted
In the devout tone of prayer:
　Ave Maria!

The light of faith seeks to depart;
Now, the night of doubt is falling.
Youth's trust in God
Is to be taken from me.
In old age, Madonna, please preserve
In me my youth's happy confidence.
Shelter my harp and my psalter,
You are my salvation, you are my light!
　Ave Maria!

The light of life seeks to depart;
Now, death's night is falling.
The soul seeks to spread its wings
And die I must.
Madonna, into your hands
I place my last, fervent plea:
Please solicit for me a trusting end
And a blissful resurrection from the dead!
　Ave Maria!

I read, whispered and prayed this poem so often that I can still recite it from memory today. It seemed as if it had been written especially for me. The 'light of life' had also been taken away from me, and in dark hours I saw no way out of my dungeon other than death.

*

88

The kidnapper knew how dependent I was on a continuous supply of films, music and reading matter, which gave him a new instrument of power over me. By withholding these things, he was able to exert pressure.

Whenever I had behaved 'improperly' in his eyes, I had to count on him slamming shut the door on the world of words and sounds that promised at least somewhat of a diversion. This was particularly awful at the weekend. By now, the kidnapper usually came to my dungeon every day in the morning, and mostly once again in the afternoon or evening. But at the weekend, I was all alone. I wouldn't see him from noon on Friday, sometimes even from Thursday evening, until Sunday. He would bring me two days of ready-to-eat meals, some fresh food and mineral water that he brought from Vienna. And videos and books. During the week I received a video cassette full of television serials, two hours, and when I really begged, four. It wasn't a lot. Every day, I had to get through twenty-four hours all by myself, interrupted only by the kidnapper's visits. At the weekend, I was given four to eight hours of entertainment on cassette, and the next book in the series that I was currently reading. But only if I met his demands. Only when I was 'good' did he give me that vitally important sustenance for my mind. He was the only one who knew what he understood by 'being good'. Sometimes only a minor infraction was enough for him to punish my behaviour.

'You've used too much air freshener. I'm going to take it away from you.'

'You were singing.'

You did this, you did that.

With the videos and books, he knew exactly which button to push. Having torn me away from my real family, it felt as if he had then taken hostage my replacement family, made up of novels and television series, in order to make me do what he said.

The man who had in the beginning made such an effort to

make my life in the dungeon 'pleasant' and who had driven to the other side of Vienna just to get a particular audio story starring the character Bibi Blocksberg, had undergone a gradual transformation since he had announced that he would never let me go.

At this time, the kidnapper began to dominate me more and more. Of course, he had had me completely under his control from the very beginning. Locked in his cellar, cooped up in only five square metres of space, I really couldn't do much to oppose him anyway. However, the longer I remained in captivity, the less this obvious manifestation of his power satisfied him. Now he wanted to bring every gesture, every word and every function of my body under his control.

It started with the timer switch. The kidnapper had had the power over light and darkness from the very beginning. When he came down to my dungeon in the morning, he turned on the electricity, and when he left in the evening, he turned it off again. Now he installed a timer switch which controlled the electric power in the room. While in the beginning I had been allowed now and then to have the light on for longer, now I had to submit to a merciless rhythm I had no control over. At seven in the morning, the electricity was turned on. For thirteen hours, I was able to lead a cheap imitation of life in a tiny, airless room: seeing, hearing, feeling warmth and cooking. Everything was synthetic. A light bulb can never replace the sun, ready-to-eat meals are only distantly reminiscent of family dinners around a shared table, and the flat people flickering across the television screen are only an empty substitute for real humans. But as long as the power was on, I could at least maintain the illusion that there was life outside myself.

The electricity was turned off at eight o'clock in the evening. From one second to the next I found myself in total darkness. The television would cease working in the middle of a series, and I had to put my book down in the middle of a sentence. And if I was not already lying in bed, I had to feel my way on all fours to my lounger. Light bulb, television set, the recorder, radio, computer, hotplate, cooker and heat – everything that brought life into my dungeon was turned off. Only the sounds of the ticking alarm clock and the excruciating whirring of the fan filled the room. For the next few hours, I was dependent on my imagination to prevent me from going crazy and keep my fear at bay.

It was a daily rhythm similar to life in a penitentiary, strictly prescribed from the outside, with no second of deviation, no consideration for my needs. It was a demonstration of power. The kidnapper loved schedules, and with the timer switch he imposed them on me.

In the beginning I still had my battery-operated Walkman, which allowed me to keep the leaden darkness at bay somewhat, when the timer switch had decreed that I had exhausted my ration of light and music. But the kidnapper did not like the fact that I could use my Walkman to circumvent his divine command of light and darkness. He began to monitor my battery status. If he thought that I used my Walkman too long or too often, he would take it away from me until I promised to behave better. One time he had apparently not yet closed the outer door to my dungeon, before I was already sitting on my lounger, wearing the headphones from my Walkman and loudly singing along to a Beatles song. He must've heard my voice and came back to the dungeon in a wild rage. Priklopil punished me for singing so loudly by taking away my light and my food. In the next few days I was forced to fall asleep without music.

His second instrument of control was the intercom system. When he came to my dungeon to install the cable, he told me, 'From now on you can ring upstairs and call me.' In the beginning I was very happy about that and I felt as though a great weight of fear had lifted off my chest. The thought that I would suddenly

be faced with an emergency had plagued me since the beginning
of my imprisonment. Over the weekend at least I was often alone
and couldn't even get the attention of the only person who
knew where I was, the kidnapper. I had played out innumerable
situations in my head. A cable fire, a burst pipe, a sudden allergy
attack . . . I could even have died a miserable death in the dungeon
by choking on some sausage skin, while the kidnapper was at
home upstairs. After all, he only came when he wanted to. For
that reason the intercom seemed to be a lifeline. It wasn't
until later that the real significance of the device dawned on me.
An intercom works in both directions. The kidnapper used it to
control me. To demonstrate his omnipotence and to assure me
that he could hear every sound I made and could comment on
everything.

The first version the kidnapper installed consisted essentially
of a button that I was to press if I needed something. Then a red
light would light up upstairs in a hidden place in his house. However, he wasn't able to see the light every time, nor was he willing
to undertake the complicated procedures necessary to open the
dungeon without knowing what exactly I wanted. And he couldn't
come down at all at the weekends. It was only much later that I
found out this was due to his mother's weekend visits, when she
would stay overnight in the house. It would have been too much
trouble and too conspicuous to remove the many obstacles
between the garage and my dungeon as long as she was there.

Shortly thereafter, he replaced the temporary device with
another system you could talk through. By pressing the button,
he could now issue his instructions and questions to my dungeon.

'Have you rationed your food?'

'Have you brushed your teeth?'

'Have you turned the television off?'

'How many pages have you read?'

'Have you done your maths exercises?'

I jumped out of my skin every time his voice pierced the stillness. He threatened me with consequences because I had been too slow in answering. Or had eaten too much.

'Have you already eaten everything ahead of schedule?'

'Didn't I tell you that you were only allowed to eat one piece of bread in the evening?'

The intercom was the perfect instrument for terrorizing me – until I discovered that it afforded me a little bit of power as well. Looking back today, it seems surprising to me that the kidnapper, with his manifest need to control everything, never figured out that a ten-year-old girl would inspect the device very carefully. But that's exactly what I did after a few days.

The intercom had three buttons. When you pressed 'Speak', the line was open on both ends. This was a setting that he had shown me. If the intercom was on 'Listen', I could hear his voice, but he couldn't hear me. And then there was a third button: when you pressed it, the line was open on my end, but up above everything was silent.

In my direct confrontations with him I had learned to let what he said go in one ear and out the other. Now I had a button that did just that. When these questions, control attempts and accusations got too much for me, I pressed the third button. It gave me deep satisfaction when his voice fell silent and it was I who had pressed the button to make that happen. I loved that button because it enabled me to shut the kidnapper out of my life for a short time. When Priklopil found out about my small, index finger-led rebellion, he was stunned at first, then indignant and angry. It took him nearly an hour to open the many doors and locks every time he wanted to speak to me face to face. But it was clear that he would have to think of something else.

In fact, it wasn't long before he removed the intercom with the wonderful third button. Instead, he came into the dungeon carrying a Siemens radio. He took the insides out of the case and began to tinker with it. At the time I didn't know a thing about the kidnapper, and it was only much later that I found out that Wolfgang Přiklopil had been a communications engineer at Siemens. However, the fact that he understood how alarms, radios and other electrical systems worked was something that was not news to me.

This rebuilt radio became a terrible instrument of torture for me. It had a microphone that was so powerful it could broadcast up above every noise I made in my room. The kidnapper could simply listen in on my 'life' without warning and monitor me every second to check whether I was following his orders. Whether I had turned off the television. Whether the radio was on. Whether I was still scraping my spoon across my plate. Whether I was still breathing.

His questions pursued me even under my blanket:

'Have you not eaten your banana?'

'Have you been a greedy pig again?'

'Have you washed your face?'

'Did you turn off your television after one episode?'

I couldn't even lie to him because I didn't know how long he had been eavesdropping. And if I did it one more time anyway, or failed to answer right away, he yelled into the loudspeaker until everything in my head hammered. Or he came into my dungeon unannounced and punished me by taking away my prized possessions: books, videos, food. I had to provide a penitent account of my misconduct, of every moment of my life in the dungeon, no matter how minute. As if there was anything that I could have concealed from him.

Yet another way for him to make sure I felt that he had total control over me was to leave the headset hanging upstairs. Then, in addition to the whirring of the fan, distorted, unbearably loud static permeated my prison, filling up every last inch of space and forcing me to feel him in every corner of the tiny cellar room.

He is here. Always. He is breathing at the other end of the line. He could begin to bellow at any time, and I would recoil, even if I was anticipating it at any second. There was no escape from his voice.

Today I'm not surprised that as a child I believed he could see me in the dungeon. After all, I didn't know whether or not he had installed cameras. I felt watched every second of the day, even while I was sleeping. Perhaps he had installed a heat-imaging camera so that he could monitor me even as I lay on my lounger in complete darkness. The thought paralysed me and I hardly dared turn over in my sleep at night. During the day, I looked round ten times before I went to the toilet. I had no idea whether or not he was watching me – and whether perhaps others were there as well.

In total panic, I began to search the entire dungeon for peepholes or cameras, always afraid that he would see what I was doing and come downstairs immediately. I filled the tiniest cracks in the wood panelling with toothpaste until I was sure that there were no more gaps. Still, the feeling of constantly being watched remained.

I believe that very few men are capable of estimating the immense amount of torture and agony which this dreadful punishment, prolonged for years, inflicts upon the sufferers; and in guessing at it myself, and in reasoning from what I have seen written upon their faces, and what to my certain knowledge they feel within, I am only the more convinced that there is a depth of terrible endurance in it which none but the sufferers themselves can fathom, and which no man has a right to inflict upon his fellow-creature. I hold this slow and daily tampering with the mysteries of the brain to be immeasurably worse than any torture of the body; and because its ghastly signs and tokens are not so palpable to the eye and sense of touch as scars upon the flesh; because its wounds are not upon

the surface, and it extorts few cries that human ears can hear;
therefore the more I denounce it.

Charles Dickens, *American Notes for General Circulation*

The author Charles Dickens wrote these words about solitary
confinement in 1842, which had set a precedent in the US and is
still in use today. My solitary confinement, the time that I spent
exclusively in the dungeon without once being able to leave those
five square metres of space, lasted over six months; my total
imprisonment 3,096 days.

The feeling that that time spent in complete darkness or constant artificial light created in me was not something I was able to
put into words at the time. When I look at the many studies today
examining the effects of solitary confinement and sensory deprivation, I can understand precisely what happened to me back then.

One of the studies documents the following effects of solitary
confinement:

Significant Decrease in the Ability of the Vegetative Nervous System Function
- Significant disruptions in hormone levels
- Absence of menstruation in women with no other
  physiological, organic cause due to age or pregnancy
  (secondary amenorrhoea)
- Increased feeling of having to eat: Zynorexia/crav-
  ings, hyperorexia, compulsive overeating
- In contrast, reduction or absence of thirst
- Severe hot flushes and/or sensations of coldness
  not attributable to any corresponding change in the
  ambient temperature or to illness (fever, chills, etc.)

Significantly Impaired Perception and Cognitive Ability
- Serious inability to process perceptions
- Serious inability to feel one's own body

- Serious general difficulties in concentrating
- Serious difficulty, even the complete inability, to read or register what has been read, comprehend it and place it within a meaningful context
- Serious difficulties, even the complete inability, to speak or process thoughts in written form (agraphia, dysgraphia)
- Serious difficulties in articulating and verbalizing thoughts, which is demonstrated in problems with syntax, grammar and word selection and can even extend to aphasia, aphrasia and agnosia.
- Serious difficulties or the complete inability to follow conversations (shown to be the result of slowed function in the primary acoustic cortex of the temporal lobes due to lack of stimulation)

Additional Limitations
- Carrying out conversations with oneself to compensate for the social and acoustic lack of stimulation
- Clear loss of intensity of feeling (e.g. vis-à-vis family members and friends)
- Situatively euphoric feelings which later transform into a depressed mood

Long-term Health Consequences
- Difficulties in social contacts, including the inability to engage in emotionally close and long-term romantic relationships
- Depression
- Negative impact on self-esteem
- Returning to imprisonment situation in dreams
- Blood pressure disorders requiring treatment
- Skin disorders requiring treatment

- Inability to recover in particular cognitive skills (e.g. in mathematics) the prisoner had mastered before solitary confinement

The prisoners felt that the effects of living in sensory deprivation were particularly horrible. Sensory deprivation has an effect on the brain, disrupts the vegetative nervous system and turns self-confident people into dependants who are wide open to being influenced by anyone they encounter during this phase of darkness and isolation. This also applies to adults who voluntarily choose such a situation. In January 2008 the BBC broadcast a programme called *Total Isolation* which affected me deeply: six volunteers allowed themselves to be locked up in a cell in a nuclear bunker for forty-eight hours. Alone and deprived of light, they found themselves in my situation, confronted by the same darkness and loneliness, albeit not the same fear or length of time. Despite the comparatively short time span, all six reported later that they had lost all sense of time and had experienced intense hallucinations and visions. When the forty-eight hours were over, all of them had lost the ability to perform simple tasks. Not one of them could think of the right answer when asked to come up with a word beginning with the letter 'F'. One of them had lost 36 per cent of his memory. Four of them were much more easily manipulated than before their isolation. They believed everything the first person they met after their voluntary imprisonment said to them. I only ever encountered the kidnapper.

When I read about such studies and experiments today, I am amazed that I managed to survive that period. In many ways the situation was comparable to the one that the adults had imposed upon themselves for the purposes of the study. Aside from the fact that my time in isolation lasted much, much longer, my case included yet another aggravating factor: I had absolutely no idea why I of all people had come to find myself in this situation. While political prisoners can hold tight to their mission, and even those who have been wrongly condemned know that a justice system, with its laws, institutions and procedures, is behind their seclusion, I was unable to discern even any kind of logical hostility in my imprisonment. There was none.

It may have helped me that I was still just a child and could adapt to the most adverse circumstances more easily than adults would ever have been able to. But it also required of me a self-discipline that, looking back, seems nearly inhuman. During the night, I used fantasy voyages to navigate the darkness. During the day, I stubbornly held tight to my plan to take my life into my own hands on my eighteenth birthday. I was firmly resolved to obtain the necessary knowledge to do so, and asked for reading matter and schoolbooks. In spite of the circumstances, I clung stubbornly to my own identity and the existence of my family.

As the first Mother's Day drew near, I made my mother a gift. I had neither glue nor scissors. The kidnapper gave me nothing I could use to hurt either myself or him. So I took my crayons from my school bag and drew several large red hearts on paper, carefully tore them out and stuck them on top of each other using Nivea lotion. I vividly imagined myself giving the hearts to my mother when I was free again. She would then know that I hadn't forgotten Mother's Day even though I couldn't be with her.

In the meantime, the kidnapper reacted more and more nega-tively when he saw that I spent time on such things, when I talked about my parents, my home and even my school. 'Your parents don't want you. They don't love you,' he repeated again and again. I refused to believe him, saying, 'That's not true, my parents love me. They told me so.' And I knew down in the deepest recesses of my heart that I was right. But my parents were so inaccessible that I felt as if I were on another planet. And yet only eighteen kilometres separated my dungeon from my mother's flat. Twenty-five minutes by car, a distance in the real world that was, in my mad world, subjected to a dimensional shift. I was so much further away than eighteen kilometres, in the midst of a world ruled by the despotic King of Hearts, in which the playing card people recoiled every time his voice boomed out.

When he was with me, he controlled my every gesture and facial expression: I was forced to stand the way he ordered me to, and I was never allowed to look him directly in the face. In his presence, he barked at me, I was to keep my gaze lowered. I was not permitted to speak if not asked to. He forced me to be submissive in his presence and demanded gratitude for every little thing he did for me: 'I saved you,' he said over and over, and seemed to mean it. He was my lifeline to the outside – light, food, books, all of these I could only get from him, and all of these he could deny me at any time. And he did so later with the consequence that I was forced to the brink of starvation.

Increasingly worn down as I was by the constant monitoring and isolation, still I did not feel any gratitude towards him. To be sure, he had not killed me or raped me, as I had feared at the beginning and had nearly expected. But at no time did I forget that his actions were a crime that I could condemn him for whenever I wanted to – and for which I never had to be thankful to him.

One day he ordered me to call him 'Maestro'.

At first I didn't take him seriously. It seemed much too ridiculous for words that someone should want to be called 'Maestro'. Yet he insisted on it, again and again: 'You will address me as "Maestro"!' At that point I knew that I mustn't give in. Those who resist continue to live. Those who are dead can no longer defend themselves. I didn't want to be dead, not even inside, which is why I had to defy him.

It reminded me of a passage from *Alice in Wonderland*: '"Well! I've often seen a cat without a grin," thought Alice; "but a grin without a cat! It's the most curious thing I ever saw in my life!"' Before me stood someone whose humanity shrank, whose façade crumbled, revealing a glimpse of a weak person. A failure in the real world, who drew his strength from his oppression of a small child. A pitiful picture. A grin that demanded that I call him 'Maestro'.

When I recall the situation today, I know why I refused to call him that at the time. Children are masters at manipulation. I must have instinctively felt how important it was to him – and that in my hand I held the key to exercising a certain power over him myself. At that moment I didn't think of the possible consequences that my refusal could entail. The only thing that crossed my mind was that I had already been successful with such behaviour before.

Back home in the Marco-Polo-Siedlung, I had sometimes walked the attack dogs belonging to my mother's customers. Their owners had impressed upon me never to allow the dogs to have too much leash – they would have exploited having too much room to move about. I should keep the leash close to their collar to show them at all times that any attempt at escape would be met with resistance. And I was never permitted to show them any fear. If you could do that, the dogs, even in the hands of a child as I was at the time, were tame and submissive.

When Priklopil now stood before me, I resolved not to allow myself to be intimidated by the frightening situation and keep the leash close to his collar. 'I'm not going to do that,' I told him to his face in a firm voice. He opened his eyes wide in surprise, protested and demanded from me again and again that I call him 'Maestro'. But finally he dropped the issue.

That was a key experience, even if that wasn't perhaps that clear to me at the time. I had demonstrated strength and the kidnapper had backed down. The cat's arrogant grin had disappeared. What was left was a person who had committed an evil deed, on whose moods my existence depended, but who in a way was also dependent on me.

In the following weeks and months I found it easier to deal with him when I pictured him as a poor, unloved child. Somewhere in the many crime stories and made-for-television films that I had watched before, I had picked up that people were evil if they had not been loved by their mothers and had had too little warmth at home. Today I realize that it was a protective mechanism necessary to my survival that I tried to see the kidnapper as a person who was not essentially evil, but had only become so in the course of his life. In no way did this mitigate what he had done, but it helped me to forgive him. By imagining on the one hand that he had perhaps had terrible experiences as an orphan in a home, from which he was still suffering today. And on the other hand by telling myself again and again that he surely also had a positive side. That he gave me the things I asked for, brought me sweets, took care of me. I think that in my complete dependence on him this was the only way for me to maintain the relationship with the kidnapper so necessary for me to survive. Had I met him only with hatred, that hatred would have eaten me up and robbed me of the strength I needed to make it through. Because I could catch at that moment a glimpse of the small, misguided and weak person behind the mask of the kidnapper, I was able to approach him.

Then there came the actual moment when I told him that. I looked at him and said, 'I forgive you, because everybody makes mistakes sometimes.' It was a step that may seem strange and sick to some people. After all, his 'mistake' had cost me my freedom. But it was the only right thing to do. I had to get along with this person, otherwise I would not survive.

Still, I never trusted him; that was impossible. But I came to terms with him. I 'consoled' him for the crime he had committed against me and appealed at the same time to his conscience, so that he would regret what he had done and at least treat me well. He paid me back by fulfilling small requests: a magazine about horses, a pen, a new book. Sometimes he would even say to me, 'I'll give you anything you want!' Then I would answer him, 'If you'll give me anything I want, why won't you let me go? I miss my parents so much.' But his answer was always the same, and I knew what it would be: my parents didn't love me – and he would never let me go.

After a few months in the dungeon, I asked him for the first time to embrace me. I needed the consolation of a touch, the feeling of human warmth. It was difficult. He had great problems with closeness, with touching. I myself on the other hand fell immediately into a blind panic and claustrophobia when he held me too tightly. But after several attempts we managed to find a way – not too close, not too tight, so that I could bear the embrace, and yet tight enough so that I could imagine feeling a loving, caring touch. It was my first physical contact with another human being in many months. For a ten-year-old child, it had been an endlessly long time.

5

Falling into Nothingness

How My Identity Was Stolen

In the autumn of 1998, over half a year since my abduction, I became completely discouraged and saddened. While my schoolmates had embarked on a new phase of their lives after the fourth grade, I was stuck here, crossing off the days on the calendar. Lost time. Lonely time. I missed my parents so much that I rolled myself up into a little ball at night, longing to hear a loving word from them, longing for an embrace. I felt small and weak, and was on the brink of capitulation. My mother had always drawn me a hot bath whenever I felt dejected and discouraged as a small child. She would put colourful bath beads that shone like silk and bubble bath in the water so that I sank under piles of crackling, fragrant clouds of foam. After my bath, she would wrap me in a thick towel, dry me, then lay me in bed and tuck me in. I always associated that with a profound feeling of security. A feeling I had had to do without for so long.

The kidnapper found it difficult to cope with my depression. When he came to the dungeon and found me sitting pathetically on my lounger, he eyed me agitatedly. He never directly addressed my mood, but tried to cheer me up with games, an extra piece of fruit or an additional episode of a television show on video. But my dark mood continued. How could I help it? After all, I was not suffering from a lack of entertainment media, but rather from the fact that I was chained through no fault of my own to the fantasy of the man who had already long ago sentenced me to life in prison.

I longed for the feeling that had always coursed through me after such a hot bath. When the kidnapper visited me in my dungeon during that time, I began to attempt to persuade him. A bath. Couldn't I take a bath just once? I asked him over and over. I don't know whether or not I got on his nerves at some point, or whether he decided for himself that perhaps it was really high time for a full bath. In any case, after a few days of asking and begging, he surprised me with the promise that I would be allowed to take a bath. If I was good.

I was allowed to leave the dungeon! I was allowed to go upstairs and bathe!

But what was this 'upstairs'? What would await me there? I vacillated between happiness, uncertainty and hope. Maybe he would leave me alone and maybe I could seize the opportunity to flee . . .

It wasn't until several days had gone by that the kidnapper came to let me out of the dungeon. And he used those days to quell any thoughts of escape in me: 'If you scream, I will have to hurt you. All of the windows and exits have been secured with explosive devices. If you open a window, you will end up blowing yourself up.' He impressed upon me that I had to stay away from windows and to make sure that I was not seen from outside. And if I failed to follow his orders down to the last detail, he would kill me on the spot. I did not doubt him for a minute. He had kidnapped me and locked me up. Why should he not also be capable of killing me?

When he finally opened the door to my dungeon one evening and ordered me to follow him, I could only hesitate in taking my first steps. In the diffuse light behind the door to my prison, I recognized a small, somewhat elevated and obliquely designed anteroom with a chest. Behind that was a heavy wooden door through which you entered a second anteroom. There my gaze fell on a massive, round-bodied monster on the narrow side of the wall on the left. A door made of reinforced concrete. Weighing 150 kilograms. Inserted in a nearly fifty-centimetre thick wall and locked from the outside with an iron-threaded bolt inserted into the masonry.

That is what it says in the police files. I can hardly put into words the feelings that surfaced in me when I got a look at that door. I had been encased in concrete. Hermetically sealed. The kidnapper warned me over and over of the explosive devices, the alarm systems, the cables with which he could electrify the entrance to my dungeon. A maximum-security prison for a child. What would become of me if something happened to him? My fear of choking on sausage skin seemed utterly ridiculous when I imagined him falling, breaking his arm and being taken to the hospital. Buried alive. Full stop.

I couldn't breathe. I had to get out of here. Immediately.

The reinforced concrete door opened up to allow me to view a small passageway. Height: 68.5 centimetres. Width: 48.5 centimetres. If I stood up, the lower edge of the access way was approximately at my knee level. The kidnapper was already waiting on the other side. I saw his legs outlined against the bright background. Then I got down on my knees and crawled forward on all fours. The black walls appeared to have been tarred, and the air was stale and damp. Once I had manoeuvred myself through the passageway, I was standing in an assembly pit for cars. Directly adjacent to the passageway were a dresser and a safe that had been moved aside.

The kidnapper once again told me to follow him. A narrow staircase, with walls of grey concrete tile, the steps high and slippery. Three down, nine up, through a trap door, and I was standing in the garage.

I stood as if paralysed. Two wooden doors. The heavy concrete door. The narrow passageway. In front of it a massive safe that the kidnapper, when I was in the dungeon, pushed in front of the entrance using a crowbar, screwed into the wall and, in addition, secured electrically. A dresser that concealed the safe and the passageway. Floorboards that covered the trap door leading down to the assembly pit.

I had already known that I would not be able to break open the door to my prison, that every attempt to flee my dungeon was futile. I had suspected that I could beat my hands against the walls and scream as long as I wanted to, nobody would hear me. But at that moment up in the garage, I understood instantaneously that nobody would ever find me either. The entrance to the dungeon was so perfectly camouflaged that the likelihood that the police would discover me when searching the house was frighteningly small.

My shock did not subside until an even stronger sensation imposed itself over my feeling of fear: air that poured into my lungs. I breathed in deeply, again and again, like someone dying of thirst who has reached a life-saving oasis at the very last second and dives into the life-giving water headfirst. After months in the cellar, I had completely forgotten how good it felt to breathe air that wasn't dry and dusty, blown by a fan into my tiny hole in the cellar. The whirring of the fan, which had wedged itself in my ears as an inescapable noise, waned for a moment; my eyes carefully scanned the unfamiliar contours and my initial tension dissolved.

But it returned immediately when the kidnapper indicated with a gesture that I was not to make a sound. Then he led me through an anteroom and up four stairs into the house. It was dim, as all the blinds had been let down. A kitchen, hallway, living room, foyer. The rooms I entered one after the other seemed unbelievable to me, almost ridiculously large and spacious. Since 2 March I had been kept in surroundings in which the greatest distance measured two metres. I could keep an eye on the small room from any angle and see what awaited me next. Here, the dimensions of the rooms swallowed me up like a large wave. Here, an unpleasant surprise, or evil, could be lurking behind every door, behind every window. After all, I did not know whether the kidnapper lived alone or how many people had been involved in my abduction – and what they would do with me if they saw me 'upstairs'. He had spoken of the 'others' so often that I expected them to be behind every corner. It also appeared plausible to me that he had a family that was in on it who were only waiting to torment me. For me, any conceivable kind of crime seemed within the realm of the possible.

The kidnapper appeared excited and nervous. On the way to the bathroom, he hissed at me repeatedly, 'Don't forget the windows and the alarm system. Do what I tell you. I'll kill you if you scream.' After I had seen the access way to my dungeon, there was absolutely no doubt in my mind when he told me that the entire house was armed with explosives.

While I let myself be led to the bathroom with my eyes lowered, as he wished, my thoughts raced. I racked my brains fiercely as to how I could overpower him and escape. I could think of nothing. I was not a coward as a child, but I had always been fearful. He was so much stronger and quicker than I was – if I had tried to run away, he would have been on me in two steps. And opening the doors and windows would obviously have been suicide. I continued to believe in the ominous security measures until after my escape.

However, it was not just the outward constraints, the many insurmountable walls and doors, the physical strength of the kidnapper, which prevented me from attempting escape. The cornerstone of my mental prison, from which I was less and less able to break away over the course of my imprisonment, had already been laid. I was intimidated and fearful. 'If you cooperate, nothing will happen to you.' The kidnapper had inculcated that belief into me from the very beginning, threatening me with the worst kinds of punishment, including death, if I resisted him. I was a child and used to obeying the authority of grown-ups – all the more if disobedience entailed consequences. He was the authority present. Even if the main door had stood wide open at that moment, I don't know if I would've had the courage to run. A house cat, allowed for the first time in her life to go outdoors, will remain, frightened, at the threshold and meow pitifully, because she does not know how to cope with her sudden freedom. And behind me was not the protective house I could return to, but rather a man who was willing to follow through with his crime to the death. I was already so deeply in my imprisonment that my imprisonment was already equally deep inside me.

The kidnapper ran a bubble bath and stayed as I undressed and got in. It bothered me that he wouldn't even leave me alone in the bathroom. On the other hand, I was already used to him seeing me naked from showering in the dungeon, so I only protested meekly. Once I sank into the warm water and closed my eyes, I was able to blot out everything around me. White peaks of foam piled over my fear, danced through the dark dungeon, washed me out of the house and carried me away with them. Into our bathroom at home, into the arms of my mother, who was waiting with a large, pre-warmed towel, and ready to take me straight to bed.

The wonderful image burst like a soap bubble when the kidnapper admonished me to hurry up. The towel was rough and smelled strange. Nobody took me to bed; instead, I descended into my dark dungeon. I heard him lock the wooden doors behind me, close the concrete door and bolt it. I imagined him going through the narrow passageway, heaving the safe into the opening again, screwing it into the wall and pushing the dresser in front of it. I wished I hadn't seen how hermetically I had been sealed off from the outside world. I lay down on my lounger, curled up and tried to recreate the feeling of the bubble bath and warm water on my skin. The feeling of being at home.

*

A little while later, in the autumn of 1998, the kidnapper once again showed me his caring side. Maybe he just had a guilty conscience; whatever the reason, my dungeon was to be made somewhat more inhabitable.

The work proceeded slowly; every piece of panelling, every bucket of paint had to be carried all the way down individually. Bookcases and cupboards could only be put together once in my dungeon.

I was allowed to pick a colour for the walls and decided in favour of wood-chip wallpaper that I wanted to have painted in pastel pink. Just like the wall in my room back home. The name of the colour was '*Elba glänzend*'. Later he used the same colour for his living room. There couldn't be any leftover tin of paint in a colour not used somewhere upstairs, he explained to me, always prepared for a police raid, always eager to nip any potential suspicions in the bud. As if the police back then had still been interested in me, as if they would have investigated such things, when they hadn't once examined the abduction car despite the two tips from the public.

My memories of my first days and weeks in the dungeon vanished piece by piece with the sections of drywall he used to cover up the wooden panelling. The sketch of the hallway dresser, my family tree, the 'Ave Maria'. But what I was getting instead seemed to be much better anyway: a wall that made me feel as if I were at home. When it was finally papered and painted, my small dungeon stank so strongly of chemicals that I was nauseated for days. The fumes from the fresh paint were too much for the small fan.

Then we proceeded to install my bunk bed. Priklopil brought boards and posts made of light-coloured pine into my dungeon, which he carefully screwed together. When the bed was finished, it took up nearly the entire width of the room and had a height of approximately one metre fifty. I was permitted to decorate the ceiling above it. I decided on three red hearts, which I carefully painted on. They were meant for my mother. When I looked at them, I could think of her.

The most complicated part was installing the ladder. It wouldn't fit through the door due to the difficult angle at which the anteroom was separated from the dungeon. The kidnapper tried it again and again, until he suddenly disappeared and came back with a battery-powered screwdriver, which he used to dismantle the wooden wall subdividing the anteroom. Then he dragged the ladder into the dungeon – and that very same day put the wall back up again.

As he was putting together my new bookcases, I witnessed for the first time a side of the kidnapper that terrified me deeply. Up until that point he had yelled at me sometimes, he had denigrated me, cursed at me, and threatened me with all sorts of terrible punishments in order to force my cooperation. But never had he lost control over himself.

He stood in front of me holding the drill and was in the process of affixing a board with screws. Working together in the dungeon had made me somewhat more trusting and I simply burst out with a question: 'Why are you screwing that board on right there?' For a second I had forgotten that I was only allowed to speak when he gave me permission. In a fraction of a second, the kidnapper flew into a rage, bellowed at me – and then he threw the heavy drill at me. I managed to duck at the very last moment before it slammed into the wall behind me. I was so stunned that it took my breath away, and I stared at him wide-eyed.

The sudden outburst of anger had not touched me physically. The drill hadn't even come into contact with me. But the incident burrowed itself deep into my psyche. Because it showed a new dimension in my relationship with the kidnapper: I now knew that he would hurt me if I did not obey him. It made me even more frightened and submissive.

The first night after the kidnapper's outburst, I lay upon the thin mattress in my new bunk bed. The rattling of the fan felt as if it was directly next to my ears and boring its way into my brain, until I would have loved to scream out in desperation. The cold air from the attic blew directly on my feet. While I had always slept on my back at home, stretched out, I now had to roll myself up on my side like a foetus and wrap the blanket tightly around my feet to avoid the unpleasant draught. But the bed was much softer than the sun-lounger. I could turn over and I had more room. And most of all I had my new wood-chip wallpaper.

I stretched out my hand, touched it and closed my eyes. I let the furniture in my room at home glide by in my thoughts, the dolls and stuffed animals as well. The position of the window, the door, the curtains, the smell. If I could just imagine it all intensely enough, I could fall asleep with my hand on the wall of the dungeon – and wake up the next day, still with my hand against the wall, in my room back home. Then my mother would bring me tea in bed, I would remove my hand from the wallpaper and everything would be okay.

Now I fell asleep every evening with my hand resting on the wallpaper, and was certain that one day I would in fact wake up again in my own room. During that initial phase, I believed in it as in a magic formula that would come true at some point. Later, touching the wallpaper was a promise to myself that I renewed every day. And I kept it: eight years later, when I visited my mother for the first time after my imprisonment I lay down on the bed in my room, where nothing had changed, and closed my eyes. When I touched the wall with my hand, all of those moments were there again – especially the first: the small, ten-year-old Natascha who was trying desperately not to lose confidence in herself, placing her hand on the wall in the dungeon for the first time. 'I'm here again,' I whispered. 'You see, it worked.'

*

The more the year wore on, the deeper my sadness became. When I crossed off the first few days in December, I was so gloomy that the chocolate 'Krampus'* the kidnapper brought me for St Nicholas Day† couldn't cheer me up. Christmas was coming closer and closer. And the thought of spending the holidays alone in my dungeon was absolutely unbearable.

Just as for any other child, Christmas was one of the highlights of the year for me. The smell of cookies, the decorated tree, the anticipation of gifts, the entire family coming together to celebrate the holiday. I was picturing these images as I apathetically pulled the foil wrapper off the chocolate. It was an image of childhood days, an image that had little in common with the last few Christmases that I had spent with my family. My nephews had come to visit us like always, but they had already received their presents at home. I was the only child opening gifts. As for tree decorations, my mother had a weakness for the latest trends, so our tree glittered with tinsel and purple balls. Underneath lay a pile of presents for me. While I opened one present after the other, the grown-ups sat on the couch, listening to the radio and looking at a tattoo magazine together. These were Christmases that disappointed me deeply. I had not even been able to persuade anyone to sing a Christmas carol with me, although I was so proud of the fact that I knew the songs that we had practised at school by heart.

It wasn't until the next day, when we celebrated with my grandmother, that I began to feel the Christmas spirit. All of us gathered in an adjacent room and solemnly sang 'Silent Night'. Then I listened for the anticipated small bell to ring. The

---

* 'Krampus' is a mythical creature who is said to accompany St Nicholas during the Christmas season, warning and punishing bad children.
† A celebration on 6 December when children receive sweets for having been good during the year.

Christkind* had been there. When we opened the door to the room, the Christmas tree shimmered in the light of real beeswax candles and gave off a wonderful smell. My grandmother always had a traditional, rustic Christmas tree, decorated with straw stars and glass baubles as delicate as soap bubbles.

That's how I imagined Christmas to be – and that's how it would have been this year as well. But I was going to spend the most significant family holiday of the year without my family. The idea frightened me. On the other hand, I had to admit that Christmas with my family had always been a disappointment anyway. And that I, in my isolation, was surely romanticizing the past. But I could try to make Christmas in my dungeon as similar as possible to how I remembered the Christmas holidays spent at my grandmother's.

The kidnapper played along. Back then I was infinitely grateful to him for making some semblance of a real Christmas possible. Today I think that he probably didn't do it for me, but rather because of his own inner compulsion. For him, too, celebrating holidays was enormously important – they provided structure, they followed certain rules, and he was unable to live without rules and structures which he obeyed with ridiculous stringency. Nevertheless, he still didn't have to grant my Christmas requests. The fact that he did may have had to do with the fact that he had been raised to meet expectations and conform to the image that others wanted to have of him. Today I know that he had failed time and again, primarily in his relationship with his father, on precisely those counts. The approval that he urgently wanted to receive from his father obviously was denied to him for long periods. Towards me, this attitude surfaced only in phases, but when it did

---

* The figure in Austria believed to bring children presents at Christmas, akin to Santa Claus. The word translates directly as 'Christ child'.

he was particularly absurd. After all, he was the one who had kidnapped me and locked me in the cellar. It's not a scenario in which you take the expectations of the other person, namely your victim, into account. It was as if he were choking someone and asking them at the same time whether they were lying comfortably and if the pressure was okay. However, at the time I blocked all of that out. I was full of grateful, childish wonder that the kidnapper was making such a fuss for me.

I knew that I wouldn't be able to have a real Christmas tree, so I asked for one made of plastic. We opened the box together and put the tree on one of the small cupboards. I was given a couple of angels and some sweets, and spent a great deal of time decorating the small tree.

On Christmas Eve I was alone watching television until the light was turned off, desperately trying not to think of my family at home. The kidnapper was at his mother's house, or she was visiting his, just as would happen on all the Christmases to come. But I didn't know that at the time. It wasn't until the next day that he celebrated with me. I was amazed that he gave me everything I asked for. I had asked for a small educational computer like the one I had received from my parents the year before. It was nowhere near as good as the first one I had got, but I was overjoyed that I could study without going to school. After all, I didn't want to be completely left behind should I manage to escape. I also got a pad of drawing paper and a box of watercolours. It was the same as the one that my father had given to me once, with twenty-four colours, including gold and silver, as if the kidnapper had given me a piece of my life back. The third package contained a paint-by-numbers set with oil paints. I had had that at home too, and I looked forward to the many hours of activity that the painstaking painting promised. The only thing that the kidnapper did not give me was turpentine. He was probably afraid that it would cause harmful fumes in the dungeon.

The days after Christmas I was busy with painting and my educational computer. I tried to see the positive side of my situation and suppress all longing for my family as much as possible by recalling the negative aspects of our last Christmases together. I tried to persuade myself that it was interesting to experience the holiday the way other grown-ups celebrated it. And I was exceedingly grateful that I had even had a Christmas celebration at all.

I spent my first New Year's Eve in captivity alone in complete darkness. I lay on my bunk bed and strained to hear whether I could make out the fireworks that would be set off at midnight up in the other world. But only the monotonous ticking of the alarm clock and the rattling of the fan penetrated my ears. Later I found out that the kidnapper always spent New Year's Eve with his friend Holzapfel. He prepared meticulously, buying the largest, most expensive rockets. Once, I must've been fourteen or fifteen, I was allowed to watch from inside the house as he set off a rocket in the early evening. At sixteen I was even allowed outside in the garden to watch a rocket sprinkle a shower of silver balls across the sky. But that was at a time when my captivity had become a fixed component of my 'self'. That's why the kidnapper dared take me with him out into the garden in the first place. He knew that by then my inner prison had grown such high walls that I would not seize the opportunity to escape.

The year in which I had been abducted was over, and I was still being held captive. The world outside moved even further into the distance and my memories of my former life became dimmer and unreal. I found it difficult to believe that a year earlier I had been a primary school girl, who played in the afternoon, went on outings with her parents and led a normal life.

I tried to come to terms as best I could with the life that I had been forced to lead. It wasn't always easy. The kidnapper's control continued to be absolute. His voice in the intercom exasperated my nerves. In my tiny dungeon, I felt as though I were miles below the earth, yet at the same time living in a fishbowl where my every move could be watched.

My visits upstairs now took place on a more regular basis: about every two weeks I was allowed to take a shower upstairs, and sometimes he let me eat and watch television in the evening. I was glad of every minute I could spend outside my dungeon, but in the house I was still afraid. I now knew that he was there alone, and no strangers would be waiting to ambush me. But my nervousness barely lessened. Because of his own paranoia, he made sure that it was impossible to relax even for a moment. When I was upstairs, I felt as if I were bound to the kidnapper by an invisible leash. I was forced always to stand and walk at the same distance from him – one metre, no more, no less – otherwise he would explode in anger. He demanded that I keep my head down, never lifting my eyes.

After the endless hours and days that I had spent in my dungeon completely isolated, I was very susceptible to his orders and manipulations. The lack of light and human contact had weakened me to such an extent that I was no longer able to defy him beyond a certain basic level of resistance. I never stopped resisting him completely, which helped me draw the boundaries that I saw as indispensable. But I rarely thought of escape any more. It seemed as if the invisible leash that he put me on upstairs was becoming more and more real, as if I were in fact chained to him and not physically able to move either nearer or further away. He had anchored the fear of the world outside – where no one loved me, no one missed me and no one was looking for me – so deep inside me that it almost became greater than my longing for freedom.

When I was in the dungeon, I tried to keep myself as busy as possible. On the long weekends I spent by myself, I continued to clean and tidy up for hours until everything was clean and smelled fresh. I painted a great deal and used even the smallest bit of space on my pad for my pictures: my mother in a long skirt, my father with his fat stomach and his moustache, me laughing in between. I drew the radiantly yellow sun that I hadn't seen for many, many months, and houses with smoking chimneys, colourful flowers and playing children – fantasy worlds that for hours allowed me to forget what my reality looked like.

One day, the kidnapper gave me a book of handicrafts. It was meant for pre-school children and made me more sad than it cheered me up. Catching paper aeroplanes was simply not possible in just five square metres of space. A better gift was the Barbie doll I was given just a little while later, and a small sewing kit, the kind that you sometimes find in hotels. I was infinitely grateful for this long-legged person made of plastic that now kept me company. It was a Horse-Riding Barbie with riding boots, white trousers, a red waistcoat and a riding crop. I asked the kidnapper for days to bring me some scraps of fabric. Sometimes it could take ages for him to satisfy such requests. And then only if I followed his orders precisely. If I cried, for example, he would take away all my amenities, such as the books and videos I needed to live. In order to get something I wanted I had to show him my gratitude and praise him for everything he did – including the fact that he had locked me up.

Finally I had worked on him so much that he brought me an old top, a white polo shirt made of soft, smooth jersey with a fine blue pattern. It was the one he had worn the day of my abduction. I don't know whether he had forgotten or simply wanted to get rid of it out of paranoia. I used the material to make a cocktail dress with thin spaghetti straps made of thread and an elegant asymmetrical top for my Barbie. Using a string that I had found among my school things, I turned a sleeve into a case for my glasses. Later I was able to persuade the kidnapper to allow me to have an old cloth serviette, which had become blue in the wash and he now used as a cleaning rag. From that I made a ball gown for my Barbie, with a thin rubber band at the waist.

Later, I made trivets from wires and folded miniature artworks out of paper. The kidnapper brought me craft needles so that I could practise crocheting and knitting. Outside, as a primary school girl, I had never learned to do them properly. When I had made mistakes, people quickly lost patience with me. Now I had an infinite amount of time, nobody corrected me, and I could always start over again, until my small handcrafted projects were finished. These craft projects became a psychological lifesaver for me. They kept me from madness in the lonely inactivity I was forced to endure. And at the same time I could think of my parents while I made small gifts for them – for some day when I would be free again.

Of course, I couldn't breathe a word to the kidnapper that I was making something for my parents. I hid the pictures from him and spoke less frequently of them, because he reacted more and more indignantly whenever I talked about my life outside, before my imprisonment. 'Your parents don't love you. They don't care about you, otherwise they would have paid your ransom,' he had said in the beginning, still annoyed whenever I spoke about how much I missed them. Then, sometime in the spring of 1999, came the prohibition: I was no longer allowed to mention my parents or to speak of anything I had experienced before my imprisonment. My mother, my father, my sisters and nephews, school, my last ski trip, my tenth birthday, my father's holiday house, my cats. Our apartment, my habits, my mother's shop. My teacher, my friends from school, my room. Everything that had existed before was now taboo.

The prohibition on my past became a standard component of his visits to my dungeon. Whenever I mentioned my parents, he flew into a rage. When I cried, he turned the light off and left me in complete darkness until I was 'good' again. Being 'good' meant I was to be grateful that he had 'rescued' me from my previous life.

'I rescued you. You belong to me now,' he said over and over. Or: 'You no longer have a family. I am your family. I am your father, your mother, your grandma and your sisters. I am now your everything. You no longer have a past.' He hammered it into me. 'You're so much better off with me. You're lucky that I took you in and that I take such good care of you. You belong to me now. I have created you.'

> Pygmalion loathing their lascivious life,
> Abhorr'd all womankind, but most a wife:
> So single chose to live, and shunn'd to wed,
> Well pleas'd to want a consort of his bed.
> Yet fearing idleness, the nurse of ill,
> In sculpture exercis'd his happy skill;
> And carv'd in iv'ry such a maid, so fair,
> As Nature could not with his art compare . . .
>
> Ovid, *Metamorphoses*

Today I believe that Wolfgang Přiklopil, in committing a terrible crime, wanted to create nothing more than his own little perfect world with a person that could be there just for him. He probably would never have been able to do so the normal way and had therefore decided to force and mould someone to do it. Basically, he didn't want anything more than anyone else: love, approval, warmth. He wanted somebody for whom he himself was the most important person in the world. He didn't seem to have seen any other way to achieve that than to abduct a shy, ten-year-old girl and cut her off from the outside world until she was psychologically so alienated that he could 'create' her anew.

The year I turned eleven, he took from me my history and my identity. I was not to be anything more than a piece of blank paper on which he could pen his sick fantasies. He even denied me my reflection in the mirror. If I couldn't see myself reflected in my social interactions with anyone else other than the kidnapper, I wanted to at least be able to see my own face to keep from losing myself completely. But he refused my request for a small mirror again and again. It wasn't until years later that I received a mirrored bathroom cabinet. When I gazed into it I no longer saw the child-like features I once had, but rather an unfamiliar face.

Had he truly recreated me? Whenever I ask myself that question today, I can't answer it unequivocally. On the one hand, he had picked the wrong person when he chose me. I continued to resist his attempts to erase my identity and make me into his creature. He never broke me.

On the other hand, his attempts to make me into a new person fell on fertile ground, especially because of who I was. Just before my abduction I had been sick of my life and was so dissatisfied with myself that I had decided to change something. And just minutes before he threw me into his delivery van, I had vividly imagined throwing myself in front of a moving car – that's how much I hated the life that I saw myself forced to live.

Of course, the fact that I was not allowed to have my own history made me infinitely sad. I felt it was a gross injustice that I was not allowed to be myself any more or talk about the deep pain the loss of my parents had caused. But what actually remained of my own history? It now consisted only of memories that had very little to do with the real world that had continued to turn without me. My primary school class no longer existed; my little nephews had grown and would perhaps not even recognize me, even if I were suddenly to stand in front of them. And perhaps my parents really were relieved because they were now spared the long and tiresome arguments over me. By cutting me off from everything for so long, the kidnapper had created the perfect foundation to enable him to take my past away from me. Because even while on the conscious level and to his face I held tight to my opinion that my abduction had been a serious crime, his constantly repeated command to view him as my saviour seeped ever more deeply into my subconscious. Basically it was much easier for me to look upon the kidnapper as my saviour, not as an evil person. In a desperate attempt to force myself to see the positive aspects of my imprisonment, so as not to let it destroy me, I said to myself, 'At least it can't get any worse.' Unlike what had happened in many of the cases that I'd heard about on television, up to that point the kidnapper had neither raped nor murdered me.

The theft of my identity did, however, offer me a great deal of freedom. Today when I think back to that feeling, it seems incomprehensible and paradoxical in light of the fact that I had been so completely robbed of my liberty. But back then I felt unencumbered by preconceived opinions for the first time in my life. I was no longer just a small cog in a family where the roles had already long been doled out – and where they had assigned me that of clumsy roly-poly. A family in which I had become a pawn for the adults whose decisions I often didn't understand.

Although I was now caught up in a system of complete oppression, had lost my freedom of movement and one single person governed every detail of my life, this form of oppression and manipulation was direct and clear. The kidnapper was not the kind of person to act subtly – he wanted to exercise his power in an open and unvarnished way. In the shadow of his power, which dictated how I should do everything, I was paradoxically able to be myself for the first time in my life.

One sign of this was the fact that since my abduction I never again wet the bed. Although I was subjected to an inhuman burden, a certain kind of stress seems to have lifted from me at that time. If I had to sum it up in one sentence, I would say that by giving up my history and submitting to the kidnapper's wishes, I felt wanted – for the first time in a long time.

In late autumn 1999, the stripping of my identity was complete. The kidnapper had ordered me to pick out a new name: 'You are no longer Natascha. Now you belong to me.'

I had refused for a long time, partly because I found that using names was unimportant anyway. There was only me and him, and 'you' was enough to know who was being addressed. But saying the name 'Natascha' triggered so much anger and displeasure in him that I acquiesced. And besides, hadn't I always disliked that name? When my mother called it reproachfully, it had the ugly sound of unmet demands and expectations I could never live up to. I had always wished for one of those names that other girls had: Stefanie, Jasmin, Sabine. Anything but Natascha. 'Natascha' contained everything that I had not liked about my former life. Everything I wanted to get rid of, everything I was forced to get rid of.

The kidnapper suggested 'Maria' as my new name, because both his grandmothers were called Maria. Although I did not like his suggestion, I agreed, because Maria was my middle name anyway. However, that didn't sit well with the kidnapper because the point was I was to have a completely new name. He pressed me to suggest something different. That very minute.

I leafed through my calendar, which gave the saints' days, and on 2 December found one possibility right next to Natascha: 'Bibiane'. For the next seven years, 'Bibiane' became my new identity, even though the kidnapper never succeeded in entirely wiping out my old one.

The kidnapper had taken my family away, my life and my freedom, my old identity. The physical prison of the dungeon underground, behind the many heavy doors, was supplemented piece by piece by a psychological one, whose walls grew ever higher. And I began to thank the prison warden who had built it. Because at the end of the year, he granted me one of the wishes most dear to my heart: a moment outside under the sky.

It was a cold, clear December night. He had already communicated to me his rules for this 'outing' days before: 'If you scream, I will kill you; if you run, I will kill you; I will kill anyone who hears or sees you, if you are so dumb as to draw attention to yourself.' It wasn't enough for him any more to threaten to kill just me. He also burdened me with the responsibility for anyone I might call to for help. I believed his murderous plans immediately and without reflection. Even today I'm convinced that he would've been capable of killing an unsuspecting neighbour who had accidentally taken notice of me. Anyone who goes to so much effort to keep a prisoner in the cellar would not hesitate to commit murder.

When he grabbed me firmly by the upper arm and opened the door to the garden, a deep sense of happiness came over me. The cool air gently caressed my face and arms, the odour of rot and isolation that had taken over my nose slowly receded, and my head became lighter. For the first time in nearly two years, I felt the soft ground beneath my feet. Every blade of grass that gave way under the soles of my shoes seemed to me a precious, singular living creature. I lifted my head and looked at the sky. The infinite space that opened up before me took my breath away. The moon was low on the horizon and a couple of stars twinkled far above. I was outside. For the first time since I had been pulled into a delivery van on 2 March 1998. I tilted my head all the way back and tried with difficulty to suppress a sob.

The kidnapper led me through the garden up to the privet hedgerow. Once there, I stretched out my hand, cautiously touching the dark leaves. They smelled tangy and shone in the moonlight. It seemed like a miracle to me to touch something living with my hand. I plucked a few leaves and put them in my pocket. A souvenir of what was living in the world outside.

After a short moment, he turned me round without a word and led me back into the house. The first time I saw it in the moonlight from the outside: a yellow house with a sloped roof and two chimneys. The windows were outlined in white. The lawn we were walking across seemed unnaturally short and well maintained.

Suddenly I was beset by doubts: I saw grass, trees, leaves, a piece of the sky, a house, a garden. But was this the world as I remembered it? Everything looked too flat, too artificial. The grass was green and the sky big, but you could see that these were stage backdrops! He had placed the shrubbery and the house there in order to deceive me. I had landed in a kind of theatre production, where the outdoor scenes of a television series were filmed. There were no neighbours, no city with my family only twenty-five minutes away by car. Instead, all of them were the kidnapper's accomplices who were trying to make me believe that I was outside, while they watched me on huge monitors and laughed at my naivety. I closed my hand firmly around the leaves in my pocket, as if they could prove something to me: that this was real, that *I* was really real. But I felt nothing. Only a large emptiness that reached mercilessly for me like a cold hand.

6

Torment and Hunger

The Daily Struggle to Survive

My childhood was over when I was abducted at the age of ten. I ceased being a child in the dungeon in the year 2000. One morning I woke up with a cramping pain in my abdomen and found spots of blood on my pyjamas. I knew immediately what was happening. I had been waiting for my period to start for years. I knew the particular brand of sanitary pads I wanted from a commercial that the kidnapper had recorded after some of the television series. When he came into the dungeon, I asked him as matter-of-factly as possible to buy me several packets. Confronted with this new development, the kidnapper was deeply unsettled, and his paranoia reached a new level. Until then, he had painstakingly picked up every piece of lint, frantically wiped away every single fingerprint, in order to eliminate all traces of me, and now he was nearly hysterical in making sure that I wouldn't sit down anywhere upstairs in the house. If I was allowed to sit somewhere, he put down a pile of newspapers first in an absurd attempt to prevent even the tiniest spot of blood from staining his house. He continued to worry daily that the police would show up and search his house for traces of DNA.

I felt personally harassed by his behaviour, like an untouchable. It was a confusing time when I urgently needed to be able to talk to my mother or one of my older sisters about the changes taking place inside my body that had so suddenly confronted me. But the only person I had to talk to was a man who was completely out of his depth on the issue. Who treated me as if I were dirty and disgusting. And who obviously had never lived with a woman.

His behaviour towards me underwent a clear change once I entered puberty. As long as I had still been a child, I was 'allowed' to remain in my dungeon and go about my business within the narrow framework of his rules. Now, having become a woman, I had to be at his service, performing tasks in and on the house under his strict supervision.

Upstairs in the house I felt as if I were in an aquarium, like a fish in a too-small container who looks longingly at the outside world, but doesn't jump out of the water as long as it can still live in its prison. Because crossing that line means certain death.

The line demarcating where the outside began was so absolute that it appeared insurmountable to me. As if the house was in a different dimension to the world outside its yellow walls. As if the house, the garden and the garage with its dungeon were located on a different matrix. Sometimes a hint of spring would waft in through a tilted window. From time to time I could hear a distant car driving down the peaceful street. Otherwise nothing more from the world outside could be discerned. The blinds were always down and the entire house was bathed in dim light. The alarm systems on the windows were activated – at least, I was convinced that they were. There were still moments when I thought of escape. But I no longer made any specific plans. The fish does not jump over the edge of the glass bowl where only death awaits.

But my longing for freedom remained.

I was now being constantly watched. I was not allowed to take a single step without him having already ordered me to. I had to stand, sit or walk however the kidnapper wanted. I had to ask if I wanted to stand up or sit down, before I turned my head or how to hold out my hand. He told me where I was to direct my gaze and even accompanied me to the toilet. I don't know what was worse, the time I spent alone in the dungeon or the time I was no longer alone, not even for a second.

This permanent surveillance reinforced my feeling of having landed in an absurd experiment. The atmosphere in the house intensified that impression. Behind its bourgeois façade, it seemed to have fallen out of time and space. Lifeless, uninhabited, like a backdrop for a gloomy film. On the outside, it fitted perfectly into its environment: conventional, extraordinarily well maintained, with thick shrubbery around the large garden to carefully screen it from the neighbours. Curious eyes were unwanted.

Strasshof is a faceless town with no history, with no centre and no character, as you would expect with a population today of about 9,000. After the town limit sign, the houses, stooping in the flat Marchfeld plain, line a thoroughfare and a railway line, interrupted time and again by the commercial areas common to the cheap surroundings of any large city. In particular, the town's full name, 'Strasshof an der Nordbahn', or 'Strasshof on the Northern Railway Line', is a major clue that this is an area whose lifeline is its connection to Vienna. You travel away from here, you travel through here, you don't travel to here without good reason. The town's attractions include a 'locomotive monument' and a railway museum named 'Heizhaus', or 'boiler house'. A century ago, not even fifty people lived here; today its inhabitants work in Vienna, returning to their suburban houses, lined up monotonously next to one another, only to sleep. At the weekend, the lawnmowers hum, the cars are polished and the cosy living room remains hidden behind closed curtains and blinds in partial darkness. Here, the façade is what counts, not what you might discover behind it. The perfect place to lead a double life. The perfect place for a crime.

The house itself was laid out as a typical early 1970s building. On the ground floor, a long hallway in which a staircase led to the upper floor. On the left the bathroom and toilet, on the right the living room, and at the end of the hallway, the kitchen. This was an oblong room, with a kitchenette on the left with rustic cabinet fronts of dark wood veneer. On the floor, tiling with an orange-brown flowered pattern. A table, four chairs with cloth coverings, hooks in the 'Prilblume' flower design on the grey-white wall tiling with the dark green decorative flowers next to the sink.

The most striking part of the room was the mural wallpaper which covered the wall on the right: a forest of birch trees, green, with slender trunks stretching upwards, as if trying to flee the oppressive atmosphere of the room. When I looked at it properly for the first time, it seemed grotesque to me that someone who could commune with nature at any time, who could go out into life whenever he liked, would surround himself with artificial, dead nature; while I desperately tried to bring life into my bedroom in the dungeon, be it only in the form of a couple of plucked leaves.

I don't know how often I scrubbed and polished the floor and the tiling in the kitchen until they gleamed immaculately. Not the tiniest streak, not the smallest crumb was allowed to mar the smooth surfaces. And when I thought I was done, I had to lie on the floor in order to check even the furthest corner from that perspective. The kidnapper always stood behind me, giving me orders. It was never clean enough for him. On countless occasions, he took the cloth from my hand and showed me how to clean 'properly'. And he flew into a rage if I besmirched a beautiful smooth surface with an oily fingerprint, thereby destroying the façade of the untouched and pure.

For me, the worst thing was cleaning the living room. It was a large room that exuded a gloom that did not only come from the closed blinds. A dark, nearly black coffered ceiling, dark wood panelling, a green leather suite, light-brown wall-to-wall carpeting. A dark brown bookcase containing works such as Kafka's *The*

Judgement and Peter Kreuder's *Only Dolls Don't Cry*. An unused fireplace with a poker and, on the mantel above, a candle on a wrought-iron candle holder, a clock, a miniature helmet from a medieval knight's armour. Two medieval portraits on the wall above the fireplace.

Whenever I spent any long period of time in that room, I had the impression that the gloom would penetrate through my clothes into every pore of my body. The living room seemed to me the perfect mirror image of the kidnapper's 'other' side. Conservative, conformist and well adjusted on the surface, barely covering the dark layer underneath.

Today I know that for years Wolfgang Priklopil had barely changed anything in that house built by his parents in the 1970s. He wanted to renovate completely to his specifications only the upper floor, which had three bedrooms, and the attic. An attic dormer window was to allow additional light in; the dusty attic, with its bare wooden beams along the slanted roof, was to be outfitted with drywalling and transformed into a living space. For me, this meant that a new phase of my imprisonment was about to begin.

For the next months and years the upper floor under renovation was where I spent most of my time during the day. Priklopil himself no longer had a regular job, although sometimes he did disappear to do some 'business' with his friend Holzapfel. I didn't find out until much later that they renovated flats in order to rent them out. However, they can't have had too many orders coming in, because most of the time the kidnapper was busy renovating his own house. I was his only worker. A worker he could fetch from the dungeon as needed to do the back-breaking work that most people would have paid tradesmen to do, and who he then coerced into cooking and cleaning 'after the working day' before he locked her in the cellar again.

Back then I was actually much too young to do all the jobs he burdened me with. Whenever I see twelve-year-old kids today complaining and rebelling when asked to do easy chores, it makes me smile every time. I don't begrudge them that small act of rebellion at all. I couldn't rebel; I had to obey.

The kidnapper, who didn't want any strange workmen in the house, took on the entire renovation project himself and forced me to do things that were far beyond my strength and capabilities. Together with him, I dragged marble slabs and heavy doors, hauled sacks of cement across the floor, broke open concrete with a chisel and a sledgehammer. We installed the dormer window, insulated and covered the walls, poured screed, then laid heating pipes and electric cabling, plastered the drywall panels, hammered an opening between the upper floor and the new attic floor and built a staircase with marble tiling.

The upper floor was next. The old flooring was ripped out, a new one put in. The doors were removed, the door frames sanded and repainted. The old brown fibre wallpaper had to be torn off the walls and new wallpaper hung and painted. We built a new bathroom with marble tiling in the attic. I was his assistant and serf in one: I had to help him carry things, hand him tools, scrape, chisel, paint. Or hold the bowl with the filler for hours, not moving, while he smoothed out the walls. When he sat down and took a break, I had to fetch him drinks.

The work had its upside too. After two years during which I could hardly move around in my tiny room, I enjoyed the exhausting physical activity. The muscles in my arms grew, and I felt strong and useful. Most of all in the beginning I enjoyed being allowed to spend several hours a day during the week outside my dungeon. Of course, the walls around me upstairs were no less insurmountable. The invisible leash too was stronger than ever before. But at least I had a change of pace.

At the same time, upstairs in the house, I was helplessly at the mercy of the kidnapper's evil, dark side. I had evidence from the incident with the drill that he was susceptible to uncontrolled outbursts of rage if I wasn't 'good'. In the dungeon there was hardly any opportunity not to be 'good'. But now, as I worked, I could make a mistake any second. And the kidnapper didn't like mistakes.

'Hand me the putty knife,' he said on one of our first days in the attic. I gave him the wrong tool. 'You can't f— do anything, can you?' he burst out. From one second to the next his eyes went dark, as if a cloud had cast a shadow over his irises. His face became distorted. He grabbed a sack of cement lying next to him, lifted it and threw it at me with a shout. It took me unawares and the heavy sack hit me with such force that I staggered for a moment.

I froze inside. It wasn't so much the pain that shocked me. The sack was heavy, and the impact hurt, but I could have handled it. It was the sheer aggression bursting forth from the kidnapper that took my breath away. After all, he was the only person in my life; I was completely dependent on him. That outburst threatened me in an extreme way. I felt like a battered dog, who is not allowed to bite the hand that beats him because it is the same hand that feeds him. The only way out I had was to escape into myself. I closed my eyes, blocked everything out and didn't move a centimetre.

The kidnapper's burst of aggression was over as quickly as it had come. He came over to me, shook me, tried to lift my arms and tickled me. 'Please stop. I'm sorry,' he said. 'It wasn't really so bad.' I remained standing there with my eyes closed. He pinched my side and pushed the corners of my mouth up with his fingers. A tormented smile, in the truest meaning of the word. 'Be normal again. I'm sorry. What can I do to make you normal again?'

I don't know how long I stood there, motionless, silent, eyes closed. At some point my childish pragmatism won out. 'I want an ice cream and gummi bears!'

Half of me exploited the situation to get sweets. The other half wanted to render the attack less significant with my request. He reiterated that he was sorry and that it would never happen again – just as every violent husband promises his battered wife and children.

Yet that outburst seemed to open the floodgates. He began to beat me on a regular basis. I don't know what switch was thrown or if he simply believed that in his omnipotence he could do anything he wanted. I had been held captive now for over two years. He had not been discovered and had such control over me that I wouldn't run away. Who was there to punish his behaviour? In his eyes he had the right to make demands of me and punish me physically if I failed to meet those demands immediately.

From then on he reacted to even the smallest inattentions with violent outbursts of temper. A couple of days after the incident with the sack of cement, he ordered me to hand him a plasterboard panel. He thought I was too slow – he grabbed my hand and twisted it round, rubbing it so hard against one of the plasterboard panels that I had a burn on the back of my hand that took years to heal. Again and again the kidnapper would rub open the wound – on the wall, on plasterboard panels; even on the smooth surface of the sink he succeeded in rubbing my hand with such brute force that blood seeped through my skin. Today, still, that spot on my right hand remains raw.

Another time when I yet again reacted too slowly to one of his orders, he aimed a Stanley knife at me. The sharp blade, which can cut through carpeting like butter, punctured my knee and remained stuck there. The pain seared so viciously through my leg that I felt nauseated. I felt the blood running down my shin. When he saw that, he bellowed as if he had taken all leave of his senses. 'Leave it! You're making a stain!' Then he grabbed me and dragged me to the bathroom to staunch the bleeding and bind my wound. I was in shock and could hardly breathe. Indignantly he splashed water on my face and barked at me, 'Stop crying.' Afterwards I was given another ice cream.

Soon he began to abuse me verbally while I did the housework as well. He would sit in his leather chair in the living room and watch me kneel and wipe the floor, making deprecating remarks about every one of my gestures.

'You are even too dumb to clean.'

'You can't even wipe away a spot of dirt.'

I would stare silently at the floor, boiling inside. On the outside, I cleaned with twice the energy. But that still wasn't enough. Without warning I would suddenly be kicked in the side or in the shin. Until everything shone.

Once, when I was thirteen years old and hadn't cleaned the kitchen counter quickly enough, he kicked me so hard in the tailbone that I slammed against the edge of the cooker and split the skin covering my hip bone. Although I was bleeding heavily, he sent me back to my dungeon with no plaster, no bandages, indignant at the annoyance my gaping wound had caused. It took weeks to heal, because he kept pushing me against the edge of the cooker in the kitchen time and again. Unexpectedly, casually, purposefully. Again and again the thin scab that had formed over the wound on my hip bone would be ripped off.

What he would not stand for at all was when the pain made me cry. Then he would grab my arm and wipe the tears from my face with the back of his hand with such brute force that fear made me stop crying. If that didn't work, he would grab me by the throat, drag me to the sink and push me under. He would squeeze my windpipe and rub my face with cold water until I almost lost consciousness. He hated being confronted with the consequences of his mistreatment. Tears, bruises, bloody injuries, he would see none of it. What you can't see didn't happen.

It wasn't systematic beatings that he subjected me to, which I could have come in a way to expect, but rather sudden outbursts that became more and more violent. Perhaps because with every line he crossed he realized that he could do so with impunity. Perhaps because he was unable to do anything to stop the spiral of violence from escalating further.

I think I got through that period only because I separated those experiences from myself. Not based on a conscious decision that an adult would take, but rather based on the survival instinct of a child. I left my body whenever the kidnapper pummelled it, and from a distance watched a twelve-year-old girl lying on the floor being battered by his feet. And even today I can only describe these attacks from a distance, as if they never happened to me, but rather someone else. I vividly remember the pain I felt from the blows and the pain that accompanied me for days. I remember I had so many bruises that there was no position I could possibly lie in that wasn't painful. I remember the torment that I went through some days, and how long my pubic bone hurt after a kick. The skin abrasions, the lacerations. And the snapping in my cervical vertebrae when he struck my head with the full force of his fist.

But emotionally, I felt nothing.

The only feeling I was not able to split off from myself was the mortal fear that seized me in those moments. It bit into my mind, my vision went black, my ears droned and adrenaline rushed through my veins, commanding me: *Flee!* But I couldn't. The prison that in the beginning was only on the outside now held me captive on the inside.

Soon, the first signs that the kidnapper could strike out at any moment were enough to make my heart start pounding. My breathing became shallow and I went stiff with fright. Even when I sat in my comparatively safe dungeon, I was seized by mortal fear as soon as I heard in the distance that the kidnapper was unscrewing the safe blocking the passageway from the wall. The feeling of panic that the body files away in its memory bank once it has experienced mortal fear and recalls at the slightest hint of a similar threat is uncontrollable. It held me in its iron grip.

After about two years of this, when I was fourteen, I began to fight back. At first it was a kind of passive resistance. When he shouted at me and drew his hand back to strike, I hit myself in the face until he told me to stop. I wanted to force him to look. He had to see how he treated me; he himself was to take the blows that I had had to take up until then. No more ice cream, no gummi bears.

At fifteen I hit back for the first time. He looked at me, surprised and somewhat stunned, when I punched him in the stomach. I felt powerless; my arm moved much too slowly and the blow had been hesitantly executed. But I had fought back. And I struck him again. He grabbed me and put me in a headlock until I stopped.

Of course, I didn't stand a chance against him physically. He was bigger, stronger; he caught me with ease, held me at a distance, so that my punches and kicks mostly hit empty air. Nonetheless, fighting back became vital to my survival. In so doing I proved to myself that I was strong and hadn't lost my self-respect. And at the same time I showed him that there were lines I was not pre-pared to allow him to cross any more. That was a decisive moment in my relationship with the kidnapper, the only person in my life and the only one who brought me sustenance. Who knows what he would have been capable of had I not fought back.

Once I entered puberty, the terror with food began. The kidnapper brought scales down into my dungeon once or twice a week. Back then I weighed forty-five kilograms and was a pudgy child. Over the next few years, I grew – and slowly slimmed down.

After a phase where I was relatively free to 'order' what I wanted to eat, he had gradually taken control over the first year, ordering me to ration my food well. In addition to forbidding me to watch television, food deprivation was one of his most effective strategies to keep me in line. But when I was twelve and my body underwent a growth spurt, he began linking the rationing of food to insults and accusations.

'Just look at you. You are fat and ugly.'

'You are such a glutton. You are going to eat me out of house and home.'

'Those who don't work, don't need to eat.'

His words pierced me like arrows. Even before my imprisonment I had been deeply unhappy with my figure, which appeared to me to be the greatest obstacle in my path towards a carefree childhood. The awareness that I was chubby filled me with a gnawing, destructive self-hate. The kidnapper knew precisely which buttons he had to push to land blows to my self-esteem, and he pressed them mercilessly.

At the same time, he was so clever about it that in the first few weeks and months I was really grateful for his control. After all, he was helping me reach one of my greatest goals: losing weight. 'Just take me for example. I hardly have to eat anything,' he told me over and over. 'You have to see it as a kind of trip to a fat farm.' And, lo and behold, I could almost picture myself shedding the fat before my very eyes, becoming lean and wiry. Until the supposedly well-meaning food rationing turned into a terror campaign which brought me to the brink of starvation at the age of sixteen.

Today I believe that the kidnapper, who was extremely thin, was probably battling anorexia himself, which he now transferred to me as well. He was filled with a deep mistrust of food of all kinds. He believed that the food industry was capable of committing collective murder with poisoned food at any time. He never used seasonings because he had read that some of them came from India and had been subjected to radiation there. And then there was his miserliness, which became ever more pathological over the course of my imprisonment. Even milk became too expensive for him at one point.

My food rations were dramatically reduced. In the morning I was given a cup of tea and two tablespoons of cereal with a glass of milk or a slice of *Guglhupf**, which was often so thin that you could have read the newspaper through it. I was given sweets only after severe beatings. At lunch and in the evening, I received a quarter of an 'adult plate'. When the kidnapper came into my dungeon with the food his mother had made or a pizza, the following rule of thumb applied: three-quarters for him, one-quarter for me. Whenever I was to cook for myself in the dungeon, he made a list beforehand of what I was allowed to eat – for example, 200 grams of frozen vegetables to boil or half a ready-to-eat meal. Add to that, one kiwi fruit and one banana a day. If I violated his rules and ate more than I was allowed, I could count on one of his violent outbursts.

He exhorted me to weigh myself and meticulously monitored my notes recording my weight. 'Take me as an example.' *Yes, take him as an example. I am such a glutton. I am much too fat.* The constant, gnawing feeling of hunger remained.

He did not yet lock me in the dungeon for long periods of time without any food whatsoever – that wasn't until later. But the consequences of malnourishment were certainly noticeable. Hunger affects the brain. When you don't get enough to eat, you can't think of anything else but: When am I going to get my next bite to eat? How can I sneak a piece of bread? How can I manipulate him to give me at least one more bite from his three-fourths portion? I thought only of food and at the same time blamed myself for being 'such a glutton'.

I asked him to bring supermarket flyers into the dungeon, which I avidly leafed through whenever I was alone. After a while I made up a game that I called 'Tastes'. For example, I would imagine a piece of butter on my tongue. Cool and hard, slowly melting, until

---

* A kind of dry marble cake commonly eaten in Austria.

the taste pervaded my entire mouth. Then I would switch to *Grammelknödel*; in my thoughts, I would bite into one, feeling the soft potato dumpling between my teeth, the filling made of crispy bacon. Or strawberries; their sweet juice on my lips, the feeling of the small seeds on my palate, their slight acidity along the sides of my tongue.

I could play that game for hours and became so good at it that it nearly felt like real food. But the imaginary calories did nothing to fuel my body. More and more frequently I became dizzy when I suddenly stood up while working, or I had to sit down because I was so weak that my legs could hardly carry me. My stomach growled constantly and was sometimes so empty that I lay in bed all night with stomach cramps, trying to appease it with water.

It took me a long time to understand that the kidnapper was not focusing on my figure, but rather using hunger to keep me weak and submissive. He knew exactly what he was doing. He hid his true motives as well as he could. Only sometimes did he say revealing things, like: 'You are being so rebellious again. I'm probably giving you too much to eat.' If you don't get enough to eat, it's difficult to think straight, let alone to think of rebellion or escape.

One of the books on the shelves in the living room that the kidnapper placed considerable value on was Hitler's *Mein Kampf*. He spoke often and admiringly of Hitler and said, 'He was right to gas the Jews.' His contemporary political idol was Jörg Haider, the right-wing leader of Austria's Freedom Party. Priklopil liked to denigrate foreigners, who he called *Tschibesen* in the slang common to Donaustadt, Vienna's twenty-second district, where we had grown up. This was a word that I was familiar with from the racist tirades of the customers in my mother's shops. When the planes flew into the World Trade Center on 11 September, he took malicious pleasure in the sight; he saw them hitting the 'American east coast' and the 'conspiracy of global Jewish dominance'.

Even though I never fully believed that he had National-Socialist attitudes – they seemed artificial, like parroted phrases – there was something there that he had deeply internalized. To him I was someone he could order around as he pleased. He felt like a member of the master race. I was a second-class human being.

And I was to look like one as well.

In the beginning, every time he came to get me from the dungeon, I had to hide my hair under a plastic bag. The kidnapper's obsession with cleanliness was caught up in his paranoia. Every single hair was a danger to him; the police, when they showed up, could trace me and throw him in prison. As a result, I had to put my hair up with slides and pins, put a plastic bag on my head and secure it with a wide rubber band. Whenever a strand worked itself free and fell into my face while I was working upstairs, he immediately pushed it back under my plastic cap. He burned every hair of mine he found with a soldering iron or a lighter. After I was done showering, he meticulously fished out every single hair and poured half a bottle of caustic drain cleaner down the plughole to eliminate all traces of me in the sewer system as well.

It was sweaty and itchy under the plastic bag. The printed pictures on the bags left yellow and red stripes on my forehead, the pins dug into my scalp, and I had red, itchy patches everywhere. Whenever I complained about this form of torment, he would hiss at me, 'If you were bald, we wouldn't have this problem.'

I refused for a long time. Hair is an important component of personality. It seemed to me that I would be sacrificing too large a part of me if I cut it off. But one day I just couldn't take it any more. I took the household scissors I had been given, grabbed the hair on the side of my head and cut it off, strand by strand. It probably took me over an hour until it was so short my head was covered only by the fuzzy remains.

The kidnapper completed the job the next day. With a wet razor, he scraped the stubble off my head. I was now bald. The process was repeated on a regular basis over the next few years whenever he showered me off in the bathtub. Not even the minutest hair was allowed to remain. Anywhere.

I must have been a pitiful sight. My ribs stuck out, my arms and legs were covered in bruises, and my cheeks were gaunt.

The man who had done this to me obviously found my appearance pleasing. Because from then on he forced me to work in the house half-naked. For the most part I wore a cap and knickers. Sometimes a T-shirt or leggings as well. But I was never fully clothed. He most likely took pleasure in humiliating me in this way. But certainly it was also one of his perfidious ploys to keep me from escaping. He was convinced that I wouldn't dare run out on to the street half-naked. And he was right about that.

During this period, my dungeon took on a double function. Of course, I still feared it as a prison, and the many doors behind which I was locked away drove me to a claustrophobic state in which, half mad, I searched the corners for a tiny crack where I could secretly dig a tunnel to the outside. There were none. But at the same time my tiny cell became the only place where I was largely safe from the kidnapper. When he took me down towards the end of the week and supplied me with books, videos and food, I knew that at least for three days I would be spared work and beatings. I tidied up, cleaned and settled down for a pleasant afternoon of television. I often ate up almost all my weekend's rations on Friday evening. Having a full stomach at least once allowed me to forget that I would have to suffer worse hunger later.

At the beginning of 2000, I was given a radio that allowed me to receive Austrian stations. He knew that two years after my disappearance the search for me had been abandoned and that interest in the media had waned, so he could afford to allow me to listen to the news as well. The radio became my lifeline to the world outside, the announcers became my friends. I could tell you exactly when someone went on holiday or retired. I tried to form a picture of the world outside by listening to the programmes broadcast on the cultural and educational station 'Ö1'. With FM4, I learned a little bit of English. When I risked losing my grasp on reality, the mundane shows on the Ö3-Wecker morning broadcasts, where people called in from work and made requests for the morning music programming, saved me. Of course, I sometimes had the feeling that the radio as well was part of the elaborate show the kidnapper had created around me, where everyone was playing along, including DJs, callers and news announcers. But in the end, when something surprising came through the loud-speakers, that brought me back down to earth.

The radio was perhaps my most important companion in those years. It gave me the certainty that, away from my martyrdom in the cellar, there was a world that continued to turn – a world that was worth returning to some day.

My second great passion became science fiction. I read hundreds of Perry Rhodan and Orion pulp booklets where heroes travelled to distant galaxies. The possibility of switching space, time and dimension from one moment to the next fascinated me deeply. When I received a small thermal printer at the age of twelve, I began to write my own science-fiction novel. The figures were similar to the crew on the Starship Enterprise (*Next Generation*), but I spent many hours and put great effort into developing particularly strong, self-confident and independent female characters. Making up stories involving my characters, whom I equipped with the wildest technological advancements, saved me during the dark nights in the dungeon for months at a time. For hours, my words became a protective cocoon that enveloped me and allowed nothing or no one to hurt me. Today only empty pages remain from my novel. Even during my imprisonment, the letters on the thermal paper faded away, until they disappeared entirely.

It must have been the many series and books full of time travel that gave me the idea of undertaking such a journey through time myself. One weekend, when I had just turned twelve, the feeling of loneliness hit me so hard that I was afraid of losing my grip. I awoke bathed in sweat and carefully climbed down the narrow ladder of my bunk bed in complete darkness. The unoccupied floor space in my dungeon had shrunk to about two or three square metres. I stumbled around in a circle with no sense of direction, continuously bumping against the table and the bookcase. Out of space. Alone. A weakened, hungry and frightened child. I longed for an adult, a person who would come to rescue me. But nobody knew where I was. The only possibility open to me was to be my own adult.

Earlier I had found comfort in imagining how my mother would encourage me. Now I took on her role and tried to transfer a little of her strength to myself. I imagined Natascha as a grown-up, helping me. My whole life lay stretched out before me like a shining beam of time that extended far into the future. I stood on the number twelve. Far out in front of me I saw my eighteen-year-old self. Big and strong, self-confident and independent like the women in my novel. My twelve-year-old self moved slowly forward along the beam, while my grown-up self came towards me. In the middle, we each reached for the other's hand. Her touch was warm and soft, and at the same time I felt the strength of my grown-up self being transferred to my younger self. Grown-up Natascha embraced the smaller Natascha, which was no longer even her name, and comforted her, saying, 'I will get you out of here, I

143

promise you that. Right now you cannot escape. You are still too small. But when you turn eighteen I will overpower the kidnapper and free you from your prison. I won't leave you alone.'

That night I made a pact with my own, older self. I kept my word.

7

Caught Between Visions of Madness and a Perfect World

The Two Faces of the Kidnapper

There are nightmares where you wake up and know that everything was just a dream. During the first period I spent in the dungeon, I clung to the possibility of waking up that way, and spent many of my lonely hours planning my first few days in the world outside. During this time the world that I had been ripped away from was still real. It was still peopled by real persons whom I knew were worrying about me every second and doing their utmost to find me. I could picture every single detail from that world in my mind's eye: my mother, my room, my clothes, our flat.

Meanwhile, the world I had landed in had the colours and the smell of the surreal. The room was too small, the air too stale to be real. And the man who had abducted me was deaf to my arguments that originated from the world outside: that they would find me; that he would have to let me go; that what he was doing to me was a serious crime that would be punished. And yet, day by day, I increasingly realized that I was trapped in this underground world and no longer held the key to my life in my own hand. I resisted making myself at home in this unnerving environment, which had sprung from the fantasy of a criminal who had designed it down to the last detail and had placed me in it like a decorative object.

But you can't live in a nightmare forever. We humans have the ability to create the appearance of normality even in the most abnormal situations so as to avoid losing ourselves. In order to survive. Children can do this sometimes better than adults. The smallest straw can be enough for them to keep from drowning. For me, those straws were my rituals, such as our meals together, the choreographed Christmas celebration or my escape into the world of books, videos and television series. These were moments that were not wholly gloomy, even if I know today that my feelings basically originated from a psychological defence mechanism. You would go crazy if you saw only horrors for years at a time. Those small moments of purported normality are the ones that you cling to, that ensure your survival. There is an entry in my diary that clearly underlines my longing for normality:

Dear diary,

I haven't written to you for so long because I was in a difficult phase of depression. So I will report only briefly what has happened so far. In December, we put up the tiling, but we didn't install the toilet tank until the beginning of January. This is how I spent New Year's Eve: I slept upstairs from 30 to 31 December, then I spent the whole day alone. But he came shortly before midnight. He showered, and we poured lead*. At midnight, we turned the television on and listened to the Pummerin† ring out and the sounds of the Blue Danube waltz. In the meantime, we toasted and looked out of the window to admire the fireworks. However, my happiness was spoilt. When a rocket flew into our conifer, a chirping suddenly emerged. And I am certain that it was a small bird that was

---

* A traditional custom at New Year in Austria. A small amount of lead is melted over a candle then cooled in water. The shape it forms is said to predict one's fortune for the coming year.

† Austria's largest bell, the Pummerin hangs in Vienna's St Stephen's Cathedral and is sounded at midnight on New Year's Eve to ring in the New Year.

frightened to death. I wasn't pleased when I heard the little dickey twitter.
I gave him the chimney sweep that I had made for him and he gave me a
chocolate coin, chocolate biscuits and a miniature chocolate chimney
sweep. The previous day he had already given me a chimney sweep cake.
My chimney sweep contained Smarties, no, mini M&Ms, that I gave
Wolfgang.

Nothing is all black or all white. And nobody is all good or all evil. That also goes for the kidnapper. These are words that people don't like to hear from an abduction victim. Because the clearly defined concept of good and evil is turned on its head, a concept that people are all too willing to accept so as not to lose their way in a world full of shades of grey. When I talk about it, I can see the confusion and rejection in the faces of many who were not there. The empathy they felt for my fate freezes and is turned to denial. People who have no insight into the complexities of imprisonment deny me the ability to judge my own experiences by pronouncing two words: Stockholm Syndrome.

'Stockholm syndrome is a term used to describe a paradoxical psychological phenomenon wherein hostages express adulation and have positive feelings towards their captors that appear irrational in light of the danger or risk endured by the victims' – that's what the textbooks say. A labelling diagnosis that I emphatically reject. Because as sympathetic as the looks may be when the term is simply tossed out there, their effect is terrible. It turns victims into victims a second time, by taking from them the power to interpret their own story – and by turning the most significant experiences from their story into the product of a syndrome. The term places the very behaviour that contributes significantly to the victim's survival that much closer to being objectionable.

Getting closer to the kidnapper is not an illness. Creating a cocoon of normality within the framework of a crime is not a syndrome. Just the opposite. It is a survival strategy in a situation with no escape – and much more true to reality than the sweeping categorization of criminals as bloodthirsty beasts and of victims as helpless lambs that society refuses to look beyond.

To the world outside, Wolfgang Priklopil came across as a shy, courteous man who always seemed a bit too young in his well-turned-out clothes. He wore proper trousers and ironed shirts or polo shirts. His hair had always been freshly washed and neatly styled, in a cut that was a bit too old-fashioned for the start of a new millennium. He probably seemed unassuming to the few people he dealt with. It was not easy to catch a glimpse of what was behind this exterior, because he maintained it completely. For Priklopil it was less important to uphold societal conventions; he was rather a slave to keeping up outward appearances.

It wasn't just that he loved order; it was necessary for his survival. A lack of order, supposed chaos and dirt threw him completely. He spent a great deal of his time keeping his cars (in addition to the delivery van, he also had a red BMW), his garden and his house meticulously clean and well maintained. It wasn't enough for him if you cleaned up after cooking. The counter had to be wiped, every cutting board, every knife that had been used to prepare the meal, had to be washed, even while the food was on the cooker.

Rules were just as important as order. Priklopil could get wrapped up for hours in instructions on how to do something and followed them fastidiously. If the instructions for heating a ready-to-eat-meal said 'Heat for four minutes', then he took it out of the oven after exactly four minutes, no matter whether it was hot enough or not. It must have made a significant impression on him that despite adhering to all the rules he couldn't quite get his life under control. It must have bothered him so much that one day he decided to break a major rule and kidnap me. But although that had made him a criminal, he maintained his belief in rules, instructions and structures nearly religiously. At times he looked at me pensively and said, 'How ridiculous that you didn't come with instructions for use.' It must have thrown him completely that his newest acquisition, a child, didn't always function like it was supposed to, and on some days he didn't know how to get it working again.

At the beginning of my imprisonment I had suspected that the kidnapper was an orphan and that the lack of warmth in his childhood had turned him into a criminal. Now that I had got to know him better, I realized that I had created a false image of him. He had had a very sheltered childhood in a classic family setting. Father, mother, child. His father Karl had worked for a large alcoholic beverage company as a travelling salesman and was on the road a great deal, where he apparently cheated on his wife repeatedly, as I found out later. But outward appearances were maintained. His parents stayed together. Priklopil told me about their weekend outings to Lake Neusiedl, family ski holidays and walks. His mother took loving care of her son. Maybe a bit too loving.

The more time I spent upstairs in the house, the stranger the presence of his mother, hovering over everything in the kidnapper's life, seemed to me. It took me some time to figure out who the ominous person was who occupied the house at the weekends, forcing me to spend two or three days alone in my dungeon. I read the name 'Waltraud Priklopil' on the letters lying near the front door. I ate the food that she had cooked over the weekend. One meal for every day she left her son alone. And when I was allowed up into the house on Mondays, I noticed the traces she left behind: everything had been spotlessly cleaned. Not one speck of dust indicated that anyone lived there. Every weekend she scrubbed the floors and dusted for her son. Who in turn made me clean the house the rest of the week. Thursdays he drove me through all the rooms again and again with the cleaning cloth. Everything had to sparkle before his mother came. It was like an absurd cleaning competition between mother and son that I was forced to bear the brunt of. Still, after my lonely weekends I was always happy when I discovered signs that his mother had been there: freshly ironed laundry, a cake in the kitchen. I never saw Waltraud Priklopil once in all those years, but through all those small signs she became a part of my world. I liked to imagine her as an older friend and pictured being able to sit with her at the kitchen table one day drinking a cup of tea. But we never got around to doing that.

Priklopil's father died when he was twenty-four years old. The death of his father must have torn a gaping hole in his life. He seldom spoke of him, but you could tell that he had never got over the loss. He seemed to keep one room on the ground floor of the house unaltered to commemorate him. It was decorated in rustic style with an upholstered corner couch and wrought-iron lamps – what you would call a *Stüberl* in Austria, where people probably used to play cards and drink when his father was still alive. The product samples from the schnapps manufacturer he had worked for were still standing on the shelves. Even when the kidnapper later renovated the house, he left that room untouched.

Waltraud Priklopil seemed to have been hit hard by the death of her husband as well. I don't wish to judge her life or interpret things that are perhaps not true. After all, I have never met her. But from my perspective, it seemed that after the death of her husband she clung even more tightly to her son, making him her substitute partner. Priklopil, who in the meantime had moved out to his own flat, moved back to the house in Strasshof, where he could never escape his mother's influence. He constantly expected her to go through his wardrobe and dirty laundry, and paid meticulous attention to making sure that there were no traces of me to be found anywhere in the house. And he set the rhythm of his week and how he dealt with me exactly after his mother. Her exaggerated mollycoddling and his acceptance of it were some-what unnatural. She didn't treat him like an adult and he didn't act like one. He lived in his mother's house – she had moved into Priklopil's flat in Vienna – and let her take care of him in every way.

I don't know whether he lived off her money as well. He had lost his job as a communications technician at Siemens, where he had done his apprenticeship, even before my abduction. After that, he was probably registered as unemployed for years. Sometimes he told me that he would go to a job interview from time to time, but then intentionally act stupid so that they wouldn't give him the job. This allowed him to keep the Employment Service happy and hold onto his unemployment benefit at the same time. Later, as mentioned above, he helped his friend and business partner, Ernst Holzapfel, renovate flats. Ernst Holzapfel, whom I sought out after my escape, describes Priklopil as correct, proper and reliable. Perhaps socially backward, as he never had any other friends, let alone girlfriends. But, above all, unremarkable.

This well-turned-out young man, incapable of setting bound-aries vis-à-vis his mother, courteous to the neighbours, and proper in a way bordering on pedantic, also kept up outward appearances. He put his repressed feelings in the cellar, allowing them later to come up into the darkened kitchen from time to time. Where I was.

I was a witness to Wolfgang Priklopil's two sides, which were probably unknown to anyone else. One was a strong tendency to power and domination. The other was an utterly insatiable need for love and approval. He had abducted and 'shaped' me in order to be able to express both these contradictory sides.

Sometime in the year 2000, I saw, at least on paper, who was hiding behind those outward appearances. 'You can call me Wolfgang,' he casually said one day while we were working.

'What is your full name?' I asked back.

'Wolfgang Priklopil,' he answered.

That was the name I had seen upstairs in the house on the address labels of the advertisement brochures he had neatly stacked on the kitchen table. Now I had confirmation. At the same time I realized at that moment that I would not leave his house alive. Otherwise he would never have entrusted me with his full name.

From then on I sometimes called him 'Wolfgang' or even 'Wolfi', a nickname that gives the appearance of a certain kind of closeness, while at the same time his treatment of me reached a new level of violence. Looking back, it seems to me that I was trying to reach the person behind the mask, while the person before me systematically tormented and beat me.

Priklopil was mentally very ill. His paranoia went even beyond the level that you would expect from someone who puts an abducted child in a cellar. His fantasies of omnipotence blended with his paranoia. In many, he played the role of absolute ruler.

Consequently, he told me one day that he was one of those Egyptian gods from the science-fiction series *Stargate* that I liked to watch. The 'evil ones' among the aliens were modelled after Egyptian gods who sought out young men as host bodies. They penetrated the body through the mouth or the back of the neck and lived as parasites in the body, completely taking over the host in the end. These gods had a particular piece of jewellery that they used to force people to their knees and humiliate them. 'I am an Egyptian god,' Priklopil said to me one day in the dungeon. 'You must do everything I say.'

At first I was unable to tell whether this was meant as a strange joke or whether he was trying to use my favourite TV series to force even more humiliations upon me. I suspected that he really did think himself a god, in whose absurd fantasy world the only role left for me was that of the oppressed, which would simultaneously lift him up.

His references to Egyptian gods frightened me. After all, I really was trapped under the earth as if in a sarcophagus; buried alive in a room that could have become my burial chamber. I lived in the pathologically paranoid world of a psychopath. If I didn't want to lose myself completely, I had to have a part in shaping it as much as possible. Back when he had told me to call him 'Maestro', I had seen from his reaction that I was not just a pawn of his will, but that I had modest means at my disposal to define boundaries. Similar to the way the kidnapper had opened up a wound in me, into which he had for years poured the poison that my parents had left me in the lurch, I felt that I had a few grains of salt in my hand that could prove painful to him as well.

'Call me "My Lord",' he demanded. It was absurd that Priklopil, whose position of power was so obvious on the surface, was so dependent on this verbal show of humility.

When I refused to call him 'My Lord', he screamed and raged, and one time he beat me for it. But with my refusal, I not only maintained a bit of personal dignity, but had also found a lever I could use. Even if I had to pay for it with immeasurable pain.

I experienced the same situation when he commanded me for the first time to kneel in front of him. He was sitting on the couch, waiting for me to serve him something to eat, when out of the blue he ordered, 'Kneel down!' I answered him calmly, 'I won't do that.' He jumped up in anger and pressed me down to the floor. I made a quick turn so that I would land on my rear end at least instead of my knees. He wasn't to have the satisfaction, not even for a second, of me kneeling in front of him. He grabbed me, turned me on my side and bent my legs as if I were a rubber doll. He pressed my calves against the back of my thighs, lifted me like a corded package off the floor and tried to push me down into a kneeling position again. I made myself heavy and stiff and twisted desperately in his grip. He punched and kicked me. But, in the end, I had the upper hand. In all the years he vehemently demanded that I call him 'Lord', I never did so. And I never kneeled before him.

Often it would've been easier to kneel and I would have saved myself a number of blows and kicks. But in that situation of total oppression and complete dependence on the kidnapper, I had to preserve a modicum of room to manoeuvre. The roles we were to play were very clear, and as prisoner I was without question the victim. However, this battle over the word 'Lord' and the kneeling became a secondary theatre where we fought for power as if in a proxy war. I was in an inferior position when he humiliated and mistreated me as he liked. I was in an inferior position when he locked me up, turned off my electricity and used me as forced labour. But on that point, I stood up to him. I called him 'Criminal' when he wanted me to call him 'Lord'. Sometimes I said 'Honey' or 'Darling' instead of 'My Lord' in order to illustrate the grotesqueness of the situation that he had placed us both in. And he punished me every time for it.

It took immeasurable strength to remain consistent in my behaviour towards him throughout the entire period of my imprisonment. Always resisting. Always saying no. Always defending myself against attacks and always explaining calmly to him that he had gone too far and had no right to treat me that way. Even on days when I had given up on myself and felt completely worthless, I couldn't afford to show any weakness. On days like that, I told myself in my childish view of things that I was doing it for him. So that he wouldn't become an even more evil person. As if it were my responsibility to prevent him from completely falling into a moral abyss.

Whenever he had his outbursts of rage, beating me with his fists and feet, there was nothing I could do. Similarly, I was powerless to do anything about the forced labour, being locked up or the hunger and the humiliations suffered while cleaning the house. This kind of oppression formed the framework in which I lived;

they were an integral component of my world. The only way for me to deal with it was to forgive the kidnapper his transgressions. I forgave him for kidnapping me and I forgave him every single time he beat me and tormented me. This act of forgiveness gave me back the power over my experience and made it possible to live with it. If I had not adopted this attitude instinctively from the very beginning, I would probably have destroyed myself in anger and hatred – or I would have been broken by the humiliations that I was subjected to daily. In this way, I would have been eliminated; this way would have entailed even more dire consequences than giving up my old identity, my past, my name. By forgiving him, I pushed his deeds away from me. They could no longer make me small or destroy me; after all, I had forgiven them. They were evil deeds that he had committed and would rebound only on him, no longer on me.

And I had my small victories. My refusal to call him 'My Lord' or 'Maestro'. My refusal to kneel. My appeals to his conscience, which sometimes fell on fertile ground. They were vital to my survival. They gave me the illusion that I was an equal partner in the relationship within certain parameters – because they gave me a kind of counter-power over him. And it showed me something very important: namely, that I still existed as a person and had not been degraded to an object with no will of her own.

Parallel to his fantasies of oppression, Priklopil nurtured a deep longing for a 'perfect' world. I, his prisoner, was to be at his disposal for this as a prop and as a person. He tried to make me into the partner he had never had. 'Real' women were out of the question. His hatred of women was deep-seated and irreconcilable, and burst out of him again and again in little remarks. I don't know whether he had had any contact with women earlier, or even a girlfriend during his time in Vienna. During my imprisonment, the only 'woman in his life' was his mother – a dependent relationship with an over-idealized figure. Release from this dominance, which he was unable to achieve in reality, was to come about in the world of my dungeon by reversing the relationship – by choosing me to take on the role of submissive woman who acquiesced and looked up to him.

His image of an ideal family was taken from the 1950s. He wanted a hard-working little woman, who had his dinner ready for him when he came home, who did not talk back and did the housework perfectly. He dreamed of 'family celebrations' and outings, enjoyed our meals together and celebrated name days, birthdays and Christmas as if there was no dungeon and no captivity for me. It was as if he was trying to live a life through me that he couldn't manage to outside the house. As if I were a walking stick that he had collected at the side of the road to support him the moment his life wasn't going the way he wanted. 'I am your king,' he said, 'and you are my slave. You obey.' Or he would tell me, 'Your family is made up of chavs. You have no right to your own life. You are here to serve me.'

He needed that insane crime to realize his vision of a perfect, small, intact world. But in the end, he really only wanted two things from me: approval and affection. As if his objective behind all the cruelty was to force a person to love him absolutely.

When I turned fourteen, I spent the night above ground for the first time in years. It was not a liberating feeling.

I lay stiff with fright on the kidnapper's bed. He locked the door behind him and placed the key on a cabinet that was so high that only he could reach it by standing on tiptoe. For me it was absolutely unreachable. Then he lay down next to me and tied my wrists to his using plastic cord cuffs.

One of the first headlines about the kidnapper after I escaped was: 'The Sex Beast'. I will not write about this part of my imprisonment – it is the last remaining bit of privacy I would like to preserve now that my life in captivity has been picked apart in innumerable reports, interrogations, photographs, etc. But I will say this much: in their eagerness for the sensational, the journalists of the red-top press were far off the mark. In many respects, the kidnapper was a beast and more cruel than can possibly be depicted. But in this sense he was not. Naturally, he subjected me to minor sexual assaults; these were part of my daily harassment, like the thumps and punches, the kicks at my shins when he walked past. But when he manacled me to him on those nights I had to spend upstairs, it wasn't about sex. The man who beat me, locked me in the cellar and starved me, wanted to cuddle. Controlled and manacled by my plastic cuffs, I was something to hold tight to in the night.

I could have screamed at how painfully paradoxical my situation seemed. But I couldn't make a sound. I lay next to him on my side and tried to move as little as possible. My back, as so often, had been beaten black and blue. It hurt so much that I couldn't lie on it, and the cuffs cut into my skin. I felt his breath on the back of my neck and stiffened.

I remained manacled to the kidnapper until the next morning. Whenever I had to go to the toilet, I had to wake him, and he came with me with his wrist tied to mine. When he had fallen asleep next to me I reflected on whether I could break the cuffs – but I soon gave up. Whenever I turned my wrist and tightened my muscles, the plastic cut into not only my arm, but also his. He would inevitably have woken up and realized immediately my attempt to escape. Today I know that the police also use cord cuffs when they make arrests. They would never have broken under the muscle strength of a starving fourteen-year-old anyway.

So there I lay, manacled to my kidnapper, the first of many nights in his bed. The next morning I would have to eat breakfast with him. As much as I had liked that ritual as a child, I became nauseated at the hypocrisy with which he forced me to sit with him at the kitchen table, drink milk and eat two tablespoonfuls of cereal, not a single bite more. An ideal world, as if nothing had happened.

That summer I tried for the first time to take my life.

In that phase of my imprisonment I no longer had any thought of escape. At the age of fifteen my psychological prison was complete. The door to the house could have been standing wide open: I couldn't have taken a single step. Escape, that meant death. For me, for him, for everyone who could have seen me.

It is not easy to explain what isolation, beatings and humiliations do to a person. How after so much mistreatment the mere sound of a door can cause you to panic so that you cannot even breathe, let alone run. How your heart pounds, the blood in your ears drones and then suddenly a switch in your brain is flipped and you feel nothing but paralysis. You are incapable of action, incapable of reason. The feeling of mortal fear has been indelibly branded on your brain, and all the details of the time when you first felt that fear – smells, sounds, voices – are preserved in your subconscious. If one detail should reappear – a raised hand – the fear returns; without the hand even closing about your throat, you feel yourself suffocating.

Just as survivors of bombing attacks can be panic-stricken at the sound of New Year's fireworks, the same happened to me with a thousand small details. The sound I heard when the heavy doors to my dungeon were opened. The rattling of the fan. Darkness. Harsh lighting. The smell upstairs in the house. The rush of air before his hand struck me. His fingers around my throat, his breath on the back of my neck. Our bodies are programmed for survival and react by going limp. At some point, the trauma is so immense that even the outside world does not promise any relief, but rather becomes a threatening terrain associated with fear.

It may be true that the kidnapper knew what I was going

through. That he understood that I would not run away when he allowed me out in his garden for the first time. Some time before that he had made it possible for me to sunbathe for short periods. On the ground floor there was a room with windows that reached to the floor, which no one could see into from the outside when he closed one of the blinds. There I was permitted to lie on a lounger and absorb the sunshine. The kidnapper probably viewed it as a kind of 'maintenance' for me. He knew that a person cannot survive forever without sunlight and therefore made sure that I got some from time to time. For me it was a revelation.

The sensation of the warm rays on my pale skin was indescribable. I closed my eyes. The sun made red circles behind my eyelids. I slowly dozed off and dreamed I was in an outdoor pool, listening to the cheerful voices of children and feeling the cool water, the way it washes over your skin when you jump in all hot. What I wouldn't have given to go swimming, just once! Just like the kidnapper, who from time to time appeared in my dungeon in his bathing trunks. Neighbours, distant relatives of the Priklopils, had the same swimming pool as he did in their garden – only there was water in theirs and it could be used. When they weren't home and the kidnapper checked up on the house or watered their plants, he sometimes went for a swim. I envied him deeply.

One day that summer, he surprised me by saying that I could come swimming with him. The neighbours weren't home and because the gardens of the two houses were connected by a path you could reach the pool without being seen from the street.

The grass tickled my naked feet and the morning dew gleamed like miniature diamonds between the blades of grass. I followed him down the narrow path to the neighbours' garden, got undressed and slipped into the water.

It was like being reborn. Underwater, my imprisonment, the dungeon, the oppression, all fell away from me for a moment. My stress dissolved in the cool blue water. I came up and floated on the surface. The small turquoise waves sparkled in the sun. Above me stretched an infinite cerulean sky. My ears were underwater and all around me was nothing but soft splashing.

When the kidnapper nervously ordered me out of the water, it took me a minute to react. It was as if I had to return from a faraway place. I followed Priklopil into the house, through the kitchen into the hallway and from there into the garage and down to the dungeon. Then I was locked up again. For the time being that was the only occasion I was permitted to swim. He didn't allow me to go in the pool for a long while after that. But that one time had been enough to remind me that in spite of all the despair and powerlessness, I still wanted a life. The memory of that moment showed me that it was worth holding on until I could escape.

I was immeasurably grateful to the kidnapper back then for such small pleasures, like the sunbathing or swimming in the neighbours' pool. And I still am today. Even if it seems strange, I can recognize that there were small, humane moments during my time in captivity. The kidnapper was unable to completely shut himself off from the influence of the child and young girl with whom he spent so many hours. Back then, I clung to even the tiniest human gesture, because I was dependent on seeing goodness in the world in which I could change nothing; in a kidnapper with whom I had to cope simply because I was unable to escape. Those moments were there and I treasured them. Moments in which he helped me paint, draw or make something, encouraging me to start again from the beginning if I was unsuccessful. By going over the school subjects I was missing with me and giving me extra maths problems to solve, even when it gave him particular pleasure afterwards to correct my mistakes, and when he only paid attention to grammar and spelling in my essays. Rules had to be followed. But he was there. He took time, of which I had more than plenty.

I succeeded in surviving by subconsciously suppressing and splitting off the horrors I experienced. And from these terrible experiences during my imprisonment I learned to be strong. Yes, perhaps even to evolve a strength I would not have been capable of had I grown up in freedom.

Today, years after my escape, I have become cautious in saying such things. That, within the evil, at least brief moments of normality, even mutual understanding, were possible. That's what I mean when I say that there is neither black nor white, neither in reality nor in extreme situations, but rather many subtle shades in between that make the difference. For me, these nuances were decisive. In time, by detecting mood swings I was perhaps able to avoid a beating. By appealing to the kidnapper's conscience again and again, he spared me perhaps even worse. By seeing him as a human being, with a very dark and a somewhat lighter side, I was able to remain human myself. Because he was unable to break me.

This may be why I so vehemently oppose being placed in the pigeonhole of Stockholm Syndrome. The term came about after a bank robbery in Stockholm in 1973. The bank robbers had held four employees hostage for five days. Much to the amazement of the media, the hostages, once free, were more afraid of the police than they had been of the hostage-takers – and they had developed an understanding of them. Some of the victims asked for mercy for the robbers and visited them in prison. Public opinion has no understanding for the 'sympathy' they showed to the robbers and turned the victims' behaviour into a pathology. The findings: compassion with the perpetrator denoted illness. This newly created illness has been called Stockholm Syndrome ever since.

Today, I sometimes observe the reactions of small children as they look forward to being with their parents, whom they haven't seen all day, and then their parents greet them only with unpleasant words and sometimes even strike them. Each of these children could be said to be suffering from Stockholm Syndrome. They love the people with whom they live and on whom they are dependent, even if those people do not treat them very well.

I too was a child when my imprisonment began. The kidnapper had torn me from my world and placed me in his own. The person who had stolen me, who took my family and identity from me, became my family. I had no choice other than to accept him as such and I learned to derive happiness from his affection and repress all that was negative. Just like any child growing up in a dysfunctional family.

After my escape I was amazed – not that I as the victim was capable of making that differentiation, but that the society in which I landed after my imprisonment does not allow for the slightest nuance. I am not permitted to reflect at all on the person who was the only one in my life for eight and a half years. I cannot even hint that I need that outlet to work through what has happened without evoking incomprehension.

In the meantime I have learned that I idealized this society to a certain extent. We live in a world in which women are battered and are unable to flee from the men who beat them, although their door is theoretically standing wide open. One out of every four women becomes a victim of severe violence. One out of every two will be confronted by sexual harassment over her lifetime. These crimes are everywhere and can take place behind any front door in the country, every day, and barely elicit much more than a shrug of the shoulders and superficial dismay.

Our society needs criminals like Wolfgang Přiklopil in order to give a face to the evil that lives within and to split it off from society itself. It needs the images of cellar dungeons so as not to have to see the many homes in which violence rears its conformist, bourgeois head. Society uses the victims of sensational cases such as mine in order to divest itself of the responsibility for the many nameless victims of daily crimes, victims nobody helps – even when they ask for help.

Crimes such as the one committed against me form the austere, black-and-white structure for the categories of Good and Evil on which society is based. The perpetrator must be a beast, so that we can see ourselves as being on the side of good. His crime must be embellished with S&M fantasies and wild orgies, until it is so extreme that it no longer has anything to do with our own lives.

And the victim must have been broken and must remain so, so that the externalization of evil is possible. The victim who refuses to assume this role contradicts society's simplistic view. Nobody wants to see it. People would have to take a look at themselves.

For this reason, I have sparked unconscious aggression in some people. Perhaps it is what has happened to me that triggers aggression, but because I'm the only one within reach after the kidnapper's suicide, they strike out at me. Particularly violently, whenever I try to get society to see that the kidnapper who abducted me was a person too. One who lived among them. Those who are able to react anonymously in Internet postings unload their hate directly on to me. It is society's self-hate that rebounds on society itself, begging the question of why it allows something like that to happen. Why people among us are able to disappear so easily without anyone noticing. For over eight years.

Those who stand across from me in interviews and at events are more subtle. They turn me – the only person who experienced my imprisonment – into a victim for the second time with those two small words. They say only 'Stockholm Syndrome'.

8

Rock Bottom

When Physical Pain Eases the Psychological Torment

The staircase was narrow, steep and slippery. I was balancing a glass fruit bowl in front of me that I had washed upstairs and was now carrying down into my dungeon. I couldn't see my feet and groped my way forward. Then it happened: I slipped and fell. My head hit the stairs and I heard the bowl shatter into pieces with a loud crash. Then I was out for a moment. When I came to again and lifted my head, I felt sick. Blood dripped from my bald head on to the stairs. Wolfgang Priklopil was right behind me, as always. He bounded down the stairs, picked me up and carried me into the bathroom to wash off the blood. He swore at me constantly under his breath: How could I be so clumsy! All the problems I was making for him! I was even too stupid to walk! Then he ineptly put a bandage on me to staunch the bleeding and locked me in the dungeon. 'Now I have to repaint the stairs,' he barked before he bolted the door. He came back the next morning with a bucket of paint and painted the grey concrete stairs where the ugly dark stains could be seen.

My head pounded. Whenever I lifted it, a harsh, stabbing pain would shoot through my body and everything would go black. I spent several days in bed and could hardly move. I think I had concussion. But in those long nights when the pain kept me awake, I was afraid that I might have broken my skull. Nevertheless, I didn't dare ask to see a doctor. The kidnapper had never wanted to hear about my pain before and punished me this time as well for having injured myself. Over the next few weeks, he aimed directly at that spot on my head whenever he beat me.

After my fall I realized that the kidnapper would rather let me die than go for help in an emergency. Until that point I had always simply been lucky: I had no contact with the outside world and was in no danger of catching any illnesses. Priklopil was so hysterically intent on avoiding germs that I was safe from illnesses despite my contact with him. I never experienced anything more than slight colds with minimal fever in all the years of my imprisonment. But an accident could have happened at any time during all the heavy work in the house, and at times it seemed a miracle that I came away with only large bruises, contusions and abrasions from his beatings and that he never broke any of my bones. But now I was sure that any serious illness, any accident that required medical treatment, would spell certain death for me.

In addition, our 'living together' wasn't turning out to be exactly what he had imagined. My fall on the stairs and his behaviour afterwards were symptomatic of a phase of bitter struggle that would continue for the next two years of my imprisonment. A phase in which I would fluctuate between depression and thoughts of suicide on one hand and the conviction on the other that I wanted to live and everything would turn out okay in the end. A phase in which he struggled to bring his violent assaults into harmony with his dream of a 'normal' life together. He had more and more difficulty doing this, which tormented him.

When I turned sixteen, the renovation of the house, in which he had invested all of his energy and my labour, was coming to an end. The work which had given his daily routine structure over months and years was about to come to an end with nothing to replace it. The child that he had abducted had now become a young woman – in other words, the embodiment of that which he deeply hated. I didn't want to be his puppet with no will of my own, as he had perhaps hoped I would be, so that he would not feel humiliated himself. I was rebellious, while at the same time I grew more and more depressed and tried to withdraw whenever I could. Sometimes he now had to force me to come out of my dungeon at all. I cried for hours and no longer had the strength to stand up. He hated resistance and tears, and my passivity enraged him. He had nothing to counter it with. Back then it must have finally become clear to him that he had not only chained my life to his, but also his life to mine. And that any attempt to break those chains would have to end in death for one of us.

Wolfgang Přiklopil became more and more erratic from week to week, and his paranoia increased. He watched me with suspicion, always expecting me to attack him or flee. In the evening, when he would fall into a state of acute anxiety, he brought me to his bed, manacled me to him and tried to calm himself with the warmth of my body. But his moodiness continued to increase and I was the one on whom he took out every one of his mood swings. He now began to talk of a 'life together'. More frequently than in the previous years, he informed me of his decisions and talked to me about his problems. The fact that I was his prisoner and that he monitored all my movements was something that didn't even seem to register with him in his longing for an ideal world. If I would only belong to him completely one day – if he could be certain that I wouldn't escape after all – then we could both lead a better life, he would always tell me with shining eyes.

He had only vague ideas about what this better life was supposed to look like. But his role in it was clearly defined: in every version he saw himself as the ruler in the house; he had reserved various roles for me. At times the housewife and forced labourer who did all the work in the house for him, from building to cooking and cleaning. At other times the companion he could lean on, and at still other times his replacement mother, the bin for his psychological garbage, the punching bag he could use to work off his anger over his powerlessness in the real world. What never changed was his idea that I had to be fully and completely at his disposal. Me having my own personality, my own needs or even a modicum of freedom never featured in his screenplay of a 'life together'.

My reaction to his dreams was torn. On the one hand they seemed to me to be deeply abnormal. Nobody who was thinking clearly would picture a life together with the person he had kidnapped, beaten for years and locked away. But, at the same time, this distant, attractive world he painted began to take root in my subconscious. I had an all-powerful longing for normality. I wanted to meet other people, leave the house, go shopping, swimming. See the sun whenever I wanted to. Talk with someone, no matter what about. This life together in the mind of the kidnapper, in which he would allow me some freedom, in which I could leave the house under his supervision, seemed to me on many days like the most that I would be entitled to in this life. Freedom, real freedom, was something I could hardly even imagine after all those years. I was afraid of venturing outside the established framework – within that framework I had learned to play the entire keyboard in every key. I had forgotten what freedom sounded like.

I felt like a soldier who is told that everything will be okay after the war. No matter that he has lost a leg in the meantime – that's just part of what happens. For me, it had become an irrefutable truth over time that I first had to suffer before our 'better life' could begin. My better life in imprisonment. *You should be so happy that I found you. You couldn't even live outside any more. Who would want you, after all. You have to be grateful to me that I have taken you in.* My war took place in my head. And it had absorbed those words like a sponge.

But even this less stringent form of imprisonment the kidnapper had promised lay in the distant future. And he blamed me for it. One evening at the kitchen table he said, 'If you weren't so defiant, we could have such a better life. If I could be sure that you wouldn't run away, I wouldn't have to lock you up and shackle you.' The older I got, the more he transferred the entire responsibility for my imprisonment on to me. It was my fault that he had to beat me and lock me up – if I would just cooperate better, be more humble and obedient, then I could live upstairs in the house with him. I would retort, 'You're the one who has locked me away! You're keeping me prisoner!' But it seemed as if he had long ago lost the ability to see that reality. And, to a certain extent, he pulled me along with him.

On his good days, this image – his image that was to become my own – became tangible. On bad days, he became more unpredictable than ever. More frequently than before he used me as a doormat for his miserable moods. The worst were the nights when he couldn't sleep because a chronic sinus inflammation tormented him. If he couldn't sleep, then I couldn't either. If I lay in my bed in the dungeon on those nights, his voice droned through the loudspeakers for hours. He told me every detail of how he had spent the day, and asked me about every step, every word I had read, every movement: 'Have you tidied up? How did you divide up your food? What did you listen to on the radio?'

I had to answer, giving him all the elaborate details, in the middle of the night, and if I had nothing to tell him I had to make something up to calm him. Other nights he simply harassed me: 'Obey! Obey! Obey!' he would call into the intercom in a monotone. His voice boomed throughout the small room, filling it up to the very last corner: 'Obey! Obey! Obey!' I couldn't block it out, even if I hid my head under the pillows. It was always there, and it enraged me. I could not escape that voice. It signalled to me day and night that he had me in his power. It signalled to me day and night that I mustn't give up on myself. In moments of clarity, my urge to survive and to escape one day was unbelievably strong.

In my daily routine, I hardly had the strength to think those thoughts all the way to the end.

His mother's recipe lay on the kitchen table. I had read it through numerous times so as not to make any mistakes: separate the eggs; sift the flour together with the baking powder; beat the egg whites until stiff. He stood behind me, watching me nervously.

'My mother doesn't beat the eggs that way!'

'My mother does that much better!'

'You're much too clumsy. Be careful!'

Some flour had spilled on to the counter. He shouted and barked at me that everything was taking much too long. His mother, the cake . . . I did the best I could, but no matter what I did, it wasn't enough for him.

'If your mother can do it so much better, why don't you ask her to bake you a cake?' It had just slipped out. And it was too much.

He struck out like a defiant child, swept the bowl with the batter on to the floor and shoved me against the kitchen table. Then he dragged me into the cellar and locked me up. It was broad daylight outside, but he wouldn't allow me any light. He knew how to torture me.

I lay down on my bed and rocked quietly back and forth. I couldn't cry or imagine myself away. With every movement, the pain from my contusions and bruises cried out in me. But I remained mute, simply lying there in the absolute darkness, as if I had fallen out of space and time.

The kidnapper didn't come. My alarm clock ticked quietly. I must have dozed off in the meantime, but I couldn't remember having done so. Everything blended together; dreams turned into delirium, where I saw myself walking along by the sea with young people my own age. The light in my dream was glisteningly bright, the water deep blue. I flew a kite out over the water, the wind played in my hair, the sun burned down on my arms. It was a feeling of an absolute dissolution of boundaries, an intoxication from the sense of being alive. In my fantasy I was standing on a stage and my parents were in the audience; I sang a song loud and strong. My mother applauded, jumped up and hugged me. I wore a beautiful dress made of shimmering fabric, light and delicate. I felt beautiful, strong, whole.

When I awoke, it was still dark. My alarm clock ticked monotonously. It was the only sign that time hadn't stood still. The darkness remained – the whole day.

The kidnapper did not come that evening and he didn't come the next morning. I was hungry, my stomach was growling, and slowly I felt cramps beginning. I had a little bit of water in my dungeon, but that was all. But drinking didn't help any more. I couldn't think of anything other than food. I would've done anything for a piece of bread.

In the course of the day, I increasingly lost control over my body, over my thoughts. I felt the pain in my stomach, the weakness, the certainty that I had overstepped my boundaries and that he would now leave me to die a miserable death. I felt as if I were on board the sinking *Titanic*. The light had already gone out, the ship was tilting slowly but inexorably to the side. There was no escape. I felt the cold, dark water climbing higher. I felt it on my legs, my back. It sloshed over my arms, encasing my ribcage. Higher, ever higher . . . There! A glaring ray of light blinded my face momentarily. I heard something fall to the floor with a muffled sound. Then a voice: 'Here, there's something for you.' Then a door clicked shut.

Dazed, I lifted my head. I was bathed in sweat and had no idea where I was. The water that had wanted to pull me into the depths was gone. But everything swayed. I swayed. And below me was nothing, black nothingness, nothing stopping my hand from reaching out into emptiness again and again. I don't know how long I remained trapped in that vision, until I realized that I was lying in my bunk bed in the dungeon. It seemed to me an eternity before I could muster the strength to grope for the ladder, climb down it backwards, rung by rung. When I reached the floor, I crawled forward on all fours. My hand brushed against a small plastic bag. I ripped it open greedily and with shaking fingers, so clumsily that the contents fell out and rolled across the floor. I fumbled around in a panic, until I felt something long and cool under my fingers. A carrot? I wiped it with my hand and bit into it. He had thrown a bag of carrots into my dungeon. On my knees, I slid across the ice-cold floor until I had found all of them. Then I carried each one individually up to my bunk bed. Each time on the way up the ladder seemed to me to be like climbing a massive mountain, but it pumped up my blood pressure. Finally, I devoured them, one after the other. My stomach grumbled loudly, contracting and cramping. The carrots rolled around like rocks in my stomach and the pain was terrible.

It wasn't until two days had passed that the kidnapper allowed me to come upstairs again. Even on the stairs in the garage I had to close my eyes. That's how much the dim brightness blinded me. I breathed in deeply in the certain knowledge of having survived once again.

'Are you going to be good now?' he asked me, once we had reached the house. 'You have to be better, otherwise I will have to lock you up again.' I was much too weak to contradict him. The next day I saw that the skin on the inside of my thighs and on my stomach had turned yellow. The beta-carotene in the carrots had been deposited in the last few remnants of fat under my transparently white skin. I weighed only thirty-eight kilograms, was sixteen years old and was one metre seventy-five tall.

Weighing myself daily had become second nature to me and I watched as the needle moved backwards day by day. The kidnapper had lost all sense of proportion and still accused me of being too fat. And I believed him. Today I know that my body mass index back then came to 14.8. The World Health Organization has said a body mass index of fifteen is an indicator of starvation. Mine was lower than that.

Hunger is an extreme physical experience. At first, you still feel good. When nourishment is cut off, the body stimulates itself. Adrenaline pours into the system, you suddenly feel better, full of energy. It is probably a mechanism the body uses to signal: I still have reserves, you can use them to search for food. However, locked underground there's no way to find food. Rushes of adrenaline go nowhere. Next comes a growling stomach and fantasizing about eating. Thoughts focus only on one's next bite of food. Later, you lose all touch with reality, sliding into delirium. You no longer dream, but simply drift between worlds. You see buffets, large plates of spaghetti, cakes and sweets, all there for the taking. A mirage. Cramps shake your whole body, that feel as if your stomach is devouring itself. The pain that hunger can cause is unbearable. You can't understand that if you have known hunger as only a slight growling of the stomach. I wish I had never come to know cramps like that. Finally, the weakness comes. You can hardly lift your arm any more, your blood pressure plummets, and when you stand up, your vision goes black and you fall over.

My body showed clear signs of lack of food and light. I was only skin and bones. Blue-black marks appeared on the white skin on my calves. I don't know whether they were from hunger or from my extended periods with no light. But they looked worrying, like marks on a corpse.

Whenever he starved me for a longer period, the kidnapper would then slowly feed me again until I had enough strength to work. It would take some time, because after a longer starvation phase I could only eat a few spoonfuls of food. Although I had fantasized about nothing else for days, the smell of food turned my stomach. When I once again became 'too strong' for him, he once again began to deny me food. Priklopil used starvation in a very targeted way: 'You are too rebellious, you have too much energy,' he would say sometimes, before he took away the last morsel of my tiny meals. At the same time, his own eating disorder, which he transferred to me, also intensified. His compulsive attempts to eat healthily took on absurd forms.

'We are going to drink a glass of wine every day to prevent heart attack,' he announced one day. From then on, I had to drink a glass of red wine a day. I only had to take a few sips, but the taste disgusted me. I choked the wine down like bitter medicine. He didn't like wine either, but forced himself to drink a small glass with his meal. For him it was never about the pleasure, but rather the introduction of a new rule that he – and therefore I – had to follow strictly.

Then he declared carbohydrates his enemy: 'We are now going to follow a ketogenic diet.' Sugar, bread and even fruit were forbidden. I was given only food rich in fats and proteins, still only in small portions, and my gaunt body coped with this treatment worse and worse. Mostly when I had been locked up for days in the dungeon with no food, I was given fatty meats and an egg upstairs. Whenever I ate with the kidnapper, I devoured my ration as quickly as possible. If I was finished before him, I could maybe hope that he would give me another bite, because he found it unpleasant when I watched him eat.

The worst thing was having to cook when I was completely starving. One day he put one of his mother's recipes and a package containing pieces of codfish on the counter. I peeled the potatoes, floured the cod, separated eggs and put the pieces of fish in the yolk. Then I heated a bit of oil in a pan, rolled the fish in breadcrumbs and fried it. As always, he sat in the kitchen, commenting on what I did:

'My mother can do that ten times faster.'

'You can see that the oil is getting much too hot, you stupid cow.'

'Don't peel too much off the potato. That's wasting it.'

The scent of fried fish permeated the kitchen, driving me half crazy. I lifted the pieces out of the pan and put them on a paper towel to drip. My mouth watered. There was enough fish for a real feast. Maybe I could eat two pieces? And maybe some potatoes as well?

I don't remember exactly what I did wrong at that moment. I only know that Priklopil suddenly jumped up, tearing the serving dish I had wanted to put on the kitchen table out of my hand and barking at me, 'You aren't getting anything today!'

At that moment, I completely lost control. I was so hungry that I could've committed murder for a piece of fish. I grabbed for the plate with one hand, took a piece of fish and tried hastily to stuff it into my mouth. But he was faster and slapped the fish out of my hand. I tried to nab a second piece, but he grabbed my wrist and squeezed it so hard that I had to let go. I dropped to the floor to pick up the remains that had fallen during our struggle. I managed to put a tiny bit in my mouth. But, immediately, he had his hand on my throat, lifting me up, dragging me to the sink and pushing my head down. With his other hand, he forced my teeth apart and choked me until the forbidden fish came back up again. 'That will teach you.' Then he slowly removed the serving dish from the table and took it to the hallway. I stood in front of the kitchen cabinets, humiliated and helpless.

The kidnapper kept me weak using such methods – and trapped me in a mixture of dependence and gratitude. You don't bite the hand that feeds you. For me there was only one hand that could save me from starvation. It was the hand of the very same man who was systematically starving me. In this way, the small rations of food seemed to me like generous gifts sometimes. I remember so vividly the sausage salad that his mother prepared from time to time at the weekend that even today it seems to me to be a particular delicacy. When I was allowed to come back upstairs after two or three long days in the dungeon, sometimes he gave me a small bowl of it. Mostly, only the onions and a few pieces of tomato were still swimming in the dressing. He had previously fished out the sausage and the hard-boiled eggs. But the leftovers seemed like a feast to me. And when he gave me an additional bit from his plate, or sometimes even a piece of cake, I was overjoyed. It is so easy to bind to you someone from whom you are withholding food.

On 1 March 2004 the trial of the serial killer Marc Dutroux began in Belgium. I can still vividly remember his case from my childhood. I was eight years old when the police stormed his house in August 1996, freeing two girls – the twelve-year-old Sabine Dardenne and the fourteen-year-old Laetitia Delhez. The dead bodies of four other girls were also found.

For months, I followed news about his trial on the radio and on television. I heard about Sabine Dardenne's martyrdom and suffered with her when she confronted the perpetrator in the courtroom. She too had been thrown into a delivery van and kidnapped on her way to school. The cellar dungeon where she had been locked up was even smaller than mine and her story of imprisonment was different. She had lived the nightmare that the kidnapper had threatened me with. Yet even though there were significant differences, the crime that had been discovered two years before my own abduction could definitely have served as a blueprint for Wolfgang Priklopil's sick plan. However, there is no proof of that.

The trial stirred me up even though I couldn't see myself reflected in Sabine Dardenne. She had been freed after eighty days in captivity. She was still angry and knew that she was right. She called her abductor 'monster' and 'bastard' and demanded an apology, which she did not receive in court back then. Sabine

Dardenne's imprisonment had been too short for her to lose herself. At the time, I had already been held captive for 2,200 long days and nights. My perception had begun to alter long ago. Intellectually, I certainly knew that I was the victim of a crime. But, emotionally, the long period of contact I had had only with the kidnapper, who was necessary to my survival, had caused me to internalize his psychopathic fantasies. They had become my reality.

I learned two things from that trial. First of all, that victims of violent crime are not always believed. All of Belgium seemed to be persuaded that Marc Dutroux was merely a front man for a large-scale network, a network that reached up to the highest levels. On the radio I heard of the revilement Sabine Dardenne was being subjected to because she refused to support these theories, always insisting that she had never seen anyone else other than Dutroux. And, secondly, that people do not empathize with victims and give them limitless sympathy, but can very quickly switch to aggression and rejection.

At about the same time, I heard my own name on the radio for the first time. I had turned on the Austrian cultural station Ö1 to listen to a broadcast on non-fiction works when I suddenly jumped: 'Natascha Kampusch'. For six years, I had heard nobody speak that name. The only person who could have said it had forbidden me my name. An announcer on the radio mentioned it in connection with a new book written by Kurt Totzer and Günther Kallinger entitled *Spurlos – die spektakulärsten Vermisstenfälle der Interpol*, or *Without a Trace – Interpol's Most Spectacular Missing Persons Cases*. The authors talked about the research they had done – and about me. A mysterious case where there was no hot trail and no body, they said. I sat in front of the radio and wanted only to scream: *Here I am! I'm alive!* But nobody would hear me.

After that radio broadcast my own situation seemed more hopeless than ever. I sat on my bed and suddenly I saw everything very clearly. I knew I couldn't spend my whole life this way. I also knew that I would no longer be rescued and that escaping seemed completely impossible. There was only one way out.

That day wasn't the first time I had attempted suicide. Simply disappearing into the distant nothingness where there was no pain and no more feelings – back then I thought it an act of empowerment. Otherwise I had very little power to make any decisions about my life, my body, my actions. Taking my own life seemed my last trump card.

At the age of fourteen I had tried several times without success to strangle myself using articles of clothing. At the age of fifteen I wanted to slit my wrists. I had sliced open my skin with a large sewing needle and had continued to bore into my skin until I couldn't stand it any more. My arm burned unbearably, but at the same time it released the inner pain that I felt. It is sometimes a relief when physical pain drowns out the psychological torment for a few moments.

This time I wanted to choose another method. It was one of those evenings when the kidnapper had locked me in the dungeon and I knew that he wouldn't come back until the next day. I tidied up my room, folded my few T-shirts properly and took one last look at the flannel dress he had kidnapped me in, which now hung on a hanger under the bed. In my thoughts I said farewell to my mother. 'Forgive me for leaving now. And for leaving once again without saying a word,' I whispered. *What could happen anyway?*

Then I walked slowly to the hotplate and turned it on. When it began to get hot, I put paper and toilet rolls on it. It took some time for the paper to begin smoking – but it worked. I climbed the ladder to my bed and lay down. The dungeon would fill with smoke and I would gently drift away, as I determined, out of a life that was no longer my own.

I don't know how long I lay on the bed waiting for death to come. It seemed like the eternity I had prepared myself for.

But it all probably happened relatively quickly. When the acrid smoke reached my lungs, I initially inhaled deeply. But then the will to survive that I believed to have lost, resurfaced in full force. Every fibre of my being was prepared to flee. I began to cough. I held my pillow in front of my mouth and stormed down the ladder. I turned on the tap, held cleaning cloths under the stream of water and threw them on top of the blistering cardboard rolls on the hotplate. The water hissed, the acrid smoke became thicker. Coughing and with tears in my eyes, I swung my towel around in the room to disperse the smoke. I feverishly racked my brains as to how to hide from the kidnapper my attempt to suffocate myself. Suicide, the ultimate act of disobedience, the worst imaginable offence.

But the next morning the dungeon still smelled like a smoke-house. Priklopil came in, inhaled, the air irritated him. He yanked me out of bed, shook me and shouted at me. How dare I try to escape him! How dare I abuse his trust in such a way! His face reflected a mixture of limitless anger and fear. Fear that I could ruin everything.

9

Afraid of Life

My Psychological Prison is Complete

Punches and kicks, choking, scratching, contusion on wrist, squeezing of
the same, shoved against the door frame. Hit with hammer (heavy
hammer) and fists in stomach area. I have bruises on: right hip bone,
right upper (5 x 1 cm) and lower (c. 3.5 cm in diameter) arm, on my left
and right outer thigh (left c. 9–10 cm long and deep black to purple,
c. 4 cm wide) as well as on both shoulders. Abrasions and scratches on
both thighs, my left calf.

Diary entry, January 2006

I was seventeen when the kidnapper brought a video of the film
Pleasantville into the dungeon. The story is about a brother and a
sister who grow up in the US in the 1990s. At school the teachers
talk about gloomy job prospects, AIDS and the threat of the
destruction of the planet due to climate change. At home, the
divorced parents fight on the phone over who is to take the kids
for the weekend. And there's nothing but problems with their
friends. The brother escapes into the world of a television series
from the 1950s: 'Welcome to Pleasantville! Morals and decency.
Warm welcomes: "Hi honey, I'm home!" The right food. "Do you
want some biscuits?" Welcome to the perfect world of Pleasantville. Only on TV Time!' In Pleasantville the mother serves
dinner exactly when the father comes home from work. The
children are nicely dressed and always hit the basket when playing
basketball. The world consists only of two streets and the fire

brigade has only one job: rescuing cats from trees. Because there are no fires in Pleasantville.

After a fight over the remote control, the brother and sister suddenly land in Pleasantville. They are trapped in this strange place where there are no colours and the inhabitants live according to rules that the two find incomprehensible. When they adapt and integrate themselves into this society, it can be very nice in Pleasantville. But when they break the rules, the friendly inhabitants turn into an angry mob.

The film was a parable of the life I was living. For the kidnapper, the outside world was synonymous with Sodom and Gomorrah: dangers, dirt and vice lurked everywhere. A world which for him had become the epitome of what he had failed at and what he wanted to keep his, and my, distance from. Our world behind the yellow walls was supposed to be like Pleasantville: 'Do you want some more biscuits?' – 'Thank you, dear.' It was an illusion that he conjured up again and again in his chitchat: we could have such a nice life. In that house with the gleaming surfaces that shone too much and with the furniture that nearly choked on its own conventionality. But he continued to work on the façade, investing in his – our – new life, which he then battered with his fists the next minute.

In *Pleasantville* there is a scene where someone says, 'My reality is only what I know.' When I leaf through my diary today, I am shocked sometimes to see how well I adapted to Priklopil's screenplay with all its contradictions:

> *Dear diary,*
> *It is time to pour my heart out completely and without reservation about the pain that I have come to know. Let us begin in October. I no longer know how it all was, but the things that happened were not very nice. He planted the Brabant Thuja shrubs. They look very nice. At times he wasn't doing very well, and when he isn't doing very well, he makes my life hell.*

Whenever he has a headache and takes a tablet, he gets an allergic reaction, and that means that his nose begins to run badly. But the doctor gave him drops to swallow. In any case, it was very difficult. There were unpleasant scenes again and again. At the end of October the new bedroom furniture arrived with the sonorous name Esmerelda. The blankets, pillows and mattresses came somewhat earlier. Everything of course hypoallergenic and washable at high temperatures. When the bed had come, I had to help him take apart the old wardrobe. That took about three days. We had to take apart the pieces, carry the heavy mirrored doors over to the study, the sides and shelves we carried downstairs. Then we went into the garage and opened all of the furniture and part of the bed. The furniture consisted of two bedside tables with two drawers each and gold-coloured brass handles, two dressers, a high, narrow one with . . .
[incomplete]

Gold-coloured brass handles, polished by the perfect housewife, who put the dinner on the table, cooked according to the recipes of his even more perfect mother. When I did everything right and kept to my designated choreography between the backdrops, the illusion held up for a moment. But any deviation from the screenplay, which no one had given me ahead of time, was punished with draconian severity. His unpredictability became my greatest enemy. Even when I was convinced that I had done everything well, even when I thought I knew what prop was needed at any given moment, I was not safe from him. A look that rested on him for too long, a wrong plate on the table that had been the right one yesterday, and he flew into a rage.

Sometime later I wrote in my notes:

Brutal punches to the head, my right shoulder, my stomach, my back and my face, as well as to my ear and eye. Uncontrolled, unpredictable, excessively sudden outbursts of rage. Screaming, insults, pushing me while climbing the stairs. Choking, sitting on me and holding my mouth and

> *nose closed, suffocating me. Sitting on my arm joints, kneeling on my*
> *knuckles, wringing my arms with his fists. On my forearms I have*
> *finger-shaped bruises and a scratch and abrasion on my left forearm. He*
> *sat on my head or, kneeling on my torso, beat my head against the floor*
> *with full force. This several times and with all his strength, giving me a*
> *headache and making me feel nauseated. Then an uncontrolled shower of*
> *punches, throwing objects at me, pushing me viciously against the*
> *bedside table.*

The bedside table with the brass handles.

Then again he allowed me things that gave me the illusion that he cared. For example, he let me grow my hair again. But that was only part of his choreography. Because I then had to dye it peroxide blonde in order to conform to his image of the ideal woman: obedient, hard-working, blonde.

I spent more and more time upstairs in the house, spent hours dusting, tidying up and cooking. As always he never let me out of his sight for a second. His desire to control me completely went so far that he even took all the doors to the toilets off their hinges: I was not to be out of his sight for two minutes. His permanent presence drove me to desperation.

But he too was a prisoner of his own screenplay. Whenever he locked me in his dungeon, he had to supply me with food, etc. Whenever he fetched me to come upstairs, he spent every single minute monitoring me. His methods were always the same. But the pressure on him grew. What if a hundred blows weren't enough to keep me down? Then he would be a failure in his Pleasantville as well. And there was no turning back.

Priklopil was aware of this risk. As a result he did everything he could to make me understand what would be in store for me should I dare leave his world. I remember a scene when he humiliated me so badly that I immediately fled back into the house.

One afternoon I was working upstairs and asked him to open a window. All I wanted was a bit more air, a hint of the twittering birds outside. The kidnapper barked at me, 'You only want me to open it so that you can scream and run away.'

I swore he could believe me that I wouldn't run. 'I'll stay, I promise. I'll never run away.'

He looked at me doubtfully, then grabbed me by the upper arm and dragged me to the front door. It was broad daylight outside and, although the street was devoid of people, his manoeuvre was still risky. He opened the door and shoved me outside without ever loosening his grip on my arm. 'Go on, run! Go on! Just see how far you get the way you look!'

I was paralysed with fright and shame. I was hardly wearing anything and tried to cover my body as best I could with my free hand. My shame that a stranger might see me so emaciated, with all my bruises and the short stubbly hair on my head, was greater than the slim hope that someone could witness the scene and start to wonder.

He did that a few times, shoving me outside naked in front of the house and saying, 'Go on, run! Just see how far you get.' Each time the world outside would become more and more threatening. I was confronted with a massive conflict between my longing to know that world outside and the fear of taking that step. For months I had begged to be allowed outside for a short time and again and again I was told, 'What do you want out there? You're not missing anything. Outside is just the same as inside here. Besides, you'll scream when you're outside, and then I'll have to kill you.'

He, in turn, vacillated between his pathological paranoia, his fear of having his crime discovered, and his dream of a normal life where we would have to go out into the outside world. It was a vicious circle, and the more he felt backed into a corner by his own thoughts, the more aggressively he turned against me. Like before, he relied on a mixture of psychological and physical violence. He trampled mercilessly on what remained of my self-esteem and hammered the same words into me over and over: 'You are worthless. You should be grateful to me that I took you in. Nobody else would take you.' He told me that my parents were in jail and that nobody was living in our old flat. 'Where would you go if you ran away? Nobody out there wants you. You would come crawling back to me remorsefully.' And he reminded me insistently that he would kill anyone who happened to witness any attempt at escape. The first victims, he told me, would probably be the neighbours. And I certainly didn't want to be responsible for them, did I?

He meant the people in the house next door. Ever since I had swum in their pool from time to time, I had felt connected to them in a unique way. As if they were the ones who had enabled me to enjoy my small escape from everyday life in the house. I never saw them, but in the evening when I was upstairs in the house, I sometimes heard them calling their cats. Their voices sounded friendly and concerned. Like people who take loving care of those who are dependent on them. Priklopil tried to keep any contact with them largely to a minimum. Sometimes they brought him a cake or a trinket from their travels. One time they rang the bell while I was in the house and I had to hide quickly in the garage. I heard their voices as they stood in front of the door with the kidnapper, giving him some homemade food. He always threw such things away immediately. Given his obsession with cleanliness, he never would have eaten any of it because they disgusted him.

When he took me out for the first time, I had no sense of liberation. I had looked forward so much to finally being allowed to leave my prison. However, I sat in the passenger seat and was paralysed with fear. The kidnapper had drilled into me precisely what I was to say if someone were to recognize me: 'First of all you are to act as if you don't know what they're talking about. If that doesn't help, you say, "No, you've got the wrong person." And if somebody asks me who you are, you are my niece.' Natascha had ceased to exist long ago. Then he started the car and drove slowly out of the garage.

We drove down Heinestrasse in Strasshof: front gardens, hedgerows with family houses behind them. The street was empty of people. I could feel my heart beating in my throat. For the first time in seven years I had left the kidnapper's house. He drove through a world I knew only from my memories and from short video films the kidnapper had made for me years ago. Small snapshots that showed Strasshof, occasionally a few people. When he turned on to the main street and queued up in traffic, I saw a man walking down the pavement out of the corner of my eye. He walked in a strangely monotonous way, never stopping, never making a surprising movement, like a wind-up toy soldier with a key sticking out of his back.

Everything I saw seemed unreal. It was like the first time I stood in the garden at night at the age of twelve; doubts struck me about the existence of all these people who moved so matter-of-factly and nonchalantly through an environment which I knew, but which had become completely alien to me. The bright light that bathed everything seemed as if it came from a gigantic spotlight. At that moment I was certain the kidnapper had arranged everything. It was his film set, his own gigantic *Truman Show*. All the people here were extras, everything was only play-acted in order to make me believe that I was outside, while in reality I remained trapped in an expanded prison cell. I didn't understand until later that I was caught in my own psychological prison.

We left Strasshof, drove cross-country for a bit and stopped in a small forest. I was allowed to get out of the car briefly. The air smelled tangy, of wood, and below me dappled sunlight skimmed across the dry pine needles. I knelt down and carefully laid my hand on the ground. The needles pricked me, leaving behind red dots on the heel of my hand. I took a few steps towards a tree and placed my forehead against a tree trunk. The craggy bark was warm from the sun and exuded the intense odour of resin. Just like the trees I remembered from my childhood.

On the way back, neither of us said a word. When the kidnapper let me out of the car in the garage and locked me in my dungeon, a deep sadness welled up within me. I had looked forward to the world outside for so long, had pictured it in the most vivid colours. And now I had moved through it as if it were an imaginary world. My reality had become the birch wallpaper in the kitchen. This was the environment in which I knew how I was supposed to move. Outside, I stumbled around as if caught in the wrong film.

That feeling ebbed somewhat the next time I was allowed out. The kidnapper had become emboldened by my submissive and frightened attitude in my first tentative steps outside the house. Just a few days later he took me to a chemist's in town. He had promised to allow me to pick something nice there. The kidnapper parked the car in front of the shop and hissed at me once again, 'Not a word. Otherwise everyone in there will die.' Then he got out, walked around the car and held the door open for me.

I walked ahead of him into the shop. I could hear him softly breathing right behind me and imagined his hand in his jacket pocket closing around a pistol, ready to shoot everyone if I made a single wrong move. But I would be good. I would endanger no one. I wouldn't run away. I wanted nothing more than to snatch a small slice of the life that other girls my age took for granted: walking through the cosmetics section at the chemist's. Although I wasn't allowed to put on make-up – the kidnapper wouldn't even allow me to wear normal clothes – I had been able to wring a concession out of him. I was permitted to choose two items that were part of the normal life of a teenager.

To my mind, mascara was an indispensable must. I had read that in the teen magazines the kidnapper had brought to my dungeon from time to time. I had read the pages of make-up tips over and over, imagining making myself pretty for my first trip to a club. Laughing and preening with my girlfriends in front of the mirror, trying on one blouse and then the other. *Is my hair okay? Come on, let's go!*

And now, there I stood between the long shelves of innumerable little bottles and tubes I was unfamiliar with. They held a magical attraction for me, but also unsettled me. It was so much at once, I didn't know what to do, and I was afraid I would drop something.

'Come on! Hurry up!' I heard the voice behind me say. I hastily grabbed a tube of mascara and selected a small bottle of essential mint oil from a wooden shelf. I wanted to keep it open in my dungeon in the hope that it would mask the mouldy smell. The whole time the kidnapper stood right behind me. He made me nervous; I felt like a criminal who had not yet been recognized, but could be discovered at any moment. I made an effort to walk up to the checkout as easily as possible. A round woman was sitting there, probably around fifty years old, her grey curls somewhat crooked. When she addressed me with a friendly *Grüss Gott!**, I jumped. They were the first words a stranger had addressed to me in over seven years. The last time I had spoken to anyone other than myself or my kidnapper was when I had still been a small, pudgy child. Now the cashier greeted me like a real grown-up customer. She addressed me with the formal *Sie* and smiled while I silently laid the two items on the conveyor belt. I was so grateful

---

* A typical greeting in Austria.

to that woman for taking note of me, for seeing that I actually existed. I could have remained standing at the checkout counter for hours, simply to feel the closeness of another person. It never occurred to me to ask her for help. The kidnapper stood, armed I was convinced, only centimetres away. I never would have endangered that woman, who had, just for a short moment, given me the feeling that I was actually alive.

Over the next few days, my beatings increased. Again and again the kidnapper angrily locked me up, and again and again I lay on my bed covered in bruises, struggling with myself. *I mustn't allow myself to be swallowed up in my pain. I mustn't give up. I mustn't give in to the thought that this imprisonment was the best thing that would ever happen to me.* I had to tell myself, over and over, that I wasn't lucky having to live with the kidnapper, despite what he had hammered into me time and again. His words had closed around me like mantraps. Whenever I lay balled up in pain in the dark, I knew that he was in the wrong. But the human brain quickly represses injuries. Already the next day I was happy to submit to the illusion that it wasn't all that bad, and believed his flights of imagination.

But if I ever wanted to escape the dungeon, I had to get rid of these mantraps.

> *I want once more in my life some happiness*
> *And survive in the ecstasy of living*
> *I want once more see a smile and a laughing for a while*
> *I want once more the taste of someone's love* *
>
> *Diary entry, January 2006*

---

* Written by Natascha Kampusch in English.

Back then I began to write short messages to myself. When you see something in black and white, things become more tangible. They become reality on a level that your mind finds more difficult to escape from. From then on I wrote down every beating, soberly and without emotion. I still have these records today. Some of them were entered into a simple school notebook in A5 format in precise, clean handwriting. Others I wrote on a green A4-sized sheet, the lines very close together. My notes back then fulfilled the same purpose as today. Because even looking back, the small, positive experiences during my imprisonment are more present in my mind than the unbelievable horrors I was subjected to for years.

20 August 2005. Wolfgang hit me at least three times in the face, shoved his knee into my tailbone about four times and once into my pubic bone. He forced me to kneel in front of him and gouged a key ring into my left elbow, giving me a bruise and an abrasion with a yellowish secretion. In addition to the screaming and tormenting. Six punches to my head.

21 August 2005. Morning grumbling. Insults for no reason. Then blows and spanking. Kicks and shoving. Seven blows to the face, a punch to the head. Insults and blows to the face, a punch to the head. Insults and blows, only breakfast with no cereal. Then darkness down below / no discussion / stupid manipulative statements. And once scratching my gums with his finger. Holding and pressing down with my chin and choking my neck.

22 August 2005. Punches to the head.

23 August 2005. At least 60 blows to the face. 10–15 punches to the head causing severe nausea, four slaps with his flat, vicious hand to the head, a punch with all his strength to my right ear and jaw. My ear turned blackish. Choking, a hard uppercut making my jaw crunch, c. 70 blows with his knee, primarily to my tailbone and my rear end. Punches to the small of my back and my spine, my ribs and between my breasts. Blows with a broom to my left elbow and upper arm (blackish-brown bruise), as well as to my left wrist. Four blows to my eye making me see blue flashes of light. And much more.

24 August 2005. Vicious blows with his knee to my stomach and genital area (wanted to get me to kneel). And to my lower spinal column as well. Slaps to the face, a vicious punch to my right ear (bluish-black discoloration). Then darkness in the dungeon with no food or air.

25 August 2005. Punches to my hip bone and my breastbone. Then utterly spiteful insults. Darkness in the dungeon. The whole day I only had seven raw carrots and a glass of milk.

26 August 2005. Vicious blows using his fist to the front side of my upper thigh and my rear end (ankle). As well as ringing slaps to my bottom, back, the side of my thighs, right shoulder, underarms and bosom leaving behind red pustules.

The horror of one single week, of which there was a countless number. Sometimes it was so bad that I shook so much I couldn't hold the pen any more. I crept into bed, whimpering, full of fear that the images from the day would come upon me at night as well. Then I spoke to my other self, who was waiting for me and would take me by the hand, no matter what was yet to happen. I imagined that she could see me in the triptych mirror that now hung above the sink in my dungeon. If I only looked long enough, I would see my strong self reflected in my face.

The next time, I had fervently promised myself, I wouldn't let go of an outstretched hand. I would have the strength to ask someone for help.

One morning, the kidnapper gave me a pair of jeans and a T-shirt. He wanted me to accompany him to a do-it-yourself centre. My courage already began to sink as we turned on to the road leading to Vienna. If he continued on that road, we would drive towards my old neighbourhood. It was the same route I had taken on 2 March 1998 in the opposite direction – cowering on the floor in the back of the van. Back then I was afraid of dying. Now I was seventeen, sat in the front seat and was afraid of living.

We drove through Süssenbrunn, just a few streets away from my grandmother's house. It seemed irretrievably lost to me, as if from a distant century. I saw the familiar streets, the houses, the cobblestones where I had played hopscotch. But I no longer belonged there.

'Lower your eyes,' Priklopil snapped next to me. I immediately obeyed. Being so close to the places of my childhood made my throat tighten and I fought back the tears. Somewhere over there, on our right, was the street leading to Rennbahnweg. Somewhere over there to our right in the large council estate, my mother was perhaps at that moment sitting at the kitchen table. Surely she now thought that I had to be dead, and here I was driving past her just a few hundred metres away. I felt beaten down and much, much further away than just those few streets that in reality lay between us.

The feeling grew when the kidnapper turned into the car park at the DIY store. My mother had waited at the red light at that corner to turn right hundreds of times. Because that was where my sister's flat was. Today I know that Waltraud Priklopil, the kidnapper's mother, also lived just a few hundred metres away.

The shop's car park was full of people. A couple queued up at a sausage stand at the entrance. Others pushed their shopping trolleys towards their cars. Blue-collar workers in their stained blue trousers carried wooden slats across the car park. My nerves were stretched to breaking point. I stared out of the window. One of these many people had to see me, had to notice that something was not right here. The kidnapper seemed to read my thoughts: 'You stay seated. You'll get out when I tell you to. And then you stay right in front of me and walk slowly to the entrance. I don't want to hear a sound!'

I went into the DIY store in front of him. He directed me with a slight pressure from one hand on my shoulder. I could feel his nervousness, the fibres in his fingers twitching.

I let my gaze sweep through the long corridor in front of me. Men in work clothes stood in front of shelves, in groups or alone, holding lists and busily absorbed in their own errands. Which one of them should I address? And what was I even to say? I eyed each one out of the corner of my eye. But the longer I looked at them, the more the people's faces distorted into grimaces. They suddenly seemed hostile and unfriendly. Heavily built people, busy with themselves and blind to their surroundings. My thoughts raced. All of a sudden it seemed absurd to ask someone for help. Who was going to believe me after all, a gaunt, confused teenager, hardly capable of using her own voice? What would happen if I were to turn to one of these men and ask, 'Please help me?'

'My niece does this all the time. The poor thing. She is unfortunately confused. She needs her medication,' Priklopil would say, and all around everyone would nod in understanding as he grabbed me by the upper arm and dragged me out of the shop. For a moment I could have heard insane cackling breaking out. The kidnapper wouldn't have to kill anyone to cover up his crime! Everything here played right into his hand. Nobody cared about me. Nobody would even think that I was telling the truth if I said, 'Please help me. I've been kidnapped.' Smile, you're on *Candid Camera*! The presenter in disguise would come out from behind the shelves and reveal the joke. Or maybe the nice uncle behind the strange girl. Voices shrilled crazily through my head: *Oh heavens. I really feel sorry for him. He has his cross to bear with someone like that . . . But so nice of him to take care of her.*

'Can I help you?' The question thundered in my ears like scorn. I needed a moment to realize that it hadn't come from the confusion of voices inside my head. A sales clerk from the bathroom section was standing in front of us. 'Can I help you?' he repeated. His gaze swept up and over me briefly and remained fixed on the kidnapper. How clueless the friendly man was! *Yes, you can help me! Please!* I began to tremble and patches of sweat formed on my T-shirt. I felt nauseated and my brain ceased to obey me. What had I wanted to say just now?

'Thank you, we're fine,' I heard a voice behind me saying. Then his hand clamped around my arm. *Thank you, we're fine. And in case I don't see you, good afternoon, good evening and good night.* Just like in *The Truman Show.*

As if in a trance, I dragged myself through the DIY store. Over, over. I had missed my opportunity. Maybe I had never really had one. I felt as if I were trapped in a transparent bubble. I could flail with my arms and legs, sink down in a gelatine-like mass, but I was unable to break through the skin. I wobbled through the corridors and saw people everywhere. But I was no longer one of them. I no longer had any rights. I was invisible.

After that experience I knew that I was unable to ask for help. What did the people outside know about the abstruse world I was trapped in? And who was I to drag them into it? That friendly sales clerk couldn't help the fact that I had appeared in his store of all places. What right did I have to subject him to the risk of Priklopil running amok? Although his voice sounded neutral and had revealed none of his nervousness, I could almost hear his heart pounding in his chest. Then there was his grip on my arm, his eyes boring into me from behind the whole way through the shop.

The threat of him going on a shooting spree. Add to that my own weakness, my inability, my failure.

I lay awake that night for a long time. I was forced to think of the pact I had made with my other self. I was seventeen. The time when I had planned to redeem my pact was drawing nearer. The incident at the DIY centre had shown me that I had to do it myself. At the same time, I felt my strength dissipating and myself slipping deeper and deeper into the paranoid, bizarre world the kidnapper had constructed for me. But how was my disheartened, fearful self to become the strong self who was to take me by the hand and lead me out of my prison? I didn't know. The only thing I knew was that I would need an immeasurable amount of strength and self-discipline. Wherever I could find them.

What helped me back then were in fact the conversations I had with my second self and my notes. I had begun a second series of pages. Now I no longer recorded the beatings, but tried to encourage myself in writing. Pep talks I could retrieve whenever I was down and read aloud to myself. Sometimes it was like shooting arrows in the dark, but it worked.

> *Don't let him get you down when he tells you that you are too stupid for anything.*
> *Don't let him get you down when he beats you.*
> *Don't answer back when he tells you that you are incapable.*
> *Don't answer back when he tells you that you can't live without him.*
> *Don't react when he turns the light off on you.*
> *Forgive him everything and don't continue to be angry at him.*
> *Be stronger.*
> *Don't give up.*
> *Never, never give up.*

Don't let him get you down, never give up. But it was easier said than done. For such a long time all my thoughts were concentrated on getting out of that cellar, out of that house. Now I had managed it. And nothing had changed. I was just as trapped on the outside as I was on the inside. The outer walls seemed to become more permeable, but my inner walls were cemented like never before. Added to that was the fact that our 'outings' pushed Wolfgang Priklopil to the brink of panic. Torn between his dream of a normal life and the fear that I could destroy everything by attempting to escape or just by my behaviour in general, he became more and more erratic and uncontrolled, even when he knew that I was safely ensconced in the house. His outbursts of rage became more frequent. He naturally blamed me and fell into an utterly paranoid delusional state. He refused to be appeased by my timid and anxious demeanour in public. I don't know if he secretly suspected me of pretending to be apprehensive. My inability to play-act in such a way became evident on another outing to Vienna, which actually should have put an end to my captivity.

We were driving straight ahead on Brünnerstrasse when traffic slowed. A stop-and-search operation by the police. I saw the police car and the officers waving vehicles to the side of the road from far away. Priklopil drew a sharp breath. He didn't shift his position one millimetre, but I did observe his hands grasping the steering wheel tightly until his knuckles turned white. Outwardly he was completely calm as he stopped the car on the side of the street and opened the window.

'Driving licence and vehicle registration please!'

I cautiously lifted my head. The police officer's face seemed surprisingly young under his cap; his tone was firm, but friendly. Priklopil dug around for the papers, while the policeman eyed him. His eyes grazed me only briefly. A word formed in my head, a word I saw floating in the air as if in a large bubble like in the comic strips: *HELP!* I could see it so clearly before my very eyes that I could hardly believe the policeman wouldn't react immediately. But he took the documents, unperturbed, and checked them.

Help! Get me out of here! You are checking a criminal! I blinked and rolled my eyes as if communicating in Morse code. It must have looked as if I was having some kind of seizure. But it was nothing more than a desperate SOS, blinked out by the eyelids of a scrawny teenager crouching on the passenger seat of a white delivery van.

Thoughts swirled around in my head. Perhaps I could just jump out of the van and start running? I could run over to the police car. After all, it was standing directly in front of me. But what should I say? Would they hear me? What would happen if they turned me away? Priklopil would collect me again, apologize profusely for the trouble and for his niece who was holding everything up. And besides: an escape attempt – that was the worst taboo I could break. If it failed, I didn't want even to imagine what was in store for me. But what would happen if it worked? I pictured Priklopil flooring the accelerator and pulling away with squealing tyres. Then he would flip the car into oncoming traffic. Screeching brakes, shattering glass, blood, death. Priklopil hanging lifeless over the steering column; sirens approaching from a distance.

'Thank you. Everything's in order! Drive safely!' The policeman smiled briefly, pushing Priklopil's documents through the window. He had no idea that he had just stopped the van in which a small girl had been abducted nearly eight years ago. He had no idea that this small girl had been held captive for nearly eight years in the kidnapper's cellar. He had no idea how close he had come to uncovering a crime – and becoming a witness to Priklopil's mad attempt at a car chase. One word from me would have been enough, a brave assertion. Instead I cowered in my seat and closed my eyes as the kidnapper started the engine.

I had probably missed my greatest opportunity to leave this

nightmare behind. It wasn't until later that I realized that one option had never crossed my mind: simply addressing the policeman. My fear that Priklopil would do something to anyone I came into contact with had become totally paralysing.

I was a slave, subordinate. Worth less than a household pet. I no longer had a voice.

During my imprisonment I had dreamed many times of going skiing in the winter just once. The blue sky, the sun shining on the glistening snow enshrouding the landscape in a pure, flaky blanket. The crunching under your shoes, the cold that turns your cheeks red. And afterwards a hot chocolate, just like after ice-skating.

Priklopil was a good skier who had gone on repeated daytrips to the mountains in the last few years of my imprisonment. While I packed his things, going through his meticulously drawn-up lists, he was very excited. Ski wax. Gloves. Granola bar. Sunscreen. Lip balm. Ski cap. Every time I burned with longing when he locked me in my dungeon and left the house to glide over the snow in the mountains in the sun. I couldn't have imagined anything more wonderful.

Just before my eighteenth birthday he spoke more often of taking me on such a ski trip one day. For him that was the biggest step towards a normal life. It might have been that he wanted to grant me one of my requests. But most of all he wanted to achieve confirmation that his crime was crowned with success. If I didn't break my tether in the mountains, in his eyes he would have done everything right.

The preparations took several days. The kidnapper went through his old ski equipment, laying out a number of items for me to try on. One of the anoraks fitted me, a fluffy thing from the 1970s. But I still needed ski trousers. 'I'll buy you a pair,' the kidnapper promised. 'We'll go shopping together.' He sounded excited and seemed happy for a moment.

The day we drove to the Donauzentrum shopping centre, my body had shut down to a bare minimum. I was severely undernourished and could hardly stand up when I got out of the car. It was a peculiar feeling to go back to the shopping centre I had so often strolled through with my parents. Today it is located only two underground stops from Rennbahnweg. Back then you took the bus a couple of stops. The kidnapper obviously felt very, very secure.

The Donauzentrum is a typical shopping centre on the outskirts of Vienna. Shops are lined up, one next to the other, over two floors. It smells of chips and popcorn, and the music is much too loud, and yet hardly drowns out the buzzing voices of innumerable teenagers who congregate in front of the shops for lack of any other place to meet. Even those who are used to such masses of people pretty soon find it too much and yearn for a moment of peace and fresh air. The noise, the lights and the crowds of people felt like a wall, like an impenetrable thicket where I was unable to get my bearings. With effort I tried to remember. Wasn't that the shop I was once in with my mother? For a fleeting moment I saw myself as a small girl trying on a pair of tights. But the images of the present pushed to the front. There were people everywhere: teenagers, grown-ups with large, colourful bags, mothers with prams, jumbled chaos. The kidnapper directed me towards a large clothing shop. A labyrinth, full of clothes racks, rummage tables and mannequins sporting expressionless smiles and displaying the fashions of the winter season.

The trousers in the adults' section didn't fit me. While Priklopil handed me one pair after another in the changing room, a sad figure looked back at me from the mirror. I was as white as a sheet, my blonde hair stood scraggily away from my head and I was so emaciated that I was swimming even in a size XS. The constant dressing and undressing was torture and I refused to repeat the entire procedure in the children's department. The kidnapper had to hold the ski trousers up in front of my body to check the size. When he was finally satisfied, I could hardly stand any longer.

I was greatly relieved to be in the car again. On the way back to Strasshof my head felt as if it was splitting. After eight years in isolation I was no longer capable of processing so much stimulation.

The ongoing preparations for our ski trip also dampened my happiness. There was primarily an atmosphere of buzzing tension. The kidnapper was agitated and irritated, remonstrating with me about the costs he was incurring on my behalf. He had me work out on the map the exact number of kilometres to the ski resort and calculate how much petrol would be needed for the trip. In addition to the lift pass, ski rental fees, maybe something to eat. In his pathological miserliness these were incredible sums he was squandering. And what for? So that I would probably act up and abuse his trust.

When his fist came crashing down on the tabletop next to me, I dropped the pen in fright. 'You are only exploiting my benevolence! You are nothing without me. Nothing!'

Don't answer back when he says that you can't live without him. I lifted my head and looked at him. And was surprised to see a hint of fear in his contorted face. This ski trip was an enormous risk. A risk that he wasn't undertaking in order to fulfil a long-standing wish of mine. It was choreographed to enable him to live out his fantasies. Gliding down the slopes with his 'partner', she admiring him for being able to ski so well. Perfect outward appearances, a self-image nourished by my humiliation and oppression, by the destruction of my 'self'.

I lost all desire to play along in this absurd drama. On the way to the garage I told him I wanted to stay home. I saw his eyes darken, then he exploded. 'What do you think you're doing!' he bellowed at me and raised his arm. He was holding the crowbar that he used to open the passageway to my dungeon. I took a deep breath, closed my eyes and tried to withdraw into myself. He brought down the crowbar on my upper thigh with all his strength. My skin split open immediately.

He was completely wound up as we drove along the motorway the next day. I, on the other hand, felt only emptiness. He had starved me and turned off my electricity again to discipline me. My leg burned. But now I was okay again, everything was okay, we were going to the mountains. Voices shrilled chaotically in my head:

You somehow have to get hold of the granola bar in the ski jacket.
There's something left to eat in his bag.

In between, very softly, a small voice said, *You have to escape. You have to do it this time.*

We exited the motorway near the town of Ybbs. Slowly the mountains emerged from the mist ahead of us. In Göstling we stopped at a ski rental shop. The kidnapper was especially afraid of this step. After all, he had to walk with me into a shop where contact with the employees was unavoidable. They would ask me whether the ski boots fitted, and I would have to answer them.

Before we got out, he barked at me with particular emphasis that he would kill anyone I asked for help – and me as well.

When I opened the car door, a strange feeling of foreignness came over me. The air was cold and tangy, and smelled of snow. The houses stooped along the river and with the caps of snow on their rooftops they looked like pieces of cake with whipped cream. The mountains jutted upwards to the left and right. If the sky had been green I wouldn't have batted an eyelash. That's how surreal the entire scene seemed to me.

When Priklopil shoved me through the door to the ski rental shop, the warm, humid air hit me in the face. Perspiring people in down jackets stood at the cashier counter, expectant faces, laughter, in between the clacking of the buckles as ski boots were tried on. A sales clerk came up to us. Tanned and jovial, a ski instructor type with a rough, loud voice, who rattled off his standard jokes. He brought me a pair of boots, size 37, and kneeled in front of me to check the fit. Priklopil didn't take his eyes off me for a second as I told the clerk that they didn't pinch. I couldn't have imagined a more unfitting place to call attention to a crime than that shop. Everyone cheerful, everything great; it was all joyful efficiency at the service of leisure-time fun. I said nothing.

'We can't ride the ski lift. That's too dangerous. You could talk to someone,' said the kidnapper when we had reached the car park of the Hochkar ski resort at the end of a long, winding road. 'We'll drive straight up to the slopes.'

We parked the car somewhat further away. The snowy slopes rose steeply to the left and right. Ahead I could see a chair lift. Faintly, I could hear the music from the bar at the lower station in the valley. Hochkar is one of the few ski resorts that is easily accessible from Vienna. It is small; six chair lifts and a couple of shorter tow lifts take the skiers up to the three peaks. The ski runs are narrow; four of them are marked 'black', the most advanced category.

I struggled to remember. When I was four, I had been here once with my mother and a family we were friends with. But nothing called to mind the small girl who back then had tramped through the deep snow in a thick pink ski-suit.

Priklopil helped me put my ski boots on and step into the bindings. Uncertain, I slid across the slippery snow on the skis. He pulled me over the piles of snow at the side of the road and pushed me over the edge, directly on to the slope. It seemed murderously steep to me and I was terrified at the speed at which I was hurtling downwards. The skis and boots probably weighed more than my legs. I didn't have the necessary muscles to steer, and had likely even forgotten how to go about doing that. The only ski course I had taken in my life was during my time in afterschool care – one week that we had spent at a youth hostel in Bad Aussee. I had been afraid, hadn't initially wanted to go along, so vivid were my memories of my broken arm. But my ski instructor was nice and cheered me on every time I managed to make a turn. I slowly made progress and even skied in the big race down the practice slope on the last day of the course. At the finish line I threw my arms up and cheered. Then I let myself fall backwards into the snow. I hadn't felt so free and proud of myself in ages.

Free and proud – a life that was light years away.

I tried desperately to brake. But at my first attempt the ski jammed, toppling me into the snow. 'What are you doing?' criticized Priklopil, when he stopped next to me and helped me up. 'You have to ski in curves! Like this!'

It took me a while to be able to stay on my skis at least for a little and for us to move forward a few metres. My helplessness and weakness seemed to soothe the kidnapper enough to make him decide to buy lift passes for us. We queued up in the long line of laughing, jostling skiers who could hardly wait for the lift to spit them out again at the next peak. In the midst of all these people in their colourful ski-suits, I felt like a creature from another planet. I recoiled when they pushed past me so closely, touching me. I recoiled whenever our skis and poles became enmeshed, when I became suddenly wedged in among strangers who very likely didn't even notice me, but whose stares I thought I could feel. *You don't belong here. This is not your place.* Priklopil shoved me from behind. 'Wake up. Move it, move it.'

After what seemed like an eternity, we were finally sitting in the air. I floated through the wintry mountain landscape – a moment of peace and stillness, which I tried to savour. But my body rebelled against the unfamiliar strain. My legs trembled and I froze miserably. When the chair lift entered the upper station, I panicked. I didn't know how to jump off and got tangled in my poles in my agitation. Priklopil swore at me, grabbed me by the arm and pulled me off the lift at the last moment.

After a couple of runs, a modicum of self-assuredness slowly returned. I could keep myself upright long enough to enjoy the short runs before I fell into the snow again. I felt my life force returning, and for the first time in ages I experienced something like bliss. I stopped as often as I could to view the panorama. Wolfgang Priklopil, proud of his knowledge of local geography, explained which mountains we saw all around. From the Hochkar summit you could see over to the massive Ötscher; behind it, mountain chains upon mountain chains vanished into the fog.

'That over there is even Styria,' he lectured. 'And there, on the other side, you can almost see all the way to the Czech Republic.'

The snow glittered in the sun and the sky was an intense blue. I took deep breaths and wanted most of all to stop time. But the kidnapper pushed me to hurry up: 'This day has cost me a fortune. We have to take full advantage of it now!'

'I have to go to the toilet!' Priklopil looked at me, annoyed. 'I really have to go!' There was nothing left for him to do other than ski with me to the next lodge. He decided in favour of the lower station, because the toilets there were located in a separate building, making it possible to avoid having to go through the restaurant area. We unstrapped our skis. The kidnapper took me to the toilets and hissed at me to hurry up. He would wait for me and keep a close eye on the time. Initially, it puzzled me that he didn't come with me. After all, he could have said that he had got the wrong door. But he stayed outside.

The toilets were empty when I walked in. But as I was in the stall, I heard a door opening. I was terrified – I was certain that I had taken too long and the kidnapper had come into the ladies to get me. But when I hurried back out into the small anteroom, a blonde woman stood in front of the mirror. For the first time since my imprisonment began I was alone with another person.

I don't remember exactly what I said. I only know that I gathered all my courage together and spoke to her. But all that came out of my mouth was a soft squeak.

The blonde woman smiled at me in a friendly way, turned round – and left. She hadn't understood what I'd said. That was the first time that I had spoken to someone. And it was just like in my worst nightmares. People couldn't hear me. I was invisible. I mustn't hope for help from others.

It wasn't until after I escaped that I found out that the woman was a tourist from the Netherlands and simply hadn't understood what I was saying to her. At the time, her reaction came as a blow to me.

I have only a hazy memory of the rest of the ski trip. I had once again failed to seize an opportunity. When I was locked in my dungeon again that evening, I was more desperate than I had been in ages.

Soon after that, the decisive date was drawing near: my eighteenth birthday. It was the date that I had feverishly anticipated for ten years, and I was determined to celebrate my day properly – even if it had to be in captivity.

In the years before, the kidnapper had allowed me to bake a cake. This time I wanted something special. I knew that his business partner organized parties in a remotely located warehouse. The kidnapper had shown me videos depicting Turkish and Serb weddings. He wanted to use them to make a video compilation to promote the event venue. I had greedily absorbed the images of the celebrating people, who jumped around in a circle holding hands, doing the strangest dances. At one celebration, an entire shark lay on the buffet, and at another, bowl upon bowl full of unfamiliar foods were lined up. But the cakes fascinated me most of all. Works of art built of several layers, featuring flowers made of marzipan or sponge cake and cream in the shape of a car. I wanted a cake like that – in the shape of an '18', the symbol of my adulthood.

When I came up into the house on the morning of 17 February 2006, there it stood on the kitchen table: a '1' and an '8' made of fluffy sponge cake, covered in a sugary pink foam and decorated with candles. I don't remember what other gifts I received that day. There were certainly several more, because Priklopil loved celebrating such special days. However, for me that '18' was the focal point of my little celebration. It was a symbol of freedom. It was *the* symbol, the sign that it was high time for me to keep my promise.

For One, Only Death Remains

My Escape to Freedom

That day began like any other – at the behest of the timer switch. I lay in my bunk bed when the light in my dungeon turned on, waking me from a confused dream. I remained in bed for some time and tried to decipher its significance from the slivers of my dream. However, the harder I tried to reach for them, the more they slid away from me. Only a vague feeling remained that I reflected on wonderingly. Deep resolve. I hadn't felt that way in a long time.

After a while, hunger motivated me to get out of bed. There had been no dinner and my stomach was rumbling. Driven by the thought of eating something, I climbed down the ladder. But before I reached the bottom, I remembered that I didn't have anything more to eat. The previous evening, the kidnapper had given me a tiny piece of cake to take with me to my dungeon for breakfast, which I had already devoured. Frustrated, I brushed my teeth in order to rid my mouth of the slightly sour taste of empty stomach. Then I looked around, uncertain as to what to do. That morning my dungeon was a big mess. Articles of clothing lay strewn all over the place and paper was stacked on my desk. Other days I would have begun tidying up immediately, making my tiny room as comfortable and organized as possible. But that morning, I had no desire to. I felt a strange, distanced feeling towards those four walls that had become my home.

In a short orange-coloured dress I was very proud of, I waited for the kidnapper to open the door. Other than that I had only leggings and paint-stained T-shirts, a turtleneck jumper formerly belonging to the kidnapper for cold days and a couple of clean, simple things for the few outings he had taken me on over the past few months. In that dress I was able to feel like a normal girl. The kidnapper had bought it for me as a reward for my work in the garden. In the spring after my eighteenth birthday, he had allowed me to work outside now and again under his super-vision. He had grown less cautious; there was a constant danger that the neighbours could see me. Twice already I had been greeted from across the fence while I was weeding in the garden. 'Temporary help,' the kidnapper once said by way of brief ex-planation, when the neighbour waved at me. He seemed satisfied with the information and I had been incapable of saying anything anyway.

When the door to my dungeon finally opened, I saw Priklopil from below standing on the forty-centimetre step. A sight that could still frighten me after all that time. Priklopil seemed so big, an overpowering shadow, distorted by the light bulb in the ante-room – just like a jailer in a horror film. But that day he didn't seem threatening to me. I felt strong and self-assured.

'May I put on a pair of knickers?' I asked him, even before I greeted him. The kidnapper looked at me, amazed.

'Out of the question,' he answered.

In the house I always had to work half-naked, and in the garden I was principally not allowed to wear any knickers. It was one of his ways to keep me down.

'Please, it's much more comfortable,' I added.

He shook his head energetically.

'Absolutely not. What made you think of that? Come on now!'

I followed him into the anteroom and waited for him to crawl through the passageway. The rounded, heavy concrete door, which had become a permanent fixture in my life's scenery, stood open.

Whenever I saw in front of me that colossus of a door made of reinforced concrete, a lump always came to my throat. Over the last few years I had had damn good luck. Any accident the kidnapper might have had would have been a death sentence for me. The door couldn't be opened from the inside and couldn't be found from the outside. I pictured the scene vividly. How I would realize after a couple of days that the kidnapper had disappeared. How I would run amok in my room and how mortal fear would grip me. How I would manage with my last ounce of strength to kick down the two wooden doors. But that concrete door would be the decisive factor of life or death. Lying in front of it, I would die of hunger and thirst. It was a relief every time I slipped through the narrow passageway behind the kidnapper. Once again a morning had broken when he opened that door, when he hadn't left me in the lurch. Again I had escaped my underground grave. When I climbed the stairs into the garage, I sucked the air deep into my lungs. I was upstairs.

The kidnapper ordered me to get him two pieces of bread with jam from the kitchen. I watched him bite into the bread with pleasure as my stomach growled. His teeth left no marks. Delicious, crispy bread with butter and apricot jam. And I was given nothing – after all, I'd had my cake. I never would have dared tell him that I had already eaten the dry slice the evening before.

After Priklopil had eaten breakfast, I washed up and went over to the tear-off calendar in the kitchen. As I did every morning, I tore off the page with the bold-face number and folded it into small pieces. I stared at the date for a long time: 23 August 2006. It was the 3,096th day of my imprisonment.

That day, Wolfgang Priklopil was in a good mood. It was to be the beginning of a new era, the dawn of a less difficult period with no money worries. That morning two decisive steps were to be taken. First of all, he wanted to get rid of the old delivery van he had used eight and a half years ago to abduct me. And, secondly, he had placed an advert on the Internet for a flat we had spent the last few months renovating. He had purchased it six months before in the hope that the rental income would alleviate the constant financial pressure his crime had put him under. The money, so he told me, was from his business activities with Holzapfel.

It was shortly after my eighteenth birthday that he had excitedly filled me in one morning.

'There's a new remodelling job. We are going to leave presently for Hollergasse.'

His delight was catching and I was in urgent need of a change of scenery. The magical date of my adulthood had passed and barely anything had changed. I was just as oppressed and monitored as all the years before. Except that a switch had been activated within me. My uncertainty about whether the kidnapper wasn't in fact right after all and I was better off in his care than outside was slowly disappearing. I was now an adult. My other self held me tight, and I knew precisely I didn't want to continue living this way. I had survived the period of my youth as the kidnapper's slave, punch bag and companion, and made myself at home in this world, as long as I had no other choice. But now that period was over. Whenever I was in my dungeon, I recalled over and over all the plans I had made as a child for this time in my life. I wanted to be independent. Become an actress, write books, make music, experience other people, be free. I no longer wanted to accept the fact that I was to be the prisoner in his fantasy for all eternity. I just had to wait for the right opportunity. Maybe that would be the new remodelling job. After all the years I had spent chained to the house, I was allowed to work at another location for the first time. Under the kidnapper's strict supervision, but still.

I remember our first trip to the flat on Hollergasse exactly. The kidnapper didn't take the fastest route via the motorway – he was too miserly to pay the toll fee. Instead, he queued up in the traffic jam on Vienna's Gürtel. It was morning and the last commuters of the rush-hour pressed in on both sides of the delivery van. I observed the people behind their steering wheels. Men with tired eyes looked at us from the van next to ours. They sat tightly squeezed in, obviously labourers from Eastern Europe, picked up by Austrian construction companies 'kerb crawling' in the morning along the arterial roads, only to dump them out there again in the evening. At once I felt a kinship with those day-labourers: no documents, no work permit, totally exploitable. That was the reality I found so hard to bear that morning. I sank deep into my seat and gave myself over to my daydream: I was on my way to a normal, regular job with my boss – just like all the other commuters in the cars next to us. I was an expert in my field and my boss placed great importance on my opinion. I lived in a grown-up world where I had a voice that was heard.

We had crossed nearly the entire city when Priklopil turned on to the Mariahilfer Strasse at the West Railway Station, driving outwards from the city centre and rolling alongside a small market where only half the stands were occupied. Then he turned on to a small side street. There he parked the car.

The flat was on the first floor of a rundown house. The kidnapper waited a long time before he allowed me to get out. He was afraid that someone would see us, and only wanted to let me scurry across the pavement once the street was empty of people. I let my eyes sweep down the street: small car repair shops, Turkish greengrocers, kebab stands and dodgy, tiny bars were scattered among the scenery of grey older buildings constructed during Vienna's Age of Promotorism in the late 1800s, which had served as tenements for the masses of poor workers from the Austrian Empire's crown lands. Even now the area was inhabited primarily by immigrants. Many of the flats still had no bathroom; the toilets were out in the corridor and were shared among neighbours. The kidnapper had purchased one of these flats.

He waited until the street was clear, then he shooed me into the stairwell. The paint was peeling off the walls and most of the letter boxes were bent open. When he opened the wooden door to the flat and shoved me inside, I could hardly believe how tiny it was. Nineteen square metres – just four times larger than my dungeon. A room with a window looking out on to the back courtyard. The air smelled stale, like body odour, mildew and old cooking oil. The wall-to-wall carpet, which had probably been dark green at some point, had taken on an indefinable grey-brown colour. A large damp stain teeming with maggots could be seen on one wall. I breathed in deeply. Hard work awaited me here.

From that day on, he took me with him to the Hollergasse flat several times a week. Only when he had longer errands to run did he lock me in my dungeon the whole day. The first thing we did was to drag the old, worn-out furniture out of the flat and on to the street. When we stepped out of the building an hour later, it was gone: taken by neighbours who had so little that even that furniture was good enough for them. Then we began the renovation work. It took me two whole days just to tear up the old carpet. A second carpet came to light under it and a thick layer of dirt. The adhesive had become so stuck to the floor underneath over the years that I had to scrape it up centimetre by centimetre. Then we poured a layer of concrete screed, on which we laid laminate flooring – the same as in my dungeon. We stripped the old wallpaper from the walls, filled the cracks and holes and put up fresh paper, which we painted white. We added the cabinets for a miniature fitted kitchen and a tiny bathroom, hardly larger than the shower tray and the new mat in front of it.

I toiled like a heavy labourer. Chiselling, carrying, sanding, smoothing, hauling tiling. Wallpapering the ceiling, standing on a narrow board balanced between two ladders. Lifting furniture.

The work, the hunger and the constant struggle against my dropping blood pressure took so much out of me that any thought of escape was a very distant notion. In the beginning I had hoped for a moment in which the kidnapper would leave me by myself. But there were none. I was under constant surveillance. It was amazing the efforts he made to prevent me from fleeing. Whenever he went out into the corridor to go to the toilet, he pushed heavy boards and beams in front of the window so that I couldn't open it quickly and scream. When he knew he would have to be outside for more than five minutes, he screwed the boards on. Even here he constructed a prison for me. When the key turned in the lock, I was transported back to my dungeon in my mind. The fear that something would happen to him and that I would have to die in that flat seized me here as well. I breathed a sigh of relief every time he came back.

Today that fear seems strange to me. After all, I was in a building with flats and could have screamed or beat against the walls. Unlike in the cellar, I would have been found quickly here. There were no rational reasons for my fear. It crept up from my insides, straight out of the dungeon within me.

One day, a strange man suddenly appeared in the flat.

We had just hauled the laminate for the floor up to the first floor. The door was only slightly ajar, when an older man with salt-and-pepper hair entered and greeted us loudly. His German was so bad that I could hardly understand him. He welcomed us to the house and obviously wanted to launch into a neighbourly chat about the weather and our renovation work. Priklopil pushed me behind him and shook him off with terse replies. I felt the panic welling up within him and let it infect me as well. Although that man could have meant my rescue, I felt almost harassed by his presence. That's how much I had internalized the kidnapper's perspective.

That evening I lay on my bunk bed in my dungeon and replayed the scene in my head over and over. Had I acted wrongly? Should I have screamed? Had I missed yet another decisive opportunity? I had to try to train myself to act with resolve the next time. In my thoughts I imagined the path from my position behind the kidnapper towards the strange neighbour like a leap across a yawning chasm. I could picture myself exactly taking a run at it, speeding towards the edge of the abyss and jumping. But I never saw myself landing on the other side. As hard as I tried, I couldn't get the image to form. Even in my fantasy, the kidnapper snatched at my T-shirt again and again, yanking me back. The few times I eluded his grasp, I hovered in the air above the chasm for a few seconds before plunging into the abyss. It was an image that tormented me the whole night through. A symbol that I was on the verge of doing it, but would again fail at the deciding moment.

Just a few days later, the neighbour came back. This time he was holding a pile of photographs. The kidnapper pushed me aside surreptitiously, but I was able to catch a quick glimpse. There were family photographs depicting him in his former home in Yugoslavia and a group photo of a football team. He talked incessantly while holding the photographs under Priklopil's nose. Again I understood only bits of conversation. No, jumping over the chasm was impossible. How was I supposed to make myself understood to this friendly man? Would he understand what I whispered to him in an unobserved moment, which would probably never happen anyway? Natascha who? Who's been abducted? Even if he did understand me, what would happen next? Would he call the police? Did he even have a telephone? And then? The police would hardly believe him. Even if a police car came to Hollergasse, the kidnapper would have plenty of time to grab me and spirit me inconspicuously back to the car. I didn't even want to imagine what would happen next.

No, this house would offer me no chance of escape. But the

chance would come. Of that I was convinced like never before. I only had to recognize it in time.

That spring, in the year 2006, the kidnapper sensed that I was trying to pull away from him. He was uncontrollable and short-tempered, and his chronic sinus infection tormented him primarily in the night. During the day he redoubled his efforts to oppress me. They became ever more absurd. 'Don't talk back!' he would spit as soon as I opened my mouth, even when he had asked me something. He demanded absolute obedience. 'What colour is that?' he barked at me once, pointing to a bucket of black paint.

'Black,' I answered.

'No, that's red. It's red because I say it is. Say that it's red!'

Whenever I refused, an uncontrollable rage possessed him and went on for longer than ever before. The blows followed in quick succession. Sometimes he beat me so long it felt like hours. More than once I almost lost consciousness before he dragged me down the stairs again, locked me away and turned out the light.

I noticed how difficult I again found it to resist a fatal reflex, namely to repress the beatings faster than it took for my injuries to heal. It would have been so much easier to give in. It was like an undertow that dragged me down unremittingly into the depths once it had got hold of me, while I heard my own voice whispering, 'Perfect world, perfect world. Everything is okay. Nothing has gone wrong.'

I had to fight that undertow with all my might and set out small life rafts for myself – my notes, where I once again recorded every single assault. Today when I hold the lined notepad where I entered all those brutalities in proper handwriting and complete with detailed drawings of my injuries, I feel light-headed. Back then I wrote them down while keeping them at a great distance from me, as if I were sitting a test at school:

15 April 2006. Once he beat my right hand so long and so hard that I could literally feel the blood pooling inside. The entire back of my hand was blue and reddish, the bruise extended through to the palm of my hand, spreading out to encompass my entire palm. Moreover, he gave me a black eye (also on the right side) that was originally located in the outer corner and turned reddish, bluish and green, then travelled upwards across my upper eyelid.

Other assaults that took place recently, provided that I still remember them and haven't repressed them – In the garden he attacked me with pruning shears because I was too afraid to climb the ladder. I had a greenish-coloured cut above my right ankle, my skin peeled away easily. Then he once threw a heavy bucket of dirt at my pelvis so that I had an ugly reddish-brown bruise. Once I refused to come upstairs with him out of fear. He ripped the sockets out of the wall, threw the timer switch at me and anything else that he could get his hands on along that wall. I had a deep, red, bloody mark on my right outer knee and my calf. In addition, I have a blackish-violet bruise on my left upper arm measuring about eight centimetres, I don't know how I got it. Several times he kicked and punched me again and again, even my head. Twice he bloodied my lip, once giving me a pea-sized swelling (slightly bluish) on my lower lip. Once he hit me, giving me a crimped swelling on the right side below my mouth. Then I also have a cut on my right cheek (I don't remember how I got it). Once he threw a toolbox on my feet, giving me pastel green bruises. He beat the back of my hand often with a spanner, wrench or similar. I have two symmetrical blackish bruises below both of my shoulder blades and along my spine.

Today he punched my right eye, making me see a flash of light, and my right ear, where I felt a stabbing pain, a ringing and a crunching. Then he continued to beat my head.

On better days he would again paint a picture of our future together.

'If I could only trust you not to run away . . .' he sighed one evening at the kitchen table. 'I could take you everywhere with me. I would take you to Lake Neusiedl or Lake Wolfgang and buy you a summer dress. We could go swimming and go skiing in the winter. But I would have to be able to count on you one hundred per cent – otherwise you'd just run away.'

At moments like this I felt infinitely sorry for the man who had persecuted me for over eight years. I didn't want to hurt him and wanted him to have the rosy future he desired so badly. He would seem so desperate and alone with himself and his crime that I sometimes forgot that I was his victim – and not responsible for his happiness. But I never allowed myself to succumb totally to the illusion that everything would be okay if only I cooperated. You can't force anyone to be eternally obedient and you certainly can't force anyone to love you.

Nevertheless, at such moments I swore to him that I would always stay with him, and comforted him, saying, 'I won't run away, I promise you. I'll always stay with you.' Of course he didn't believe me and it broke my heart to lie to him. We both vacillated between reality and appearances.

I was present in body, but in my mind I was already on the run. I still couldn't imagine landing safely on the other side though. The notion of suddenly surfacing in the real world outside frightened me unspeakably. Sometimes I even went so far as to believe that I would commit suicide immediately, as soon as I had left the kidnapper. I couldn't bear the thought that my freedom would put him behind bars for years on end. Of course, I wanted others to be protected from this man who was capable of anything. I was still providing that protection by absorbing his violent energy myself. Later it would have to be up to the police and the justice system to keep him from committing any more crimes. Still, the thought gave me no satisfaction. I was unable to find any desire for revenge within me – just the opposite. It seemed as if I would only reverse the crime he had committed against me if I delivered him into the hands of the police. First he had locked me up, then I would make sure that he was locked up. In my twisted world view, the crime would not have been cancelled out, but rather intensified. The evil in the world would be no less, but indeed would multiply.

All these reflections were in a way the logical culmination of the emotional insanity I had been subjected to for years. By the two faces of the kidnapper, by the rapid switch between violence and pseudo-normality, by my survival strategy to block out what threatened to kill me. Until black is no longer black, and white is no longer white, but everything is only a grey fog causing you to lose your bearings. I had internalized all of that to such an extent that at times the betrayal of the kidnapper carried more weight than the betrayal of my own life. Perhaps I should just give in to my fate, I thought more than once whenever I was in danger of being sucked under and losing sight of my life rafts.

Other days I racked my brains, thinking about how the world outside would react to me after all those years. The images from the Dutroux trial were still very present in my mind. I never wanted to be presented like the victims in that case, I thought. I had been a victim for eight years and I didn't want to spend the rest of my life as a victim. I pictured exactly how I would deal with the media. Most preferable was that they would leave me alone. But when they reported on me, then never to use my first name. I wanted to re-enter life as a grown-up woman. And I wanted to select the media that I would talk to myself.

It was an evening at the beginning of August, when I was sitting at the kitchen table with the kidnapper eating supper. His mother had put a sausage salad in the refrigerator. He gave me the vegetables and piled the sausage and cheese on his own plate. I slowly chewed on a piece of pepper in the hope of being able to suck every last bit of energy from every single red fibre. In the meantime I had gained a bit of weight and now weighed forty-two kilograms, but the work in the Hollergasse flat had exhausted me and I felt physically drained. My mind was wide awake. Now that the renovation work was finished, yet another phase of my imprisonment was over. What was to come next? The normal insanity of everyday life? Summer retreat on Lake Wolfgang, begun with severe beatings, accompanied by humiliations and, as a special treat, a dress? No, I didn't want to live this life any more.

The next day we were working in the assembly pit. From a distance I could hear a mother calling loudly for her children. Now and again a short puff of air carried a hint of summer and freshly mown grass into the garage where we were overhauling the underneath of the old white delivery van. It was the vehicle he had abducted me in, and now he wanted to sell it. Not only had the world of my childhood moved out of reach into the distance – now all of the set pieces from the first years of my imprisonment were disappearing as well. This van was my connection to the day of my abduction. Now I was working towards making it vanish. With every brushstroke I seemed to be cementing my future in the cellar.

'You have brought a situation upon us in which only one of us can make it through alive,' I said suddenly. The kidnapper looked at me in surprise. I wouldn't be deterred. 'I really am grateful to you for not killing me and that you have taken such good care of me. That is very nice of you. But you can't force me to stay with you. I am my own person, with my own needs. This situation must come to an end.'

In response Wolfgang Priklopil took the brush from my hand without a word. I could see from his face that he was deeply frightened. All the years he must have feared this very moment. The moment it became clear that all his oppression had borne no fruit. That when it came right down to it, he hadn't been able to break me. I continued: 'It is only natural that I have to go. You should have counted on that from the beginning. One of us has to die; there is no other way out any more. Either you kill me or you let me go.'

Priklopil slowly shook his head. 'I will never do that. You know that too well,' he said softly.

I waited for pain soon to explode in some part of my body and mentally prepared myself for it. *Never give up. Never give up. I will not give up on myself.* When nothing happened, when he only remained standing motionless in front of me, I took a deep breath and spoke the words that changed everything: 'By now I have tried to kill myself so many times – and here I am, the victim. It would actually be much better if you would kill yourself. You won't be able to find any other way out anyway. If you killed yourself, all of these problems would suddenly be gone.'

At that moment something inside him seemed to die. I saw the despair in his eyes as he mutely turned away from me and I could hardly bear it. This man was a criminal – but he was the only person I had in the world. As if on fast-rewind, specific scenes from the past few years whizzed before my eyes. I wavered and heard myself say, 'Don't worry. If I run away, I'll throw myself in front of a train. I would never put you in any danger.' Suicide seemed to me to be the greatest kind of freedom, a release from everything, from a life that had already been ruined long ago.

At that moment I would've really liked to have taken back my words. But now it had been said: I would run at the next opportunity. And one of us wouldn't come through it alive.

Three weeks later I stood in the kitchen, staring at the calendar. I tossed the paper I had torn off into the dustbin and turned away. I couldn't afford to reflect on things for longer periods. The kidnapper was calling me to work. The day before I'd had to help him finish the advertisements for the flat on Hollergasse. Priklopil had brought me a map of Vienna and a ruler. I measured the route from the flat on Hollergasse to the nearest underground station, checked the scale and calculated how many metres it was on foot. After that he'd called me into the corridor and ordered me to walk quickly from one end to the other. He timed me with his watch. Then I calculated how long it would take to get from the flat to the underground station and to the next bus stop. In his pedantry, the kidnapper wanted to know down to the second how far the flat was from public transport. When the advertisements were finished, he called his friend who was to put them on the Internet. I took a deep breath and smiled. 'Now everything will be easier.' He appeared to have completely forgotten our discussion about escape and death.

Just before noon on 23 August 2006, we went into the garden. The neighbours weren't there and I picked the last strawberries from the bed in front of the privet hedgerow and collected all of the apricots lying on the ground around the tree. Then I washed the fruit off in the kitchen and put it in the refrigerator. The kidnapper went with me every step of the way and at no time did he take his eyes off me.

Around noon he took me to the little garden hut at the back of the property on the left. The hut was separated from a small path by a fence. Priklopil was meticulous about always closing the garden gate. He locked it even when he left the property for only a short moment to knock the dirt out of the floor mats of his red BMW. The white van was parked between the hut and the garden gate, which was to be picked up in the next few days.

Priklopil fetched the vacuum cleaner, plugged it in and ordered me to clean thoroughly the interior, the seats and the floor mats. I was in the middle of doing so when his mobile rang. He walked a couple of steps away from the car, covered his ear with his hand and asked twice, 'Excuse me please?' From the brief fragments I picked up through the noise of the vacuum cleaner, I concluded that it must be somebody on the line interested in the flat. Priklopil was overjoyed. Absorbed in his conversation, he turned round and moved several metres away from me towards the pool.

I was alone. For the first time since the beginning of my imprisonment the kidnapper had let me out of his sight while outside. I stood frozen in front of the car for a brief second holding the vacuum cleaner a feeling of paralysis spread through my legs and arms. My ribcage felt as if it were encased in an iron corset. I could hardly breathe. Slowly my hand holding the vacuum cleaner sank. Disordered, confused images raced through my head. Priklopil coming back and finding me gone. Him looking for me and then going on a shooting spree. A train speeding along. My lifeless body. His lifeless body. Police cars. My mother. My mother's smile.

Then everything happened so fast. With superhuman strength I tore myself out of the paralysing quicksand that was tightening around my legs. The voice of my other self hammered in my head: *If you had just been abducted yesterday, you would run now. You have to act as if you didn't know the kidnapper. He is a stranger. Run. Run. Damn it, run!*

I dropped the vacuum cleaner and bolted to the garden gate. It was open.

I hesitated for a moment. Should I go left or right? Where could I find people? Where were the railway tracks? I mustn't lose my head now, mustn't be afraid. *Don't turn round, just go*. I hurried down the small pathway, turned on to Blasselgasse and ran towards the housing estate that lay alongside the street – small allotment gardens, in between mini houses built on the erstwhile parcels of land. In my ears was only a droning noise; my lungs hurt. And I was certain that the kidnapper was coming closer every second. I thought I heard his footsteps and felt his eyes on my back. Briefly I even thought I felt his breath on the back of my neck. But I didn't turn round. I would realize it soon enough whenever he threw me to the ground from behind, dragged me back to the house and killed me. Anything was better than going back in the dungeon. I had chosen death anyway. Either by train or by the kidnapper. The freedom to choose, the freedom to die. My thoughts shooting through my head were all jumbled up, while I rushed onwards. It wasn't until I saw three people coming towards me in the street that I knew I wanted to live. And that I would.

I bolted towards them and panted at them, 'You have to help me! I need a mobile to call the police! Please!' The three of them stared at me in surprise: an older man, a child, maybe twelve years old, and a third person, perhaps the boy's father.

'We can't,' he said. Then the three of them went round me and continued walking.

The older man turned back once more and said, 'I'm sorry. I don't have my mobile on me.'

Tears suddenly came to my eyes. What was I, after all, to the world outside? I had no life in it. I was an illegal, a person with no name and no history. What would happen if nobody believed my story?

I stood on the pavement trembling, my hand gripping a fence. Where to? I had to get off this street. Priklopil had surely noticed already that I was gone. I took a few steps back, pulled myself up over a low fence, landed in one of the gardens and rang the doorbell. But nothing happened, there was nobody to be seen. I ran further, climbed over hedges and flowerbeds, from one garden to the next. Finally I caught sight of an older woman through an open window in one of the houses. I knocked on the window frame and called softly, 'Please help me! Call the police! I've been abducted. Call the police!'

'What are you doing in my garden? What do you want here?' a voice snapped at me through the windowpane. She eyed me mistrustfully.

'Please call the police for me! Quick!' I repeated breathlessly. 'I'm the victim of an abduction. My name is Natascha Kampusch . . .

Please ask for the Vienna police. Tell them it's about an abduction case. They should come here in an unmarked car. I am Natascha Kampusch.'

'Why did you come to me of all people?'

I started. But then I saw that she hesitated for a moment.

'Wait by the hedge. And don't walk on my lawn!'

I nodded mutely as she turned away and disappeared from sight. For the first time in seven years I had spoken my name. I was back.

I stood by the hedgerow and waited. Seconds passed. My heart beat in my throat. I knew that Wolfgang Priklopil would be looking for me and was in a panic that he would go completely berserk. After a while I saw two police cars with blue flashing lights over the fences of the allotment gardens. Either the woman had not passed on my request for an unmarked car or the police had disregarded it. Two young police officers got out and entered the small garden.

'Stay where you are and put your hands in the air!' one of them barked at me.

This was not the way I had imagined my first encounter with my newfound freedom. With my hands raised like a criminal, standing beside the hedge, I told the police who I was.

'My name is Natascha Kampusch. You must have heard about my case. I was abducted in 1998.'

'Kampusch?' replied one of the two officers.

I heard the kidnapper's voice: *Nobody will miss you. They are all glad that you're gone.*

'Date of birth? Registered domicile?'

'Seventeenth of February 1988, domiciled in Rennbahnweg 27, stairway 38, floor 7, door 18.'

'Abducted when and by whom?'

'In 1998. I have been held captive in the house at Heinestrasse 60. The kidnapper's name is Wolfgang Priklopil.'

There couldn't have been any greater contrast between the

sober ascertaining of fact and the mixture of euphoria and panic that was literally coursing through me.

The voice of the officer, who was radioing to confirm my claims, penetrated my ears only with difficulty. The tension was nearly tearing me apart inside. I had run only a couple of hundred metres; the kidnapper's house was only a hop, skip and a jump away. I tried to breathe in and out evenly to get a grip on my fear. I didn't doubt for a second that it would be a piece of cake for him to eliminate these two young police officers. I stood by the hedge as if frozen and strained to hear. Twittering birds, a car in the distance. But it seemed like the calm before the storm. Shots would be fired presently. I tensed my muscles. I had taken the leap. And had finally landed on the other side. I was prepared to fight for my new-found freedom.

SPECIAL REPORT

Case: Natascha Kampusch – Woman claiming to be missing person.

Police attempting to ascertain identity.

Vienna (APA) – The case of Natascha Kampusch, now missing for over eight years, has taken a surprising turn. A young woman is claiming to be the girl who went missing on 2 March 1998 in Vienna. The Austrian Federal Criminal Police Office has begun an investigation into ascertaining the identity of the woman. 'We do not know whether she is in fact the missing Natascha Kampusch or just disorientated,' Erich Zwettler from the Federal Criminal Police Office told the Austria Press Agency. The woman was at the police station in Deutsch-Wagram in Lower Austria.

23 August 2006

I wasn't a disorientated young woman. It was painful to me that something like that would even be considered. But for the police, who had to compare the missing person photographs from back then, which showed a small, pudgy primary school child, to the emaciated young woman who now stood before them, that was probably a distinct possibility.

Before we went to the car, I asked for a blanket. I didn't want the kidnapper to see me, because I thought he was still in the vicinity, or that somebody was making a video of the scene. There was no blanket, but the police officers shielded me from view.

Once in the car, I ducked down low in the seat. When the police officer started the engine and the car began to move, a wave of relief washed over me. I had done it. I had escaped.

At the police station in Deutsch-Wagram I was received like a lost child. 'I can hardly believe that you're here! That you're alive!' The officers who had worked on my case crowded around me. Most of them were convinced of who I was; only one or two wanted to wait for a DNA test. They told me how long they had looked for me. That special task forces had been formed and then replaced by others. Their words rushed past me left and right. I was trying to focus, but I hadn't spoken to anyone for so long that I was overwhelmed. I stood helplessly in the middle of all these people, feeling infinitely weak, and began to shake in my thin dress. A female police officer gave me her jacket.

'You're cold. Put this on,' she said caringly. I immediately took her into my heart.

Looking back, I am amazed that they didn't take me straight to a quiet place and wait at least a day before interrogating me. After all, I was in a complete state of panic. For eight and a half years I had believed the kidnapper when he told me that people would die if I ran. Now I had done exactly that and nothing of the sort had happened. Nevertheless, I could feel fear breathing down my neck so that I couldn't feel safe or free at the police station. I had no idea how to cope with the storm of questions and sympathy. I felt completely without protection.

Today I think that they should have let me rest a bit under gentle care. Back then, I didn't question the hubbub. Without stopping for breath, without a second of respite, I was taken to an adjacent room after they had noted down my personal information. The friendly female police officer who had given me her jacket was entrusted with questioning me.

'Sit down and tell me about it calmly,' she said.

I glanced around the room uncertainly. A room with innumerable police files and slightly stale air, which exuded busy efficiency. The first room in which I spent any amount of time after my imprisonment. I had prepared myself for this moment for so long, but the whole situation still seemed surreal.

The first thing the police officer asked me was whether it was okay for her to use the informal *du* with me. She said that it might be easier, for me as well. But I didn't want that. I didn't want to be 'Natascha', who could be treated like a child and pushed around. I had escaped, I was grown-up, and I was going to fight to be treated as such.

The police officer nodded, asked me inconsequential questions and had sandwiches brought in. 'Eat something. You're nothing but skin and bones,' she suggested.

I held the sandwich she had given me and didn't know what to do. I was so befuddled that the ministrations, the well-meant suggestion, seemed like an order I couldn't follow. I was too wound up to eat and had gone without food for so long anyway that I knew I would have terrible stomach cramps if I ate an entire sandwich right now. 'I can't eat anything,' I whispered. But the habit of obeying orders kicked in. Like a mouse, I nibbled along the edge of the sandwich. It took some time for my tension to ease enough so I could concentrate on the conversation.

The female officer immediately made me feel I could trust her. While the male officers intimidated me and I regarded them extremely warily, I felt that I could let my guard down a bit with a woman. I hadn't been close to a woman for such a long time that

I stared at her, fascinated. Her dark hair was parted on the side and a lighter-coloured strand softened her look. A heart-shaped gold pendant dangled on her necklace; earrings sparkled at her ears. I felt safe with her.

Then I began to tell her my story. From the beginning. The words literally poured out of me. I felt a weight drop from me with every sentence I spoke about my imprisonment. As if putting it in words in this sober police room, dictating it into a police report, could take the awfulness away from the horror. I told her how much I was looking forward to an adult life where I would make the decisions; that I wanted my own flat, a job, later my own family. Eventually I almost had the feeling that I had made a friend. At the end of my questioning the officer gave me her watch. It made me feel that I was actually the mistress of my own time once again. No longer dictated to by another, no longer dependent on the timer switch that decreed when it was to be light and when it was to be dark.

'Please don't give any interviews,' I asked her as we said good-bye. 'But if you do talk to the media, please say something nice about me.'

She laughed. 'I promise that I won't give any interviews – who's going to ask me anything anyway!'

The young police officer to whom I had entrusted my life only kept her word for a few hours. By the next day she could no longer withstand the pressure from the media and went on television, revealing details of my questioning. Later she apologized to me for it. She was terribly sorry, but like everyone else, she was completely overwhelmed by the situation.

Her fellow police officers in Deutsch-Wagram also approached the situation with remarkable naivety. Nobody was prepared for the media circus that broke out when news of my escape leaked. After my initial questioning I followed the plan that I had been drawing up for months, but the police had no strategy ready.

'Please do not inform the press,' I repeated over and over.

They just laughed, 'The press isn't going to come here.'

But they were badly mistaken. By the time I was due to be taken to police headquarters in Vienna that afternoon, the building was already surrounded. Fortunately I had enough presence of mind to ask them to place a blanket over my head before I left the police station. But even under the blanket I could make out the storm of flash photography. 'Natascha! Natascha!' I heard on all sides. Assisted by two police officers, I stumbled, as best as I could, towards the car. The picture of my white, bruised legs under the blue blanket, which revealed only a strip of my orange dress, went round the world.

On my way to Vienna I found out that the search for Wolfgang Priklopil was in full swing. The police had called at the house but found no one. 'A manhunt is under way,' one of the officers told me. 'We don't have him yet, but every able-bodied officer is working on it. There is nowhere the kidnapper can run, certainly not abroad. We will catch him.' From that moment on I waited for the news that Wolfgang Priklopil had killed himself.

I had set off a bomb. The fuse was lit and there was no way to put it out again. I had chosen life. Only death remained for the kidnapper.

I recognized my mother immediately when she walked into police headquarters in Vienna. A total of 3,096 days had gone by since that morning I had left the flat on Rennbahnweg without saying goodbye. Eight and a half years, during which it had torn my heart apart that I had never been able to apologize. My entire youth without my family. Eight Christmases, my birthdays from the eleventh to the eighteenth, innumerable evenings when I would have liked to have had a word from her, a touch. Now she stood before me, almost unchanged, like a dream that has suddenly become reality. She sobbed loudly and laughed and cried at the same time as she ran towards me and hugged me. 'My child! My child! You're here again! I always knew that you'd come back again!' I breathed in her scent deeply. 'You're here again,' whispered my mother, over and over. 'Natascha – you're here again.'

We hugged, holding each other tightly for a long time. I was so unused to such close physical contact that so much closeness made my head spin.

Both my sisters had walked into police headquarters right behind her. They too burst into tears when we hugged. My father came a bit later. He rushed up to me, stared disbelievingly and first looked for the scar I had from an injury suffered as a child. Then he embraced me, lifted me up and sobbed, 'Natascha! It's really you!' The big and strong Ludwig Koch was crying like a baby, and I cried too.

'I love you,' I whispered when he had to leave again too soon – just like the many times he had dropped me off at home after a weekend together.

It is strange how after such a long separation all we wanted to ask were trivial questions. 'Are my cats still alive?' 'Are you still together with your boyfriend?' 'How young you look!' 'How grown-up you are!' As if it was a conversation with a stranger to whom – out of politeness or because you don't have anything else to talk about – you don't want to get too close. As if we had to slowly get to know each other again. For me, in particular, it was an unbelievably difficult situation. I had got through the last few years only by withdrawing into myself. I couldn't simply flip the switch and, despite the physical closeness, I still felt as if there was a wall between me and my family. As if from under a bell jar, I watched them laugh and cry while my tears dried. I had lived in a nightmare too long; my psychological prison was still there and stood between me and my family. In my perception they all looked exactly the same as eight years ago, while I had gone from being a school-aged child to an adult woman. I felt as if we were prisoners in different time bubbles that had briefly touched and were now drifting apart at top speed. I had no idea how they had spent the last few years, what had happened in their world. But I knew that for everything I had experienced there were no words – and that I couldn't let the emotions causing my inner turmoil show. I had locked them away for so long that I couldn't tear open the door to my own emotional dungeon that easily.

The world I had returned to was no longer the world I had left. And I was no longer the same. Nothing would be as before – never. That became clear to me when I asked my mother, 'How is Grandmother?'

My mother looked at the floor awkwardly. 'She passed away two years ago. I'm very sorry.'

I swallowed and immediately tucked the sad news behind the thick armour I had built up during my imprisonment. My grandmother. Bits of memories swirled through my head. The scent of *Franzbranntwein* and Christmas tree candles. Her apron, the feeling of closeness and the knowledge that thinking of her had got me through so many nights in my dungeon.

Now that my parents had done their duty by identifying me, they were escorted out. My own duty was to make myself available to the police apparatus. I still had not yet had a moment of peace.

The police organized a psychologist to offer me support over the next few days. I was asked again and again how they could get the kidnapper to give himself up. I had no answer. I was certain that he would kill himself, but I had no idea how or where. In Strasshof, I overheard, the house was examined for explosives. Late in the afternoon officers discovered my dungeon. While I was sitting in the station, specialists in white suits rummaged through the room that had been my prison and my refuge for eight years. Just a few hours ago I had woken up there.

That evening I was taken to a hotel in the province of Burgenland

in an unmarked police car. After the Vienna police had been unsuccessful in locating me, a special task force in Burgenland had
taken over my case. I was now given over to their supervision. Night
had already fallen long ago when we arrived at the hotel. Accompanied by the police psychologist, the officers led me into a room
with a double bed and a bathroom. The entire floor had been
cleared and was guarded by armed police officers. They were afraid
that the kidnapper, who was still at large, would attempt revenge.

I spent my first night of freedom with a police psychologist
who talked incessantly and whose words rippled over me in a
constant stream. Again I was cut off from the outside world – for
my own protection, the police assured me.

They were probably right, but in that room I nearly went off
the rails myself. I felt locked up and wanted only one thing: to
listen to the radio. To find out what had happened to Wolfgang
Priklopil. 'Believe me, that isn't good for you,' the police psychologist shook me off again and again. Inside, I was in a spin, but
I heeded her instructions. Late that night I took a bath. I sank into
the water and tried to relax. I could count on two hands how often
I had been allowed to take a bath in all the years of my imprisonment. Now I could run my own bath and put in as much bubble
bath as I wanted. But I couldn't enjoy it. Somewhere out there was
the man who had been the only person in my life for eight and a
half years, looking for a way to kill himself.

I heard the news the next day in the police car that took me
back to Vienna.

'Is there any news of the kidnapper?' was my first question as
I climbed into the car.

'Yes,' said the officer cautiously. 'The kidnapper is no longer
alive. He committed suicide, throwing himself in front of a train
at 8:59 p.m. near Vienna's northern railway station.'

I lifted my head and looked out of the window. Outside, Burgenland's flat, summery landscape glided past me on the motorway.

A flock of birds rose up out of a field. The sun stood low on the sky, bathing the late summer meadows in warm light. I took a deep breath and stretched out my arms. A feeling of warmth and safety coursed through my body, moving outwards from my stomach to the tips of my toes and fingers. My head felt light. Wolfgang Priklopil was no more. It was over.

I was free.

Epilogue

I spent the first few days of my new life in freedom at Vienna's General Hospital in the Psychiatric Ward for Children and Adolescents. It was a long and wary return to normal life – and also a taste of what awaited me. I received the best care but, placed in the closed ward, I was not allowed to leave. Cut off from the outside world I had just escaped to, I talked in the common room to anorexic young girls and children who self-harmed. Outside, on the other side of the protective walls, a media feeding frenzy raged. Photographers climbed trees to get the first picture of me. Reporters tried to sneak into the hospital disguised as nurses. My parents were bombarded by interview requests. My case was the first, say media experts, in which the otherwise restrained Austrian and German media let it all hang out. Pictures of my dungeon appeared in the newspapers. The concrete door stood wide open. My precious few possessions – my diaries and the few items of clothing – had been uncaringly thrown around by the men in white protective suits. Yellow markers with numbers could be clearly seen on my desk and my bed. I was forced to watch as my tiny private world, locked away for so long, was splashed across the front pages. Everything I had managed to hide even from the kidnapper had now been dragged out into the public eye, which cobbled together its own version of the truth.

Two weeks after my escape I resolved to put an end to the speculation and tell my story myself. I gave three interviews: to the Austrian Broadcasting Corporation, Austria's most widely read daily, the *Kronenzeitung*, and the magazine *News*.

Before taking this step into the public sphere I had been advised by many people to change my name and go into hiding. They told me that I would otherwise never have the opportunity to lead a normal life. But what kind of life is it when you cannot show your face, cannot see your family and have to deny your name? What kind of life would that be, especially for someone like me, who during all those years in captivity had fought not to lose herself? Despite the violence, the isolation, being locked up in darkness and all the other torments, I had remained Natascha Kampusch. Never would I now, after my escape, relinquish this most important asset: my identity. I stepped in front of the camera with my full name and my undisguised face and provided a glimpse into my time in captivity. But despite my openness, the media wouldn't let go. One headline followed the next, and more and more absurd speculations dominated the reports. It seemed as if the horrible truth by itself wouldn't be horrible enough, as if it had to be embellished above and beyond any bearable degree, thereby denying me the authority to interpret what I had experienced. The house in which I had been forced to spend so many years of my youth was surrounded by curious onlookers. Everybody wanted to feel the cold shudder of terror. For me it was an absolute horror that a perverse admirer of the kidnapper might purchase that house, that it might become a place of pilgrimage for those who saw their darkest fantasies transformed into reality there. That is why I made sure that it was not sold, but was granted to me as 'damages'. By so doing, I had reconquered and reclaimed a part of my past.

At first, the wave of sympathy was overwhelming. I received thousands of letters from absolute strangers who rejoiced at my escape. After a few weeks I moved to a nurses' residence near the hospital, and after a few months to my own flat. People asked me why I wasn't living with my mother again. But the question seemed so odd that I couldn't think of an answer. After all, it had been my plan to be self-sufficient once I turned eighteen that had sustained me all those years. Now I wanted to make it reality, standing on my own two feet and finally taking charge of my own life. I had the feeling that the world was my oyster: I was free and could do anything I wanted. Anything. Go for some ice cream on a sunny afternoon, dance, take up my schooling again. I strolled through this large, colourful, loud world that both intimidated me and made me felt euphoric, greedily soaking up even the tiniest detail. There were many things I did not yet understand after having been isolated for so long. I had to learn how the world works, how young people interact, what codes they use, their gestures and what they want to express with their clothing. I enjoyed my freedom and learned, learned, learned. I had lost my entire youth and had such an infinite amount to catch up on.

Only gradually did I notice that I had slipped into a new prison. Inch by inch, the walls that replaced my dungeon became visible. These are more subtle walls, built of excessive public interest, which judged my every move, making it impossible for me to take the underground like other people or to go shopping in peace. In the first few months after my escape a staff of advisers organized my life for me, giving me little space to reflect on what I actually wanted to do now. I had believed that by accommodating the media I would be able to gain the upper hand in telling my story. It wasn't until later that I understood such an attempt could never be successful. In this world that was clamouring for me, it wasn't about me. I had become a prominent person as a result of a terrible crime. The kidnapper was dead – there was no Priklopil Case. I was the case: the Natascha Kampusch Case.

The sympathy extended to a victim is deceptive. People love the victim only when they can feel superior to him or her. Already in the initial flood of correspondence, I received dozens of letters that provoked a queasy feeling. There were many stalkers, love letters, marriage requests and the perverse anonymous letter. But even the offers of help were indicative of what was going on inside many. It is a human reflex that makes you feel better about your-self when you can help someone weaker, a victim. That works as long as the roles are clearly defined. Gratitude to the giver is won-derful; but when it is abused to prevent the other from developing his or her full potential, the whole thing takes on a hollow ring. 'You could live with me and help me with the housework. I'm offering board, wages and lodging. Although I'm married, I'm sure we'll find an arrangement,' wrote one man. 'You can work at my house so that you can learn to clean and cook,' wrote another woman for whom that 'consideration' appeared to be sufficient. Over the last few years I had truly had enough of cleaning. Don't get me wrong. I was deeply touched by all the genuine expressions of sympathy and all the honest interest in my person. But it becomes difficult to be reduced to a broken girl in need of help. That is a role I have not acquiesced to, nor is it one I would like to assume in the future.

I had withstood all Wolfgang Priklopil's psychological garbage and dark fantasies and had not allowed myself to be broken. Now I was out in the world, and that's exactly what people wanted to see: a broken person who would never get back up again, who would always be dependent on help from others. But the moment I refused to bear that mark of Cain for the rest of my life, the mood turned.

Disapprovingly, the helpful people who had sent me their old clothes and had offered me a job cleaning their houses took note of the fact that I wanted to live according to my own rules. It quickly got around that I was ungrateful and would certainly try to capitalize on my situation. People found it strange that I could afford my own flat. Fairy tales of horrendous sums paid for inter-views swirled. Gradually, the sympathy turned to resentment and envy – and sometimes to open hate.

What people could least forgive me for was that I refused to judge the kidnapper the way the public expected me to. People didn't want to hear from me that there is no absolute evil, no clear black and white. Of course, the kidnapper had taken my youth away from me, locked me up and tormented me – but during the key years between the eleventh and nineteenth years of my life, he had been my only attachment figure. By escaping I had not only freed myself from my tormentor, but I had also lost a person, who was, by force of circumstances, close to me. But grief, even if it may seem difficult to comprehend, was not something I was entitled to. As soon as I began to paint a more nuanced picture of the kidnapper, people rolled their eyes and looked away. It makes people uncomfortable whenever categories of Good and Evil begin to topple, and they are confronted with the fact that personified Evil also had a human face. His dark side didn't simply fall from the sky; nobody is born a monster. We are all shaped by our contact with the world, with other people, all of which makes us who we are. And therefore we bear the final responsibility for what happens in our families, in our environment. Admitting that to oneself is not easy. It is all the more difficult when someone holds up a mirror that was not intended for that purpose. With my comments I have touched a nerve and with my attempts at discerning the human behind the façade of tormentor and Mr Clean, I have reaped incomprehension. After my escape I even met with Wolfgang Priklopil's friend Holzapfel to talk about the kidnapper, because I wanted to understand why he had become the person who had done that to me. But I quickly abandoned such attempts. I was not permitted to work through my experiences in this way; it was glibly dismissed as Stockholm Syndrome.

The authorities as well have begun to treat me differently over time. I got the impression that in a way they resented the fact that I had freed myself. In this case they were not the rescuers, but rather those who had failed all those years. The smouldering frustration that was likely elicited in all those responsible surfaced in 2008. Herwig Haidinger, the former director of the Federal

Criminal Police Office, revealed that political leaders and the police had actively covered up their mistakes in my case after my escape. He published the tip from the canine police officer, who six weeks after my abduction had pointed to Priklopil as the kidnapper – a tip the police did not pursue, despite having otherwise grabbed at every straw in the search for me.

The special task force, which later took over my case, knew nothing about that key piece of evidence. The file had gone 'missing'. Herwig Haidinger had been the one to find it after examining all the case files following my escape. He alerted the minister for home affairs to the blunder. But she didn't want to face a police scandal so soon after the autumn 2006 elections and instructed all investigations to cease. It wasn't until 2008, after he had been transferred, that Haidinger revealed the intervention and published the following e-mail via Austrian MP Peter Pilz, which he had written on 26 September 2006, one month after my escape:

Dear Brigadier

The tenor of the initial instructions to me was that no investigations into the second tip (i.e. canine police officer from Vienna) were to be made. In compliance with the head of the ministry I have followed these instructions – even under protest. The instructions also contained a second component: namely to wait until after the general elections. That date is this coming Sunday.

However, even after the election nobody dares touch the matter, and all pertinent information remained under wraps.

When Haidinger went public with it in 2008, his statement nearly triggered a government crisis. A new fact-finding commission was created. But, strangely enough, its efforts were not directed at investigating the blunders, but rather at questioning my statements. Once again a search for accomplices was begun, and the commission accused me of covering for them – I, who had always been at the mercy of only one person and could have known nothing about anything going on in the periphery. I was questioned for hours, even during the work on this book. They no longer treated me like a victim, but rather accused me of hushing up or hiding key details, and publicly speculated on whether I was blackmailed by accomplices. It seems to be easier for the authorities to believe in the great conspiracy behind such a crime than to admit that they overlooked a single perpetrator acting alone who appeared harmless. The new investigations were ended without success. In 2010 the case was closed. The authorities' findings: there were no accomplices. Wolfgang Priklopil acted alone. I was relieved at that conclusion.

Now, four years after my escape, I can breathe and dedicate myself to tackling the hardest chapter in dealing with what happened: coming to terms with the past myself and looking to the future. Again I see that a few people, most of them anonymous, react to me with aggression. The majority of those I meet have supported me along my path. Slowly and cautiously, I am taking it one step at a time and learning to trust again.

In these four years I have become reacquainted with my family and have once again established a loving relationship with my mother. I have got my secondary school leaving certificate and am now learning languages. My imprisonment is something I will have to cope with my whole life, but I am gradually coming to believe that I am no longer dominated by it. It is a part of me, but not everything. There are so many other facets to life I would like to experience. In writing this account I have tried to close the book on the so far longest and darkest chapter in my life. I am deeply relieved that I have found words for all that is unspeakable and contradictory. Seeing it in front of me in black and white helps me to look to the future with confidence. Because what I have experienced also gives me strength: I survived imprisonment in my dungeon, freed myself and remained intact. I know that I can master life in freedom as well. And this freedom begins now, four years after 23 August 2006. Only now can I put the past behind me with these pages and truly say: I am free.

He just wanted a decent book to read ...

Not too much to ask, is it? It was in 1935 when Allen Lane, Managing Director of Bodley Head Publishers, stood on a platform at Exeter railway station looking for something good to read on his journey back to London. His choice was limited to popular magazines and poor-quality paperbacks – the same choice faced every day by the vast majority of readers, few of whom could afford hardbacks. Lane's disappointment and subsequent anger at the range of books generally available led him to found a company – and change the world.

'We believed in the existence in this country of a vast reading public for intelligent books at a low price, and staked everything on it'
Sir Allen Lane, 1902–1970, founder of Penguin Books

The quality paperback had arrived – and not just in bookshops. Lane was adamant that his Penguins should appear in chain stores and tobacconists, and should cost no more than a packet of cigarettes.

Reading habits (and cigarette prices) have changed since 1935, but Penguin still believes in publishing the best books for everybody to enjoy. We still believe that good design costs no more than bad design, and we still believe that quality books published passionately and responsibly make the world a better place.

So wherever you see the little bird – whether it's on a piece of prize-winning literary fiction or a celebrity autobiography, political tour de force or historical masterpiece, a serial-killer thriller, reference book, world classic or a piece of pure escapism – you can bet that it represents the very best that the genre has to offer.

Whatever you like to read – trust Penguin.

read more
www.penguin.co.uk